Honda
Production
Motorcycles
1946–1980

Other Titles in the Crowood MotoClassic Series

Honda
Production
Motorcycles
1946–1980

Mick Walker

THE CROWOOD PRESS

First published in 2006 by
The Crowood Press Ltd
Ramsbury, Marlborough
Wiltshire SN8 2HR

www.crowood.com

British Library Cataloguing-in-Publication Data
A catalogue record for this book is available from the British
Library.

ISBN 1 86126 820 3
EAN 978 1 86126 820 4

Dedication
This book is dedicated to David and Eileen Livesey.

Acknowledgements
Many of the photographs in *Honda Production Motorcycles
1946–1980* come from my own camera and Japanese sources,
including the Honda Motor Company. But others who have
helped include Peter Reeve, Vic Bates, the late Don Upshaw,
CBX Owners Club, T.D. Brown, Roy Francis, Felix Apicella, Len
Thorpe, Doug Curran, Peter Fleming, Cotswold Classics, Jim
Parker, Rod Scivyer, Andrew French, Bob Hansen, Terry
Naughton and Castrol.

Designed and edited by Focus Publishing
11a St Botolph's Road, Sevenoaks,
Kent TN13 3AJ

Printed and bound in Great Britain by CPI Bath.

Contents

Preface

From exceedingly humble beginnings Honda became the world's largest motorcycle producer in a mere fourteen years – from something rather less than a moped Soichiro Honda took on not only his own domestic competitors, but also the rest of the world, to design engines that would spin to over 20,000rpm, with double-overhead cams, 4-valves-per-cylinder and in 4-, 5- and 6-cylinder guises which rocked the racing world and shattered records wherever they went.

And this progress, it must be remembered, came from a country which, when Honda began, was in financial and physical chaos – and which has never had sufficient raw materials.

Honda also can be credited with reviving a decaying motorcycle industry on a worldwide scale – giving it unheard-of sophistication, including making features such as an electric start, direction indication, overhead cam engines, horizontally split crankcases with unit construction and decent electric standard fitment.

It is also probably true to say that without the stimulus and competition provided by Honda, plus fierce determination to reach set objectives, the other Japanese manufacturers would not have developed as rapidly. Honda did have its problems from time to time (both financial and design-wise), but in the main it possessed an almost unique ability to come up with the right machines at the right time – at the same time adding a new dimension to motorcycling.

And I know from personal experience that Honda deserves the success, having ridden many of the company's motorcycles over the last forty-two years, beginning with my own CB92 Super Sport in 1963.

This, my ninety-fifth book, has given me as much pleasure in its putting together as any I have done so far.

Mick Walker
Wisbech,
Cambridgeshire

OPPOSITE: *Soichiro Honda with the 10 millionth motorcycle produced by his company in January 1968: a CB450 twin.*

1   Origins

Soichiro Honda, who was born on 17 November 1906, was without doubt one of the most influential commercial figures of the twentieth century – certainly as regards to the car and motorcycle industries. The eldest son of the village blacksmith in Komyo, long since swallowed up by the urban sprawl of modern-day Hamamatsu, from an early age the young Soichiro displayed an interest in mechanical things and at school showed a distinct leaning towards the practical approach. As a child, Soichiro helped his father repair pedal cycles.

Entering the Motor Industry

From his village Soichiro moved, at the age of sixteen, to Tokyo, joining the Art Trading Company, a motor repair garage. But this enterprise was wrecked in the devastating earthquake which hit this part of Japan in 1923 – in fact, Soichiro actually drove a car out of the wreckage to safety. Not only this, but it was the first time he had actually driven! Shortly afterwards, he rode a motorcycle for the first time as he toured the city to view the widespread damage caused by the earthquake. He later commented that, 'Driving a motor car for the first time and riding round on a motorcycle and learning how to repair automobiles – for me, the great earthquake was nearly a blessing.'

In 1928 he then returned to Hamamatsu, the city near his birthplace, for a brief period in which he repaired vehicles, but was to go back to Tokyo where he started his own car dealership. At the same time, by now well into the

1930s, he was bitten by the racing bug. At first, this saw Soichiro build his own racing car, powered by an ex-military Curtiss-Wright V8 aero engine. This was followed by other cars, one using a Ford engine with a supercharger. But all this came to an abrupt end following a serious accident in a supercharged Ford-engined car during the All-Japan Speed Rally at the Tama River circuit, near Tokyo, in July 1936.

Upon recovery, Soichiro Honda began a new career at the age of thirty, selling his dealership and entering the world of manufacturing with a piston-ring factory, Tokai Seiki Heavy Industries Company. The first attempts proved less than successful. In fact, the Honda-produced ring proved extremely brittle and thus prone to premature breakage. Eventually, after having samples analysed by a local professor, Soichiro discovered that the problem was a lack of silicone content. Realizing how little he knew about the subject, he enrolled as a student at a local engineering college. He did in fact complete the full course, but before the end had learned enough to produce his first satisfactory piston ring and thereafter made a commercial success of the venture.

With the outbreak of war in Japan in December 1941, he developed a special machine so that the piston rings could be produced by unskilled women. Later, Soichiro's company was also involved in the production of wooden aircraft propellers for the Japanese Army Air Force. Besides both army and navy contracts, he also produced for larger companies such as Toyota, but after the Japanese surrender Soichiro decided to sell the remains of his operation to Toyota and effectively took a year off.

The Honda Technical Research Institute

But such an active mind couldn't rest for long and in October 1946 Soichiro, together with a dozen employees, established the grand-sounding Honda Technical Research Institute in Hamamatsu. But the name hid the fact that this new enterprise was located in little more than a small wooden building on a levelled bombsite in the outskirts of the city – and had only a single machine tool.

Post-war Japan was hungry for any form of personal transport – provided it was cheap. Soichiro Honda was extremely fortunate to uncover a cache of 500 war-surplus 50cc Tohatsu-made two-stroke engines, which had been used by the military authorities to power small generators. Thus he took the first hesitant steps to his ultimate emergence as the largest motorcycle manufacturer in the world by adapting these tiny engines to power conventional pedal cycles. Within a short period of time, Honda was offering the first of these for sale.

The very first Honda was the 1F of 1946, made possible by the purchase of 500 war surplus 50cc two-stroke generator engines; it was popularly known as the 'bata-bata'.

In March 1947 Kiyoshi Kawashima (who was later to become Honda President in 1983, succeeding Soichiro himself) joined the fledgling company. Later that same year in November 1947, productions of the first Honda-designed engine, the A-type, began. This 50cc two-stroke engine, soon nicknamed the 'Chimney', was, like the ex-military Tohatsu unit, an auxiliary engine for fitment into conventional pedal cycles. The A-type developed

Aoi, Yamashita works, 1946.

The Honda A-type 49cc two-stroke engine (dubbed 'Chimney'), belt drive and pedal cycle-type frame, 1948.

1bhp at 5,000rpm, with the cylinder horizontal and with ignition by flywheel magneto. It also featured a reduction gear to a countershaft and from this a belt drove the rear wheel with a jockey pulley to maintain tension.

The Honda Motor Company

In September 1948 the Honda Technical Research Institute was incorporated and the Honda Motor Company Ltd began its life, capitalized with one million yen. At around the same time, the first complete Honda motorcycle was launched – the B-type. The newcomer was powered by a 90cc engine (two-stroke again) and was actually what the Italians would have called a *Moto carro*, a strange cross between a motorcycle and small goods truck, for businessmen operating on a budget. The front section of the machine was a conventional motorcycle (with single front wheel and forks), whilst the rear section (behind the engine) carried a large square 'box-like' assembly between the two rear (driving) wheels.

Also in 1948, Honda's existing A-type engine obtained a 60 per cent share of the Japanese domestic market in its class.

Honda's First Real Motorcycle

In August 1949 production began of what can be termed Honda's first real motorcycle, the D-type named the 'Dream' by Soichiro Honda. It was again powered by a piston-port induction two-stroke single-cylinder engine displacing 98cc and with bore and stroke dimensions of 50 × 50mm. Producing 3.5bhp

The Dream D-type with 98cc two-stroke engine, circa 1949.

The Dream D-type assembly line, 1951.

at 4,000rpm, the D-type had a maximum speed of just over 40mph (65km/h). Other details of the machine's specification included chain final drive (all previous Honda's had featured belt operation), telescopic forks (another first for Honda), a rigid frame (very much in the style of pre-war German designs, with its steel channel construction), 3.00 × 20 tyres, flywheel magneto ignition and a dry weight of 176lb (80kg).

Then in October 1949 Takeo Fujisawa joined the company. Together with Kiyoshi Kawashima, he was to play a pivotal role in the future development of the Honda organization. As Roland Brown said in his 1991 Crowood Moto Classics book, *Honda*:

> Designing and building good machines are all very well, but to a motorcycle manufacturer the most important thing of all is to sell them, and to make a profit in doing so. As the financial genius behind the Honda Motor Co. from 1949 to his retirement in 1973, Takeo Fujisawa was arguably as vital as Soichiro Honda himself to the firm's success.

Kiyoshi Kawashima was also a key player in Honda's growth, but worked closely with Soichiro Honda on engineering.

In November 1949 the firm's capital had been increased to two million yen, whilst the following year, 1950, saw the Tokyo plant opened in November. In this year, Japanese motorcycle production totalled 2,633 units, approximately 1,000 of these being Hondas, the other 1,600 being shared by nine other companies.

Honda's First Four-Stroke

In July 1951 a brand-new Honda was built in prototype form, undergoing tests at Hakone, where it averaged some 43mph (70km/h). The rider was none other than Kiyoshi Kawashima. The bike used a 146cc (57 × 57mm) ohv four-stroke with near vertical cylinder and three valves (two inlet, one exhaust). There were also two carburettors (one for each inlet port). Kawashima's performance testing proved the E-type's reliability and resulted in the model entering series production in October 1951. Soon, no fewer

1949 Model D Specifications

Engine	Air-cooled, piston-port, single-cylinder, two-stroke, exhaust port at rear of cylinder, alloy head, cast-iron barrel, unit construction, vertically split crankcases	Frame	Channel steel, full loop
		Front suspension	Telescopic fork
		Rear suspension	Rigid
		Front brake	SLS drum
		Rear brake	SLS drum
Bore	50mm	Tyres	3.00 × 20 front and rear
Stroke	50mm		
Displacement	98cc	**General Specifications**	
Compression ratio	5.2:1	Wheelbase	48.8in (1,240mm)
Lubrication	Petroil mixture	Ground clearance	5.5in (140mm)
Ignition	Flywheel magneto	Seat height	29.5in (749mm)
Carburettor	N/A	Fuel tank capacity	N/A
Primary drive	Gears	Dry weight	176lb (80kg)
Final drive	Chain	Maximum power	3.4bhp @ 4,500rpm
Gearbox	Two speeds; foot-change	Top speed	45mph (72km/h)

ABOVE: *The Dream E-type, Honda's first four-stroke, with 5.5bhp ohv single-cylinder engine, unit construction, telescopic forks and plunger rear suspension, 1951.*

LEFT: *The Dream E racer, which was the first Honda to race outside Japan, at Sao Paulo, Brazil, February 1954.*

than 130 E-types were leaving the Honda plant, establishing a new record for Japanese motorcycle manufacture at the time.

Japanese motorcycle production rose to 11,510 units for 1951. That same year all the other domestic motorcycle builders were petitioning the government to curb imports. However, Soichiro Honda refused to take this line, believing that a better product, good service and spares availability, plus a competitive price, would ensure the company's success.

1952 – Honda Broadens its Horizons

The Honda Motor Co. experienced a busy year in 1952. In April, Soichiro Honda was awarded the Medal of Honour with Blue Ribbon by the Japanese government for commercial services rendered to the country (the presentation being made by the Emperor). By June 1952 capital had been increased to six million yen and in that same month the new F-type Cub was launched. This was a 50cc (40 × 40mm) two-stroke engine which could be fitted easily to any standard pedal cycle within

minutes. It featured a horizontal cylinder and flywheel magneto ignition. Output was 1bhp at 3,000rpm with a reduction gear behind the crankcase and a tiny silencer; the F-type unit was mounted in the rear wheel.

The first-ever Hondas to be exported occurred in 1952, with the new F-type engine going to Taiwan in June and E-type Dream motorcycles shipped to Okinawa and the Philippines for the first time.

In November, Soichiro Honda made a visit to the USA, where he made several purchases of machine tools and also took a detailed look at the American motorcycle industry and its market (including European imports). Finally, in December 1952 production of the F-type Cub reached 7,000 units per month, accounting for 70 per cent of Japanese motorcycle output that month.

A Vast Expansion

The following year, 1953, saw a vast expansion of the Honda operation. To illustrate this, in November 1952 capital had been fifteen million yen, but thirteen months later in

---

1951 Dream Model E Specifications

Engine	Air-cooled, ohv single with three valves (two inlet, one exhaust), alloy head, cast-iron barrel, unit construction, vertically split crankcases	Frame	Channel steel, full loop
		Front suspension	Telescopic fork
		Rear suspension	Rigid (Plunger optional)
		Front brake	SLS drum
		Rear brake	SLS drum
Bore	57mm	Tyres	2.75 × 19 front and rear
Stroke	57mm		
Displacement	145cc	**General Specifications**	
Compression ratio	6.5:1	Wheelbase	51.2in (1,300mm)
Lubrication	Plunger pump, wet sump	Ground clearance	6in (152mm)
Ignition	Flywheel magneto	Seat height	29.5in (749mm)
Carburettor	Two carburettors	Fuel tank capacity	N/A
Primary drive	Gears	Dry weight	213lb (97kg)
Final drive	Chain	Maximum power	5.5bhp @ 5,000rpm
Gearbox	Two speeds; foot-change	Top speed	50mph (80km/h)

The F-Type Cub, a 49cc two-stroke engine designed in 1952 by Soichiro Honda for fitment to a conventional pedal cycle.

December 1953, this had increased four-fold to sixty million yen!

Between August and October 1953 four new models were introduced: the 89cc J-type Benly ohv lightweight motorcycle; the 145cc 3E Dream and 6E Dream models; and lastly the H-type engine for agricultural use. To cope with these newcomers and also the existing increased demands, several new production facilities came on-stream during 1953.

The J-Type Benly

Of all the new designs, the J-type, or Benly as it was commonly known, was by far the most important to Honda's future as a major motorcycle producer. And it was, as Roland Brown once described it, 'copied unashamedly from a West German NSU'. Well, at least the general concept was, with its neatly styled ohv unit construction using a slightly inclined cylinder. But the machine in question, the Fox 4, was actually of 98cc displacement and produced 3.8bhp at 6,000rpm. The Honda

had telescopic front forks in place of the NSU leading link type, a three-speed gearbox and a spine-type frame built from two steel pressings welded together. On the J-type Benly the rear suspension was unusual, as it involved both engine and swinging arm moving round a central pivot.

The J-type Benly ohv single of advanced design, based very much on the West German 98cc NSU Fox; 1953.

But there is no doubt, as we will see later, that of all the European brands, Soichiro Honda saw NSU as being at the very forefront of design at that time.

1954 – A Year of Problems

In January 1954 Honda Motor Co. shares were offered on the Tokyo Stock Exchange for the first time and Honda's first scooter, the K-type Juno, was launched, with a 200cc (68 × 57mm) ohv engine (from the end of 1954 increased to 219cc by increasing the bore size to 70mm). Interestingly, the K-type was the first Honda-designed engine not to feature square bore and stroke dimensions.

However, 1954 was to be a year of problems for the fast-growing Honda empire. The first of the glitches to hit Honda came when a works-prepared Dream, ridden by Mikio Omura, finished last in the 125cc race at the international race meeting staged at Sâo Paulo, Brazil. The race was won by Nello Pagani rid-

ing an Italian FB Mondial – and Soichiro Honda realized that there was much work to be done if his company was to make an effective challenge against the top European marques which dominated Grand Prix racing at the time.

Next, Soichiro visited Europe, leaving in May 1954. Not only did he visit several factories (including NSU in Germany and Triumph in the UK), but he also took in the Isle of Man TT. In truth, Soichiro was staggered by what he saw and for the first time he realized just how hard his task would be to become a world motorcycle power. The NSUs led the lightweight (125 and 250cc) classes that year and Honda was to hold the German marque in such high regard that it was to dominate his design thinking for the next five years, particularly in the racing field. Not only this, but as Roy Bacon stated in his 1985 book, *Honda: The Early Classic Motorcycles* (Osprey): 'His [Honda's] road models lacked the sophistication of Europe, in that components such as

Honda's first scooter, the K-type, with 200cc ohv single-cylinder engine, 1954.

1954 JA Specifications

Engine	Air-cooled, ohv single with two valves, alloy head, cast-iron barrel, pressed-up crankshaft, roller big-end bearing, vertically split crankcases	Front suspension	Telescopic forks
		Rear suspension	Swinging arm, twin shock absorbers
Bore	60mm	Front brake	SLS drum
Stroke	49mm	Rear brake	SLS drum
Displacement	138cc	Tyres	2.50 × 19 front and rear
Compression ratio	6:1		
Lubrication	Plunger pump, wet sump	**General Specifications**	
Ignition	Flywheel magneto	Wheelbase	48.4in (1,229mm)
Carburettor	N/A	Ground clearance	5.5in (140mm)
Primary drive	Gears	Seat height	29in (737mm)
Final drive	Chain	Fuel tank capacity	N/A
Gearbox	Three speeds; foot-change	Dry weight	231lb (105kg)
Frame	Spine-type, built from two pressings welded together	Maximum power	4.5bhp @ 5,000rpm
		Top speed	49mph (79km/h)

magnetos, plugs, carburettors, tyres and much more were far more developed there.' But perhaps the most amazing aspect of Honda's European visit was that everyone he met was happy to explain to the little man from Japan the hows and whys of their production techniques. In short, they told him everything he wanted to know. Soichiro Honda soaked up this information like a sponge. What he saw fired his enthusiasm and most importantly determination to return to Europe, in order to win in both the showroom and on the race circuit. To this end, Soichiro took back to Japan not only ideas, but actual components to study and analyse.

However, on the commercial front there were considerable problems – in fact, a financial crisis. Although the Honda Motor Co. had racked up record sales and there had been a truly vast expansion programme, there were serious financial risks. Soichiro's purchase of expensive American (and also German and Swiss) machine tools (at a cost of US$1.1 million) meant that the company could produce better engineered products, but it had also swal-

lowed up much-needed capital. In fact, at the time the actual capital of the company represented only US$166,000! Japan had entered a period of recession following the ending of the conflict in Korea, while the unions were growing stronger and demanding higher wages.

This situation came to a head towards the end of 1954. For example, in the trading year March 1953 to February 1954, Honda made a staggering 514 million yen, but the following financial year (March 1954 to February 1955), this figure was reduced to only sixty-eight million. Honda's financial director, Takeo Fujisawa, could see that the organization was close to bankruptcy.

In fact, this did not happen, but it was a very close-run thing. If not for the backing of the Mitsubishi Bank, the subcontractors and the workforce, the Honda story would have ended there and then. There were some six months of stress for all concerned before the good ship Honda emerged from its financial storm and entered less turbulent waters, with everyone 'strengthened by the experience' as Soichiro was later to recall the situation.

The Investment Pays Off

The huge investment in plant, labour and tooling really started to come into its own as the second half of the 1950s unfolded, helped by the introduction by the Japanese government of strict import controls on foreign motorcycles. New models introduced for 1955 were the 125cc ohv JB Benly (February), the 345cc (76 × 76mm) – SB Benly (Honda's first overhead camshaft model), the 246cc (70 × 64mm) – SA Dream and finally in November the first Benly JC56 models were built. The latter was notable because the front forks were of the Earles type, rather than the telescopics found on the earlier Benlys and the newly released 250 and 350 Dream models.

1955 was also notable because it was the year that Honda took over from Tohatsu as Japan's leading motorcycle manufacturer.

In 1956 consolidation was the buzz word. Except for the 200cc EJ motorcycle (March) and the VN general purpose industrial engine (April) there were no new products. However, attention was given to the service side of the operation, with not only an official Service Division established, but also the introduction of a one-year warranty across the product range.

The Benly JC-type 125cc ohv single with four speeds, 7bhp at 6,000rpm, and a de luxe specification, 1955.

The Honda 200 of 1956 with 219cc ohv unit construction single-cylinder engine, 10bhp at 6,000rpm, 18in wheels and full enclosed transmission.

1955 JC Specifications

Engine	Air-cooled ohv single with two valves, alloy head, cast-iron barrel, pressed-up crankshaft, roller big-end bearing, vertically split crankcases	Front suspension	Leading type of Earles pattern, with twin spring units
		Rear suspension	Swinging arm, twin shock absorbers
Bore	54mm	Front brake	SLS drum
Stroke	54mm	Rear brake	SLS drum
Displacement	125cc	Tyres	2.50 × 19 front and rear
Compression ratio	6.5:1		
Lubrication	Plunger pump, wet sump	**General Specifications**	
Ignition	Flywheel magneto	Wheelbase	49in (1,245mm)
Carburettor	N/A	Ground clearance	5.5in (140mm)
Primary drive	Gear	Seat height	736mm (29in)
Final drive	Chain	Fuel tank capacity	N/A
Gearbox	Four speeds; foot-change	Dry weight	110kg (242lb)
Frame	Spine-type, built from two pressings welded together	Maximum power	7bhp @ 6,000rpm
		Top speed	53mph (85km/h)

Into Overdrive

1957 began with Honda Motor's capital being increased to 360 million yen. Then in June that year an R & D centre was set up at the Shirako plant. In September the exciting C70 Dream went on sale. This was to be a pivotal introduction. Not only was it Honda's first overhead camshaft twin-cylinder model, but it was to lay the foundation for future Honda models that were soon to shake the motorcycling world with their innovation and sophistication.

1955 KB Juno Scooter

Engine	Air-cooled ohv single with two valves, alloy head, cast-iron barrel, pressed-up crankshaft, roller-bearing big end, vertically split crankcases	Front suspension	Leading link fork
		Rear suspension	Swinging arm, twin shock absorbers
Bore	70mm	Front brake	SLS drum
Stroke	57mm	Rear brake	SLS drum
Displacement	219cc	Tyres	5.00 × 9 front and rear
Compression ratio	6:1		
Lubrication	Plunger pump, wet sump	**General Specifications**	
Ignition	Flywheel magneto	Wheelbase	1,384mm (54.5in)
Carburettor	N/A	Ground clearance	114mm (4.5in)
Primary drive	Gears	Seat height	762mm (30in)
Final drive	Enclosed chain	Fuel tank capacity	N/A
Gearbox	Three speeds; foot-change	Dry weight	352lb (160kg)
Frame	Tubular steel construction	Maximum power	9bhp @ 5,500rpm
		Top speed	55mph (89km/h)

1957 ME/MF Specifications (MF in brackets where different)

Engine	Air-cooled, sohc single with two valves, alloy head, cast-iron barrel, chain-driven camshaft, vertically split aluminium crankcases	Rear suspension	Swinging arm, twin shock absorbers
Bore	70mm (MF: 76mm)	Front brake	SLS drum
Stroke	64mm (MF: 76mm)	Rear brake	SLS drum
Displacement	246cc (345cc)	Tyres	3.00 × 18 front and rear (MF: 3.25 rear)
Compression ratio	7.5 (MF 7:1)		
Lubrication	Plunger pump, wet sump	**General Specifications**	
Ignition	Flywheel magneto	Wheelbase	52.8in (1,341mm)
Carburettor	N/A	Ground clearance	5.5in (140mm)
Primary drive	Gear	Seat height	30in (762mm)
Final drive	Chain	Fuel tank capacity	N/A
Gearbox	Four speeds; foot-change	Dry weight	383lb (174kg) (MF: 387lb (176kg))
Frame	Cradle-type, part tubular, part metal pressings	Maximum power	14bhp @ 6,000rpm (MF: 20bhp @ 6,500rpm)
Front suspension	Leading link	Top speed	65mph (105km/h) (MF: 73mph (118km/h))

But if 1957 was a good year, 1958 was even better. In May the C71 Dream entered production – the first Honda to boast an electric starter. The following month the company's head office was relocated to No. 5–5, Yaesu, Chuo-ku, Tokyo, while in July capital had increased again, to 720 million yen. But the really big news was the launch of the 49cc (40 × 39mm) ohv C100 Super Cub. As Roland Brown put it:

> There is not much doubt that of all the brilliant bikes Honda have built – the CB750 superbike, Mike Hailwood's magnificent 6-cylinder racers, the mighty Gold Wing, you name them – the most important of them all is the C100 Super Cub of 1958. Quite simply, the humble little 40mph (65km/h) runabout changed the face of motorcycling, introducing bikes to people all over the world and providing Honda with the finance to produce so many infinitely more exciting things in the future.

And as the following chapters record, Honda simply kept expanding, introducing a myriad of ever more capable designs. But with the Super Cub, its whole commercial thrust had been given a huge fillip. The little bike sold in millions and was responsible for the now legendary marketing term, 'You meet the nicest people on a Honda' – penned by the Grays Advertising Agency in Los Angeles.

Honda was on its way and nobody would be able to stop it.

The ME 250 specification included an ohc 246cc (70 × 64mm) engine, 14bhp at 6,000rpm and a dry weight of 383lb. There was also a 343cc (76 × 76mm) version coded MF.

2 Super Cub and Other Singles

During the 1920s and 1930s Japan had become an Imperial power and a major force on the world stage. Then came Pearl Harbor and the attack on the US Fleet, which brought America into the war, and within less than four years Japan had lost both its power and influence. Going to war had been a bad mistake.

The Second World War had left Japan a shattered country, with the vast majority of its production facilities and cities little more than piles of rubble. From this scene of desolation, in only a few short years Japan was to be reborn, creating the biggest economic and industrial miracle of modern times.

The Japanese Motorcycle Industry

And so, from the ashes, the Japanese motorcycle industry marched forth. Yes, there had been a two-wheel industry with a few manufacturers in pre-war days, but during the late 1940s and throughout the 1950s there was to grow a major motorcycling powerhouse.

First into production after the war were Meguro, Miyato and Rikuo, the existing pre-war marques. Soon these were joined by Tohatsu, Pointer, Abe Star and Mishima. Other early post-war names included Mizuho, Hosk, IMC, Olympus, Showa, Cruiser, Gas Den and others with such quaint names as Pearl, Queen Bee, Jet, Pony, Hope Star and even Happy! The number of manufacturers reached a peak of around 120 companies by 1952. By the late 1950s few of these had survived. Those that did were headed by Honda, Suzuki and Yamaha,

plus the Meguro concern (later taken over by Kawasaki), Tohatsu, Pointer, Bridgestone, Lilac, Liner and Rabbit.

But although there were many fewer marques, the survivors built more bikes. The full extent of this can be gauged by recalling that in 1945 only 127 motorcycles were built in Japan, but by 1950 production had risen nearly twenty-fold to 2,633. Five years on and these figures had increased to 204,304. By 1960, the figure had reached an amazing 1,349,090 units. Much of this figure was thanks to the phenomenal success of one model, Honda's C100 Super Cub.

The Bestseller

Introduced in August 1958, the Super Cub sold in vast numbers straight away. The Cub was the inspiration of Honda's financial brains, Takeo Fujisawa. Until the arrival of this mould-breaking design, the world's motorcycle manufacturers had largely concentrated their efforts on enthusiast models – which only a limited number of people would purchase. But the new 'step-thru' enabled Honda to open up a vast new customer base consisting of both men and women, which was ultimately to stretch all around the world. The Cub gave motorcycling a new identity. It was truly a machine which anyone could consider owning.

Although the vast majority of Japanese motorcycles (including Hondas) of the 1950s were influenced by German designs – and British to a lesser extent – the C100 Super

Cub didn't owe its origins to anyone except the Honda Motor Co. As Clement Salvadori explained in *The Art of the Motorcycle* (Guggenheim Museum, 1998):

> Honda's market was the new rider; this little machine was designed to attract the non-motor-cycling crowd, which was an ingenious plan. Although the rider, both men or women, had to kick-start the engine to life, cranking a 50 was not at all difficult – you had only to start it up, roll the bike off the centre-stand, put it into gear, twist the throttle, and away you went. If you shifted to second, then third, on a good downhill, the Cub might get all the way up to 50mph – the aerodynamics were, in a word, non-existent. The Cub was not intended as a speedster, but as transportation around town.

Ease of Production

Another ace card was the Cub's minimal production costs. This was not only because of the vast number produced, but also through its use

of plastic for components such as the front mudguard and leg shields; plastic did the job just as well as metal, but at a considerably lower cost. In addition, the frame, swinging arm and front fork were all manufactured of inexpensive, easy to mass-produce, pressed steel. This and other design details ensured that the Cub's price was best described as 'budget'. However, and here again Honda scored, quality didn't suffer. Not only was build construction excellent, but the Cub had the huge advantage of having an economical ohv four-stroke engine and features such as full-width polished alloy brake hubs and a comprehensive and smart chrome-plated exhaust system. Finally, as future events were to prove, it was a timeless design, which still appeared modern decades later.

Record Sales

In its first full year of production, 1959, no fewer than 755,589 Super Cubs were sold – a record for any powered two-wheeler up to

The most successful power two-wheeler of all time, the Honda 'step-thru', began with the C100 Super Cub in 1958, with flywheel magneto ignition.

that time. Forty years later, a staggering twenty-six million of these supremely utilitarian machines had been built and sold, a figure which seems unlikely ever to be exceeded by any powered two-wheeler. Production continues up to the present time and is a basic means of transportation in many Asian, African and South American countries.

In *The Motor Cycle*, dated 24 September 1959, 'Nitor' in his On the Four Winds column, carried the following news item:

> The Honda concern of Japan comes increasingly into the news. And a colleague, Allan Robinson [now well-known for his excellent commentary at Classic Racing Motorcycle Club meetings] had the opportunity the other day to ride what is believed to be the only 49cc Honda Super Cub in Britain. The machine was purchased for David Fryer of Upminster, Essex, by his son in Australia and shipped over here at a cost of only £7 10s (although Mr Fryer had to fork out an additional £28 purchase tax before he could collect). The model features an open, spine-type frame, pressed-steel fork with leading links and a fabricated pivoted rear fork. Of overhead-valve design, the engine has a bore and stroke of 40 × 39mm. Ignition is by coil, with current fed from a 6V 2 ampere-hour battery, little bigger than a pocket diary. Transmission is by chain and through a centrifugal clutch and three-speed gearbox, with heel-and-toe change. Robinson found much to praise. The silencer is 23 times the capacity of the cylinder and emitted a subdued purr. The centrifugal clutch was foolproof, freed perfectly and took up the drive sweetly. The brakes were really potent and the handling above reproach. We shall hear a lot more of Hondas yet.

And what an understatement that was …

The Step-Thru Explained

The C100 Super Cub created its own market. It was as simple as that. And as with all the best

ideas, the formula was so simple that one can only ask why nobody had thought of it before. But in a way, it could only have come from a fledgling company, which was not set in its ways and which could produce it at a competitive price. As Roy Bacon explained in *Honda: The Early Motorcycles*:

> The format of the new machine was completely new, as was the concept for the mechanics. For far too long the aim had been to produce a cheap machine and the result was always the same. Mediocre performance, poor reliability, dreadful electrics, doubtful starting and dissatisfied riders. Honda decided that from the start his machines, and the Super Cub in particular, would be inexpensive, not cheap, and achieved this by the use of the best of mass-production techniques. Parts would be die-cast in aluminium to leave the minimum of machining, moulded in plastic to remove the need for painting, stamped out in sheet for easy machine welding. Most of all, the electrics would be built in, properly designed and made to survive their environment.

The Super Cub combined the best of moped, scooter and even full grown motorcycle features, which together with the techniques described above, created its own description, that of step-thru, and in some countries scooterette.

It was, when introduced, a unique product that deserved to do well – which it did in spectacular fashion. This design above all others really put Honda on the map, not just in Japan, but all around the world.

Engine Details

As already explained, the 49cc ohv engine had near square bore and stroke dimensions of 40 × 39mm. The single cylinder was laid almost horizontal and with a compression ratio of 8.5:1, the 1958 C100 Super Cub produced 4.5bhp at 9,500rpm. This was enough to give the machine a maximum speed of around

1958 C100 Super Cub Specifications

Engine	Air-cooled ohv single with horizontal cylinder, cast-iron head and barrel, caged roller-bearing big end, two main bearings, pressed-up crankshaft, vertically split aluminium crankcases	Front suspension	Leading link
		Rear suspension	Swinging arm, twin shock absorbers
		Front brake	Full-width alloy drum
		Rear brake	Full-width alloy drum
		Tyres	2.25 × 17 front and rear
Bore	40mm		
Stroke	39mm	**General Specifications**	
Displacement	49cc	Wheelbase	46.5in (1,180mm)
Compression ratio	8.5:1	Ground clearance	5in (127mm)
Lubrication	No oil pump; lubrication by splash; big end by rod-dip method	Seat height	29in (737mm)
		Fuel tank capacity	0.7gal (3ltr)
Ignition	Flywheel magneto	Dry weight	143lb (65kg)
Carburettor	Slide-type	Maximum power	4.5bhp @ 9,500rpm
Primary drive	Gears	Top speed	45mph (72km/h)
Final drive	Chain		
Gearbox	Three-speeds; foot-change, with centrifugal clutch		
Frame	U-type, built from tube and pressings		

The C102 model was similar except for the addition of an electric starter, an alternator instead of flywheel magneto, a larger battery and minor changes to the electrical system.

45mph (72km/h) – well above what other 50cc commuter models were capable of at the time.

The crankshaft was a pressed-up affair, with the big-end bearing comprising a series of caged rollers running directly onto the crankpin, the latter being pressed into each crank flywheel section. There were two main bearings, these being of the conventional ball race type.

The hardened gudgeon pin ran directly in the small end eye of the one-piece steel connecting rod and supported an aluminium three-ring piston, the latter with two compression and one oil scraper ring.

In these early engines both the cylinder head and barrel were manufactured in cast iron. The latter featured integral pushrod tunnels, which not only gave a neater appearance, but also did much to prevent oil leaks. A light-alloy rocker was bolted to the cylinder head. Each rocker operated on its own spindle, whilst there were screw adjusters in the outer rocker end to provide the tappets to be set. Access for this purpose was provided by a pair of circular alloy caps, these being equipped with large hexagons for removal by a spanner provided in the tool kit.

Each valve was supported by a pair of coil springs and were opened by a camshaft that ran directly in the crankcase. The latter was split vertically and in unit with the three-speed foot-change gearbox and centrifugal clutch assemblies.

Ignition was by a 6V crankshaft-mounted flywheel magneto, with the contact breaker points and condenser mounted on the stator plate. A small cover gave access to the points for adjustment purposes and the rotor incorporated a centrifugal advance mechanism.

Lubrication

Notably, the lubrication system did without an oil pump. The lubricant was common to both the engine and gearbox and of the wet sump contained in the base of the crankcases.

Simplicity was very much the order of the day, with the majority of components relying on splash for their supply. However, the all-important big-end bearing went a stage further. As in years gone by at the very dawn of the internal combustion engine, the base of the connecting rod 'dipped' into the oil contained within the crankcase. For this purpose the rod was forged with a small extension below the big-end eye. As the crankshaft rotated, the rod extension dipped beneath the oil level, which was then forced via a small drilled hole on the big-end rollers. This was more effective than it may have sounded and operated perfectly unless the engine oil level was allowed to fall below the recommended level. For such a relatively low-powered engine this system was found to have the advantage of low cost (fewer working parts) and effectiveness.

To lubricate the top end of the engine, which, as readers will remember, was laid almost horizontal to the crankcase, the camshaft (which was in the crankcase) was machined with a spiral groove at one end, the action of this pumping oil into an external pipe that ran to the top of the rocker box. Again simple, but nonetheless effective. Engine breathing was accomplished by way of a labyrinth passage, which was cast into the top of the crankcase wall and given an external pipe to pass gases into the atmosphere.

The Clutch
The clutch was a major feature of the Super Cub's design, one commentator describing it as 'quite an assembly, complex in operation but simple to put together'. An important feature of the Cub's clutch was that it was required to take up its drive as engine revolutions increased. It achieved this in the following way: weights were moved outwards by centrifugal force (in other words they were pushed outwards) and so a gear could be selected without the usual novice's biggest fear

of having to juggle with the conventional hand-operated lever, because there wasn't one! The rider simply had to select the gear by foot and open the throttle to get under way, or change to a higher or lower gear; it was that simple.

As for the drive itself, this was transferred through friction and plain plates in the conventional manner, the outer plates being lightly spring-loaded apart to ensure separation when required. Stiffer springs pressed them together so that drive could be taken up.

The clutch centre, splined to the driven plates, was not itself directly attached to the straight-cut primary drive gear. Instead, it was positioned on a section of that gear, machined into a quick-start thread. The effect of this was two-fold: first, it allowed the kick-starter lever to lock up the clutch and thus rotate the engine; secondly, it achieved a similar process on the overrun.

One other feature of the clutch was a ball-and-ramp lifting device, which was mounted outboard of the clutch and the outer engine cover. Roy Bacon said: 'Cunningly, this was linked to the gear pedal, so that regardless of which way that was moved, the clutch plates were separated and gear changing made easy.'

The Chassis
Although the engine was to be enlarged over the years to 54cc (42 × 39mm), 63cc (44 × 41.4mm), 71.8cc (47 × 41.4mm) and finally 89.5cc (50 × 45.6mm), and built in both ohv and later ohc guises, the basic chassis was to remain largely unchanged. Even the wheel size remained constant at 17in, front and rear.

Being a full unit construction design meant that the frame could be kept simple. In fact, only two bolts held the Super Cub's engine in the frame. There was one at the rear of the crankcase, the other at the top. Built from tube and pressings, the Honda frame was both neat and functional. At the steering head a tube ran rearwards to a point above the crankcase. There

The C102 Super Cub with electric starter and coil ignition, circa 1960.

it was welded to an assembly of pressings, which ran up and rearwards to form the main spine and thence to the rear mudguard. The central area was also taken down to the rear of the engine, in order to support the frame itself and also the swinging arm and the centre stand.

The centre stand was typical of the general good standard of the machine's ancillary equipment, which also included features such as a fully enclosed (steel) final drive chaincase, deeply valanced front mudguard (plastic), leg shields/engine cover (plastic), plus a single seat, rear carrier (upon which a pillion seat could be fitted), rider's mirror and a pressing that covered the control cables/electrical wiring on the handlebars.

For such a basic means of transport, the suspension was in the 'de luxe' bracket, being sprung at both ends. The front forks were of the pressed steel, leading link type (as seen on the early Honda twins), whilst the pressed-steel swinging arm was controlled by two rear shock absorbers. The level of comfort this gave the Super Cub was considerably superior to the conventional moped and the larger diameter wheels/tyres gave the little machine a definite advantage over a scooter. The latter usually only had a wheel diameter of between 10–12in, compared with 17in on the Honda.

The Export Drive

During 1959 the massive Honda export drive really began and in June that year American Honda Motor Co. Inc. was established in Gardena, California. That very same month, the Honda team took part in the Isle of Man 125cc TT, winning the team prize.

Then in March 1960 a brand-new Head Office building was completed in Tokyo, followed in April by the new Suzuka factory coming on stream at Suzuka City. And if all this was not enough, Honda launched the C102 Super Cub with electric starter as standard equipment and a change to coil ignition – but otherwise it was the same machine as the C100. In July, a Research and Development division was officially established as the Honda R&D Co. Ltd.

ABOVE: *The C114 (also known as C110D) Sports Cub arrived in 1960, with a full motorcycle specification in miniature. It used a suitably tuned version of the 49cc ohv Super Cub engine.*

LEFT: *Honda workers on the C102 Super Cub production line, circa 1961.*

BELOW: *The C110 engine (C111 shown – only difference is the single seat), showing near-horizontal alloy cylinder head and cast-iron barrel, long induction tract to carb and heel and toe gear-change pedal.*

The Sports Cub

The C110, or the 'Sports Cub', arrived in October 1960. Essentially this used an original ohv C100 engine with three-speed gearbox and flywheel magneto ignition. Additional power came by way of an increase in compression to 9.5:1, giving 5bhp at 9,500rpm and a top speed of almost 50mph (80km/h). But the main difference was its motorcycle appearance, thanks largely to a new frame (still of the spine-type, conventional motorcycle-type tank and new seat. At first, the C110 was built with a high-level exhaust which ran along the offside just in front of the side panel and rear shock absorber. This was equipped with two quite large heat shields, which covered both the silencer and the second section of the exhaust header pipe. Suspension, wheels and much of the remainder of the machine closely followed the existing C100/C102 step-thru models. Besides the basic C110, there was also the C111 (which was identical except for a tiny single seat) and the C114 with low exhaust.

The CZ100 'Monkey Bike'. This made its bow in mid-1960 and ran through to the beginning of 1967. This is the original 1960 version. Note the 5in wheels and rigid frame.

The 'Monkey Bike'

Yet another variant to use the familiar 49cc ohv three-speed engine was CZ100 (also launched in 1960). This was better known as the 'Monkey Bike' and sported 5in wheels, a rigid frame, miniature telescopic forks and weighed in (dry) at 111lb (50kg). Meant really as a means of transport from a campervan whilst on holiday, or in the race paddock, the 'Z' brought Honda considerable publicity due to its unusual looks and the convenience of being something that could be easily folded down for stowage in the 'trunk' of an American-size automobile.

Actually, the Monkey Bike attracted something of a cult following and was also copied by several other manufacturers, including Harley-Davidson (with its 65 Shortster and X90 Minibike). The concept was later further

LEFT: J Kersey dealership stand circa 1964, showing a fully kitted out C100, a C110 and a CS90 Sport.

Film stars Barbara Windsor and the late Sid James are all smiles with an ST70 Chaly, circa 1972.

imported into Great Britain by Nottingham-based Scootamatic Ltd. Alf Briggs, a former racer and vice-president of the Pathfinders Club, who had been the Scootamatic service manager for some time, was appointed technical director.

In May 1961 European Honda GmbH was established in Hamburg, West Germany. Then in the summer of 1961 the C105 Super Cub and C115 Sports Cub were launched. Essentially, these were the same as before, but with a new 54cc engine size, which was achieved by increasing the bore size by 2mm, to 42mm.

1962 was a relatively quiet year, at least for the introduction of new models, with only the C240 Port-Cub (with two-speed gearbox, modified frame and no leg shields) being

A neat trials conversion of the 49cc C110 as carried out by a British dealer, circa 1963.

developed to include the Z50 (1967) and ST70 (1969), then in the 1980s it became the Dax.

British Imports

Larger 125 and 250cc Honda twins were already imported into the UK by Maico Ltd, when in mid-October 1960 it was announced that the C100 Super Cub with the ohv, three-speed single-cylinder engine would be

Seven Days and Nights Non-Stop at Goodwood

The *Motor Cycle* dated 8 November 1962 called it 'Oriental Reliability'. This was in response to the performances of three Honda Cub 49cc machines (a C100, C102 and C110). The latter had travelled 5,896 miles (9,487km) in seven days without a break, then to sign off it did a flying lap of the Goodwood circuit in West Sussex at 51.42mph (82.74km/h). The Honda seven-day test of the three machines saw a total of 15,853 miles (25,508km) completed and relatively little in the way of maintenance during this time.

Ichiro Neuchi, chief of the European Honda organization, flagged 'three frozen riders – part of the team of 18 – over the finishing line on Wednesday of last week'. Jim Harrison, general manager of European Honda in the UK, and Geoff Monty, the team manager, were 'justifiably proud of their achievement'. Weather conditions for the final week of October could not have been worse, with torrential rain, biting winds and night-time frost throughout the seven days.

Following the successful completion of the test, European Honda announced that, by mutual agreement, Hondis Ltd (owned by Maico Concessionaires) had relinquished the rights to sell Honda motorcycles over 100cc in England, Scotland, Wales and the Channel Islands. The sole UK distributor of all Honda products from now onwards would be European Honda Motor Trading, 2 Manorgate Road, Kingston-upon-Thames, Surrey.

How the three Cubs fared:

- C110 Sports Cub: total mileage 5,896.23 (9,487km); 124mpg (2.28/100km); brake test (from 30mph) 41ft (12.5m).
- C100 Super Cub: total mileage 4,934.69 (7,940km); 140mpg (2/100km); brake test (from 30mph) 51ft (15.5m).
- C102 Super Cub (Electric Start): total mileage 5,022.1 (8,080km); 124mpg (2.28/100km); brake test (from 30mph) 44ft (13.4m).

introduced in July that year, together with the 170cc M85 twin-cylinder Juno scooter (*see* Chapter 3).

In September 1962 Honda set up a factory in Belgium to assemble and sell small machines (such as mopeds and step-thrus). Originally trading as NV Honda Motor SA, it subsequently became Honda Benelux NV.

The C200

The following year, 1963, Honda introduced the C200 ultra-lightweight motorcycle. This is best described as being similar, but not an exact copy, of the C100/C114 series. Besides the revised appearance (including a tank with chrome-plated side panels of larger size), the

The 86.7cc (49 × 46mm) C200 ohv motorcycle with four speeds, 17in wheels and fully enclosed final drive chain, which went on sale in the UK on 1 January 1964, priced £124 18s 8d including taxes.

C200 had a displacement of 86.7cc (49 × 46mm), still with ohv, cast-iron head and barrel, horizontal cylinder and unit construction. But it now had four speeds and a conventional clutch, rather than the centrifugal device on the 49/54cc engines. The C200, which had a compression ratio of 8:1, produced a maximum power output of 6.5bhp at 8,000rpm and could reach 55mph. As on the smaller mounts, the wheel size was 17in, but with wider 2.50 section tyres, dry weight was 184lb (84kg).

The CS90

Confusingly, Honda also brought out the CS90 (launched in mid-1964). This used a 89.5cc (50 × 45.6mm) overhead cam engine (with alloy head and barrel), but still employed the near horizontal cylinder configuration. Much of the CS90 was totally changed from the C200, including the frame (although still a spine-type), front forks (telescopics instead of leading link), 18in instead of 17in wheels (but still with 2.50 section tyres). The price was £142 19s.

Motorcycle Mechanics tested a CS90 in its July 1965 issue. This is a section of the test:

> The oversquare engine produced its power evenly right up the rev range to its peak of 9,000rpm where it turned out its stated maximum of 8 bhp. Top speed was 60mph, although 55 could be reached fairly easily in third gear. Suspension was a little on the soft side for a sports bike, although there was none of the tendency to wallow on fast corners that was the one-time hallmark of Japanese machines.

As for fuel consumption, the tester simply said it was 'so frugal and it used so little that one was in grave danger of running out because filling was so infrequent'.

First Ohc Step-Thru

For the 1966 model year Honda produced its first ohc step-thru model, the CM90. This replaced the C90, introduced in 1965, which had an 86.7cc (49 × 46mm) three-speed ohv power unit. With its ohc engine, the CM90 gained just over 3cc (50 × 45.6mm) and a use-

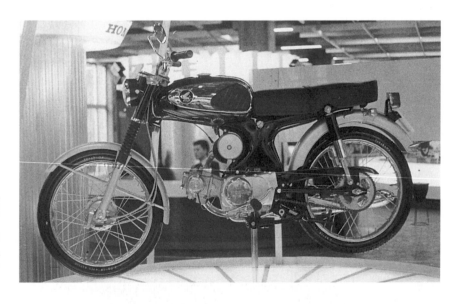

Honda's very neat looking CS90 Sport was powered by an all-alloy 89.5cc (50 × 45.6mm) overhead cam single-cylinder engine. It ran from 1964 through to 1969.

The largest version of the Super Cub was the 86.7cc (49 × 46mm) model. Coded C200 upon its debut in 1963, it became the C90 from 1965.

ful 1bhp boost in claimed power output. The latest model turned out 7.5bhp at 9,500rpm, as opposed to the pushrod's 6.5bhp at 7,500rpm.

By now, new small capacity Hondas were arriving thick and fast. Another newcomer for 1965 had been the neat little S65 sports machine with a 63cc (44 × 41.4mm) ohc, four-speeder capable of 6.2bhp at 10,000rpm.

Quite frankly, listing every new Honda single would need a book in itself. So I am concentrating my efforts on the more notable designs for the remainder of this chapter.

From 1 July 1965 the Honda S65 could be purchased in Britain for £114 19s. It had a capacity of 63cc (44 × 41.4mm) and produced 6.2bhp at 10,000rpm.

The P50 and CB125

One model that certainly deserves recognition was the P50 moped of 1967. This was a highly unusual design, with the 49.3cc (42 × 35.6mm) ohc engine being mounted in the rear wheel. Selling in the UK for only £52 4s 9d that year, it was so quiet that it was hard to tell when it was running – even when 'flat out' at 30mph (50km/h).

Another small Honda single deserving attention is the CB125S, the first of which arrived for the 1970 model year. This was quite a sporty little bike, with an ohc engine and a near-vertical cylinder, which displaced 121.9cc (56 × 49.5mm). With a compression ratio of 9.5:1, the CB125S produced a very good 12bhp at 9,000rpm. This when mated to a five-speed gearbox provided surprisingly fleet performance, especially when helped by a dry weight of only 200lb (90kg). One scribe, Ken Corkett, in describing the CB125S during a 1972 test, had this to say:

> I was going to describe the Honda 125 single as a simple, low-powered runabout for the learner rider or ride-to-work man who needs economy

transport. But when one considers the specification of the Honda: five-speed gearbox, chain-driven overhead camshaft, flashing indicators, main beam, neutral and indicator warning lights etc, it makes the old Bantam look rather sick, especially at £40 less than the Bantam price!

The CG125

The CG125 arrived in 1976. *Motorcycle Mechanic* described it as a 'Common Sense Package'. Unlike the CB125S, the CG125 was a pushrod, not an overhead cam engine. With a capacity of 124.1cc (56.5 × 49.5mm), it owed nothing to the earlier design and was much more of a budget affair. The power output was down to 11bhp at 9,000rpm, but in truth the performances of the two machines were similar. Colin Mayo reported the following after a July 1977 test:

> If city commuters are ever going to be persuaded that two wheels make more sense than steaming in a train, fuming in a car, or waiting for a bus, then it is a bike like Honda's new CG125 that will do it. And not just because it is so cheap to buy, the thing is so easy to ride. The whole package spells commonsense for the first time biker, the little Honda offering adequate performance, a high degree of manoeuvrability and astonishing fuel economy.

But whereas the CB125S cost £199 in June 1973, only four years later in July 1977 the less sophisticated CG125 cost a whopping £358 (both prices including UK taxes). This reflected the problem facing Honda (and the rest of the Japanese industry) – rising production costs. Just as the British industry had found it hard in the 1960s, the Japanese were beginning to experience the very same problems as the

The P50 moped of 1967 was a highly unusual design, the 49.3cc (42 × 35.6mm) ohc engine being mounted in the rear wheel.

The CB125S arrived in 1970, with an ohc 121.9cc (56 × 49.5mm), five-speed engine, producing 12bhp at 9,000rpm.

1970s unfolded. However, unlike the Brits, the Japanese responded by setting up local production plants in overseas export markets, certainly for the smaller capacity, lower cost models.

Even then, in later years from the early 1980s onwards, smaller Hondas dropped by the wayside to be replaced by ever larger, more expensive and complicated motorcycles. The era of the small single-cylinder commuter Honda was coming to an end, certainly in Western countries such as North America and Europe.

But one basic model bucked the trend – the original budget price, step-thru Super Cub, which was now being built in engine sizes up to the 90cc class. And as recorded earlier in this chapter the Super Cub series of single-cylinder Hondas has been produced in larger numbers than any other powered two-wheeler in history – a record of which Soichiro Honda and team could be justifiably proud.

The XR75 miniature motocrosser arrived in 1973 with a 71.8cc (47 × 41.4mm) ohc engine and four-speed gearbox. Here, road racer Paul Smart hides the Honda emblem as he was a works Suzuki rider at the time.

3 CB92 and Other Small Twins

The CB92 sportster (and its touring brother, the C92) arrived at the beginning of 1959, and in the author's opinion was one of the very best, if not the best of all early Japanese motorcycles (those built up to the 1960 model year).

It was, and still is, a true classic. This enthusiasm comes from ownership of a CB92 back in the early 1960s and my forty-five years of motorcycling experience, which has included virtually every facet of the sport. During 1958 a relatively small number of CB90 and C90 models were built, from which the CB92/C92 were developed. But it is the 92 series with which the Honda small twins' story really began in earnest. By 'small' twins, I mean those of less than 250cc, as these latter twins and above are featured in Chapter 4.

First Western News of the CB92

The first Western news of the new CB92 model appeared in the 5 February 1959 issue of *The Motor Cycle*, when 'Nitor', in his *On the Four Winds* column, presented the following news story, which although primarily concerned with Honda's arrival on the European scene, also provided an insight into the Japanese marque's existing series production machines:

The prospect of a trio of Japanese riders buzzing round the Clypse circuit on their 13,000rpm Honda twins in this year's Lightweight 125cc TT will surprise many enthusiasts. But the fact is the industry and sport are thriving much better there than many folk in Western Europe realize. When Eng. Niitsuma and adviser William Hunt [an American] called at Dorset House after their visit to the ACU last week, they brought news of mustard-hot enthusiasm, expansion and technical progress. Their own factory is the most flourishing of 30 or more manufacturers, including small builders of mopeds. Honda have been established for seven years [sic] and supply 36 per cent of the home market. There are, in fact two Honda factories. One makes a one-fifty roadster twin, with chain-driven overhead camshaft, coil ignition and electric starting, and a one-two-five twin in both roadster and sports-racing trim. The latter version has two camshafts [sic] and is claimed to develop 15bhp at 10,500rpm. The other factory turns out 247 and 305cc Dream roadster twins of similar layout to the one-fifty, and a 49cc, three-speed Super Cub ultra-lightweight with automatic clutch and, in common with the larger models, leading link front and pivoted rear forks.

Headed 'Technical Initiative', 'Nitor' continued:

Both factories use up-to-date production methods; the spine frames are made from steel pressings and plastic mouldings are extensively employed on the Super Cub. In overall appearance all models bear unmistakable evidence of West German inspiration. Incidentally, the makers seem to have a passion for high revs: the 49cc model peaks at 9,500rpm, while the 247 and 305cc Dreams are built to run at 8,400 and 8,000rpm respectively. But perhaps the most significant sign of a developing technical initiative is the fact that Hondas are experimenting with a coupled braking system incorporating an automatic anti-locking device. The factory, by the way, has its own ¾-mile tarmac test circuit.

Talk of the coupled braking system and anti-locking device is a reminder of just how technically forward-thinking Honda was, even at the end of the 1950s. BMW, during the late 1980s, may have been the first bike manufacturer to offer customers ABS, but Honda had already tested a system some three decades earlier!

'Nitor's' column was illustrated with only two photographs. These showed the standard and race kit CB92 Super Sport models. Originally, Honda had entered the Formula 1 TT with a trio of CB92s, only for the entry to be returned as the F1 class was for 350 and 500cc machines only.

The CB92 and C92 arrive in the UK

Imports of the CB92 and its touring brother, the C92 began in the UK during late 1961. One of the first dealers to stock these machines on behalf of the British concessionaires, Maico Ltd, was Patricroft Motorcycles of 344 Liverpool Road, Eccles, Manchester.

Advertising themselves as Manx GP and TT rider/agents, the firm offered the CB92 in standard trim for £207 3s 2d. But with a specially tuned engine, megaphones, racing camshaft, rev counter and dropped handlebars, they said 'Top is in excess of 103mph (with optional dolphin fairing fitted)' – whereas the standard model was claimed to give 81mph. The tuned bike being listed by Patricroft

Motorcycles at £265. Sprockets, jets, etc were also available.

Testing the CB92

Road tests of the CB92 in the British press were few and far between. But in 1964, after imports were being handled by European Honda Ltd of Power Road, West London, one machine, registration number 573PG, was put on the road test fleet. This was subsequently tested by *Motorcycle Mechanics* in February 1964 and *Motor Cycling* in the latter's 4 July 1964 issue.

The report in *Mechanics* began by saying:

A 125cc motorcycle with the performance of a 250cc machine! This one sentence briefly describes the incredible twin-cylinder, four-

One of the very first CB92 models built in early 1959. Note the guard at the rear of the head and barrel, which was dispensed with on later production versions. Note also the lack of electric starter motor (at the front of the crankcase).

speed, overhead camshaft Honda Sports 125. With a cruising speed of between 60 and 65 miles-an-hour and a top speed approaching the 80 miles-an-hour mark, Honda have completely altered the general impression that a 125cc motorcycle is an underpowered 45mph run-about machine.

At first, the *Motorcycle Mechanics* tester was 'disappointed by what seemed a very mediocre performance'. But of course small sporting Honda twins thrived on high revs – the CB92 would really show its true colours at between six and ten thousand revs, as I know from personal experience. The tester went on to say:

> In many ways this dual-personality mount is ideal, for at low engine revs about town, it is a very docile mount which one can ride at walking pace in first gear and idle at thirty-miles-an-hour in top. Then, if one wants soaring acceleration for over-taking a lorry or bus, it is simply a matter of changing down a couple of cogs to build up the revs, opening the throttle and hanging on!

First-Class Brakes

A giant twin-leading shoe front brake was fully up to pukka racing standards, whilst the CB92 also had an equally large 7.87in (200mm) full-width drum at the rear, the latter 'only' a single-leading shoe-type. The two brakes combined to provide truly first-class braking. The riding position was also excellent, with the deeply contoured tank and almost flat handlebars proving comfortable, even over quite long distances. Also, again from personal experience, the CB92 was fully capable of accommodating a pillion passenger – but this was something owners had to devise themselves, as although the little bike was equipped with a dual seat, there was no provision for passenger footrests.

Early Hondas had a reputation for over-soft suspension with almost no rear damping. But on the 1964 version of the CB92 this fault was not so apparent. If anything, the suspension was a shade too hard. But this did have the advantage of giving hairline steering and no apparent frame flex. The only thing which could be criticized was the machine's tendency to dive at the front under heavy braking, due to the leading link fork design.

Like other Honda twins of the era, the CB92 was equipped with an electric starter, and as *Motorcycle Mechanic* said 'consequently starting proves no hardship. Even on the coldest day. One simply switches on the ignition, half closes the choke (a lever being set in the carb) and then presses the starter button. No choke was needed for warm starting.'

A Detailed Examination

The *Motor Cycling* CB92 test was extremely detailed and began:

> Three years ago, the Honda CB92 Benly Super Sport established itself as the fastest 125 that *Motor Cycling* had ever tested. The current model maintains this distinction. It also shows a marked improvement in what had been the original machine's weakest feature, suspension – although this is not yet perfect. The remarkable top-end performance of the single ohc engine is paid for in flexibility; this is a motor which must be kept within a narrow rev band (which is no hardship with such a good gearbox). But there is no other concession to 'sports' specification; silencing is extremely effective and standard equipment, including an electric starter, is lavish. Brakes are excellent. Summary: A very sophisticated piece of high-class Japanese engineering.

The Jekyll and Hyde character of the CB92's motor was aptly described by the *Motor Cycling* tester, Bruce Main-Smith: 'There is a marked "step" in the output, the cut-in (from 7,000rpm) being predictable and almost savage in the briskness of the acceleration it produces.'

As before, the brakes received high praise:

Superlative under every heading, the 8-inch stoppers were among the very best we have tested. The two-leading-shoe front unit – a type which can often be fierce – was perfection itself. Exceptionally good was the brick-wall stopping when it was used to pull up hard at main wall baulks. Equally effective was the single leading shoe back brake. Neither unit had any vices. Both were waterproof and fade-free.

Six-Volt Electrics

Although 'only' of 6V, the electrics of the CB92 were good. Even prolonged use of the starter motor or lights didn't seem to matter – whilst the wind-tone horn was, *Motor Cycling* said, 'extremely effective'.

The general equipment came in for praise. According to *Motor Cycling*: 'Abounding in neat features, like the rubber padding to the tank and the very stout silencer brackets of unusual type and rigidity, the CB92 shows careful detail design.'

As for maintenance, as I know from personal experience, this was good – unless a major engine stripdown was required. It was also good at keeping its tune (helped by a single 20mm Keihin carb). Valve clearances, at around a minute per rocker, were easily set up. Contact breakers were equally accessible, via a circular cover on the nearside (left) of the engine. The spark plugs were located on the side of the head, deeply angled, at the same level as the exhaust header pipes. To the casual observers the plugs appeared much lower than on other engines. However, this was because the cylinder head on the CB92/C92 engine was very tall. The optional rev counter drove off the offside (right) and off the camshaft. Oil level for the fully unit construction, wet-sump engine was checked in an

Roy Francis racing the ex-Bill Ivy CB92 at Thruxton in 1964. It was fitted with MV Agusta telescopic front forks in place of the Honda leading link type.

A CB92 engine, with single carb, alloy head, cast-iron barrel; spine type, pressed-steel frame and rev counter drive.

instant by a car-type dipstick, but the filler orifice was unusually small. To get the best of the CB92's engine performance it was best to use the original equipment NGK spark plugs. The rear chain adjusters were marked for ease of wheel alignment, while both front and rear wheels were easy to remove – and replace. All routine maintenance tasks could be carried out with the 'as supplied' tool kit.

Technical Details

The basic engine design was shared by both the 124.7cc (44 × 41mm) and 154.6cc (49 × 41mm) sizes. The cylinders were inclined forward by some 40 degrees from the vertical on the parallel twin, sohc layout. Camshaft drive was by a chain running off the centre of the 360-degree crankshaft to a matching sprocket in the centre of the camshaft. Drive to the starter motor (situated at the front of the engine) was also by chain, whereas primary drive was by gears.

In many ways, the design mirrored that of the existing 250 and 305cc twins (see Chapter 4), including the plunger pump pressure lubrication with gravity return to the wet-sump,

The BMF Concours D'Elegance 1974 at Woburn Park, with an immaculate CB92 and Douglas fore-and-aft twin in the background.

1959 CB92 Specifications

Engine	Air-cooled sohc parallel twin with cylinders inclined 40 degrees, alloy head, cast-iron barrel, unit construction, 180- degree crankshaft, horizontally split aluminium crankcases, chain-driven camshaft	Front suspension	Leading link fork
		Rear suspension	Swinging arm, twin shock absorbers
		Front brake	2LS drum, full-width hub
		Rear brake	5LS drum, full-width hub
		Tyres	Front 2.50 × 18, rear 2.75 × 18
Bore	44mm		
Stroke	41mm		
Displacement	124.7cc		
Compression ratio	10:1	**General Specifications**	
Lubrication	Plunger pump, wet sump	Wheelbase	49.6in (1,260mm)
Ignition	6V, coil/battery, with auto advance	Ground clearance	6in (152mm)
Carburettor	Keihin 22mm	Seat height	29.5in (749mm)
Primary drive	Gears	Fuel tank capacity	N/A
Final drive	Chain	Dry weight	242lb (110kg)
Gearbox	Four speeds; foot-change	Maximum power	15bhp @ 10,500rpm
Frame	Spine-type, built from steel pressings; engine as stressed member	Top speed	80mph (130km/h)

horizontally split crankcases and a four-speed gearbox in unit with the engine.

The C92/C95

The C92 and C95 Benly touring models were identical to each other, apart from the bigger 154.6cc C95 having a 5mm larger bore size than the 124.7cc C92. The engine design at least closely followed that of the CB92 already described above. And like the sporting 125, both 125 and 150 touring models were equipped with the same electric starter motor mounted at the front of the

crankcases and driving the crankshaft through double reduction of gears and chain, and again the electric starter was supplemented by a conventional kick-starter (whose main purpose was freeing the clutch plates before the first cold start of the day). Also, and unlike the 250/305 twins, all the 125 and 150 Hondas of

The CB92's touring brother, the C92, came fully equipped with electric start, fully enclosed drive chain, comprehensive mudguarding, dual seat – note the pump at the base of the dual seat.

the late 1950s and early 1960s had a 6V electrical system. The actual layout was coil ignition with auto advance, whilst there was a 50W alternator, with the rotor mounted on the nearside end of the crankshaft, charging an 11-amp hour battery through a rectifier.

As with the CB92 Super Sport, the C92 and C95 were certainly not simply poor relations to their bigger 250/305 brothers; far from it indeed. In fact, the C92/95 were actually better balanced motorcycles than their respective C72/77 brothers, because the over-soft suspension of the early Honda touring twins was not overstretched as it was on the larger engined models. The smaller engines (like the CB92) were also considerably smoother. All in all, unless you regularly needed to carry a pillion passenger, the 125/150 Honda twins had much to offer.

Value for Money

As *The Motor Cycle* said in its 18 May 1961 issue: 'The Benly's [they were testing a C92 125] trump card is its sheer value for money. For less than £180, including purchase tax, it offers a luxury specification including push-button starting, transmission enclosure and flashing turn indicators, while its above-average road performance goes hand-in-hand with quietness, cleanliness, economy and tirelessness.'

In fact, the engine was one of the very best of its type ever offered, certainly as regards its high level of sophistication. *The Motor Cycle* lavished praise:

> Slow and dependable, idling was so unobtrusive as to make it difficult to determine whether the engine was running or not when among other vehicles at traffic stops. Never, at any engine revs from idling to valve float, did the twin silencers emit more than a very subdued drone, which was inaudible to the rider when on the move. The only indication of engine speed was the pitch of the induction hum, augmented by a little general mechanical clatter.

A mechanic working on an early C92; note the squared angles on components such as the rear shock and rear mudguard.

But as with the CB92, the C92/95 really came into its own at high engine revolutions, when the power unit was at its best for acceleration and hill climbing. Certainly to retain maximum performance the motor had to be kept on the boil. But as *The Motor Cycle* pointed out: 'This is no disadvantage since, as mentioned, silencing is really effective, rubber mountings for the power unit and handlebar insulate the rider from vibration, and the engine is happy to run at high revs indefinitely.'

Smaller Carb, Lower Compression Ratio

Whereas the sporting CB92 had a 22mm carburettor, the C92 (and C95) came with a smaller Keihin PW18H (18mm) instrument. Likewise, the C92 had a compression ratio of 8.3:1 (C95 8.6:1), whilst the CB92 had a loftier 10:1 ratio. This, of course, showed in the power output figures: C92 11.5bhp at 9,500rpm; C95 13.5bhp at 9,500rpm; CB92 5bhp at 10,500rpm.

Other major differences between the touring and sports models were wheel and brake sizes. The sportster was equipped with 18in rims, the C92/95 tourers 16in. As already described, the CB92 had huge 200mm (nearly 8in) brakes, with a 2LS at the front, whereas the lower-powered models came with much smaller 6.5in (160mm) diameter front and rear SLS full-width alloy hubs.

During its 1961 test *The Motor Cycle* achieved a highest one-way speed of 66mph (106km/h), whereas *Motor Cycling* achieved 68.6mph (110km/h) in a C92 test published on 1 August 1962. The same journal said 'The Honda C92 is something of an Oriental enigma. It packs a quart's performance into a pint pot, failing by only a few mph to match the speed of the standard 250, yet it has the economy, tractability and low cost of a practicable ride-to-work or touring mount.'

But, as with the C72/77, 'Low ground clearance and 16in tyres took their toll, however. On the right, the rear brake pedal and the footrest rubber could be grounded and on the left, the alloy propstand had a considerable amount of metal removed while the footrest took such a hammering that its tip took on a pronounced rearway setting.'

But as *The Motor Cycle* said: 'Styling is essentially a matter of taste. With continuous curves replaced by separate faces wherever possible, that of the Honda is certainly distinctive.' *Motor Cyclist Illustrated* editor, Cyril Quantrill, said of the C92 in an August 1964 test, 'Finished in blue and chrome, it looks something like an NSU.' Also that it 'looked much bigger than its 125cc capacity'.

The CB160

The next new small Honda twin was the CB160. Although this sported an unusual engine size − actually 161cc (50 × 41mm) − it was, in many ways, the best of the breed, and was to be responsible for a whole series of models which in turn grew to encompass 175, 185 and finally 200cc in future years.

The CB160 was most definitely a sports mount. Also, compared with the CB92, it had the advantage of twin carburettors (Keihin

---

1958 C95/1959 C92 Specifications (C92 in brackets where different)

Engine	Air-cooled sohc parallel twin with cylinders inclined 40 degrees, alloy head, cast-iron barrel, unit construction, 360-degree pressed-up crankshaft, horizontally split aluminium crankcase, chain-driven camshaft	Front suspension	Leading link fork
		Rear suspension	Swinging-arm, twin shock absorbers
		Front brake	SLS drum, full-width hub
		Rear brake	SLS drum, full-width hub
		Tyres	3.00 × 16 front and rear
Bore	49mm (C92: 44mm)		
Stroke	41mm		
Displacement	154.6cc (C92: 124.7cc)	**General Specifications**	
Compression ratio	8.6:1 (C92: 8.5:1)	Wheelbase	49.8in (1,265mm)
Lubrication	Plunger pump, wet sump	Ground clearance	5in (127mm)
Ignition	6V, battery/coil with auto advance	Seat height	28.5in (724mm)
Carburettor	Keihin 18mm	Fuel tank capacity	N/A
Primary drive	Gears	Dry weight kg	264lb (120kg)
Final drive	Chain	Maximum power	13.5bhp @ 9,500rpm (C92: 11.5bhp @ 9,500rpm)
Gearbox	Four speeds; foot-change		
Frame	Spine-type, built from steel pressings; engine as stressed member	Top speed	C95 65mph (105km/h) (C92: 62mph (100km/h))

Felix Apicella with his 1965 C95 (154.6cc – 49 × 41mm), the larger-engined version of the 124.7cc C92, circa 1968. The higher bars arrived from 1964.

22mm instruments) and a much-improved frame design and suspension package. In fact, the frame and suspension (telescopic forks at the front) were so good that a number of CB160s were used to house Yamaha 125 twins during the early 1970s for road racing! This was because the CB160 closely resembled the chassis of the CR93 production racer (see Chapter 9).

When Charles Deane tested the CB160 on which Honda dealer Artie Shaw had visited four capitals in one twenty-four-hour ride in the March 1965 issue of *Motor Cyclist Illustrated*, he said:

> Honda breed motorcycles quicker than a magician can pull rabbits out of a hat. They are not modified copies of what has gone before but entirely new machines, right down to the shape of the speedometer. And they are built from the experience gained not only from racing but also from the success and failings of previous models.

Deane went on:

> For example, the suspension of Honda sports models has always been too rigid, giving a rather uncomfortable ride on bumpy surfaces. This com-

The CB160 arrived in spring 1965 and sported the unusual 161cc (50 _ 41mm) engine size and was, in many ways, the best of all the sub-250cc Honda twins. The chassis and suspension provided racer-like handling and were based on the CR93 production racer.

plaint no longer applies to the new CB160. In the past, Honda sports engines have been high-revving, intractable motors which lacked power at anything below 6,000rpm. Once again, you won't find this mistake repeated in the design of the CB160. This entirely new Honda is one of the best machines ever to roll off the assembly line in Japan.

A 360-Degree Crankshaft

As before, the 360-degree crankshaft rotation allowed the pistons to rise and fall in unison and there were horizontally split light-alloy castings which formed the crankcase and gear-box shell. The oil pump was driven by an eccentric and bell-crank from behind the clutch drum, together with the centrifugal oil filter carried on the drive-side end of the four-bearing (three roller, one ball) crankshaft. The primary drive system was new and was by split, fine-tooth, straight-cut pinions, with the teeth staggered to cut out backlash and thus reduce the load on individual teeth.

Again, the drive to the single overhead camshaft was by simplex chain enclosed in a tunnel between the two cylinders, with a tensioner that automatically adjusted itself when a single lock-nut was slackened. A major change was a move from 6V to 12V electrics. The starter motor was chain-driven and was still located at the front of the engine.

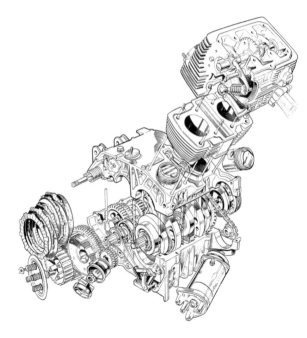

ABOVE: The 161cc (50 × 41mm) CB160 engine with dual primary drive gears, wet multi-plate clutch, four speeds and chain drives for the sohc and electric starter motor.

LEFT: Artie Shaw, a dealer in Welling, Kent, organized a 'Four Capitals in Twenty-Four Hours' ride in early 1965. Here are the two CB160s which took part, with Big Ben in the background.

All the major engine castings of the CB160 were aluminium, with the cylinder block featuring shrink-fit steel liners. Interestingly, on the other twin-carb Honda engines of the period (the 250 CB72 and 305 CB77), Honda employed a cast-in iron 'skull' into the combustion chambers and cut the valve seats in the skull. However, with the CB160 conventional inserted valve seats were used. The cylinder head also featured long manifold pipes out to the carburettors, whereas the CB72/77 had its bolted right up to the head, with rubber air-cleaner hoses providing the necessary tuned length. The CB160 arrangement was superior, also having the added advantage of keeping engine heat away from the carbs.

Boring the Cylinders Out to 50mm

The displacement of 161cc had been achieved by increasing the 125's box size from 44 to 50mm, whilst the stroke remained unchanged at 41mm. A major change was that the ignition contact breaker points had been transferred from the end of the crankshaft up to the nearside end of the camshaft. With a compression ratio of 8.5:1, the CB160 produced a maximum power output of 16.5bhp at 10,000rpm and still retained the 125s four-speed gearbox in unit with the engine, but with revised ratios.

Although of 2LS, the front (and rear brakes) of the CB160 were not the same as either the CB92 or C92/95 – in appearance, if not exact design, they were similar to the existing ones found on the CB72/77 series. This meant full-width polished aluminium hubs of a particularly neat design (*Motorcycle Mechanics* described them as 'a masterpiece of alloy and chrome with neat adjusters and rubber cable protectors'.)

The frame was generally agreed to provide the best handling of any production Honda roadster up to that time. It had a tubular design much like the CB72/77, but the tubes which braced the steering head and picked up the engine's cylinder head lugs were disposed in a manner very reminiscent of the duplex racing frames used on the works 4-cylinder two-fifty. But there was still no conventional front down-tube as one would have found on most European bikes; instead, the engine was employed as a stressed member as on the other early twin-

---

1964 CB160 Specifications

Engine	Air-cooled sohc parallel twin, alloy head and barrel, chain-driven camshaft, unit construction, 36-degree pressed-up crankshaft, horizontally split aluminium crankcase	Frame	Tubular spine frame, with engine as a stressed member
		Front suspension	Oil-damped telescopic forks
		Rear suspension	Swinging arm, twin shock absorbers
		Front brake	2LS drum, full-width
Bore	50mm	Rear brake	SLS drum, full-width
Stroke	41mm	Tyres	Front 2.50 × 18, rear 2.75 × 18
Displacement	161cc		
Compression ratio	8.5:1	**General Specifications**	
Lubrication	Plunger pump, wet sump	Wheelbase	51in (1,295mm)
Ignition	Battery powered double coil, with single contact	Ground clearance	6.5in (165mm)
		Seat height	30.6in (777mm)
Carburettor	2 × Keihin 22mm	Fuel tank capacity	N/A
Primary drive	Gears	Dry weight	246lb (112kg)
Final drive	Chain	Maximum power	16.5bhp @ 10,000rpm
Gearbox	Four speeds; foot-change	Top speed	79mph (127km/h)

cylinder Honda range (except the new CB450 dohc model).

When Charles Deane concluded his March 1965 test in *Motor Cyclist Illustrated* he commented:

> I'm British and proud of it and I reckon we produce the best biggest bangers in the world, but where, oh where, can you find a lightweight to compare with the Japanese machines? Looking at the CB160 overall, I would say that the riding position is extremely comfortable, the power and acceleration from such a small motor are surprising and that roadholding and braking are both first-class. One possible slight criticism – a little engine vibration about halfway up the rev scale. Apart from this and the tyres, I can only say it is a superb little machine and all for £227 19s 0d including purchase tax.

New 125s

In the mid-1960s a series of new 125-class machines began to appear. Effectively, this new family was to replace the C92/CB92 models. The first of the newcomers to make its bow was the CB125 (with CL and CD variants). This was then followed in mid-1967 by the SS125 (and CS).

The CB employed a semi-tubular frame, twin Keihin carburettors and telescopic front forks, with 18in wheels, whereas the SS125 had a pressed-steel frame, single Keihin CV2 21HA carb, telescopic forks with rubber gaiters and 17in wheels. And it is worth noting that all the 125 roadster twins had four-speed gearboxes until the CB125 gained five-speed from 1969. Bore and stroke dimensions of 44 × 41mm remained as before. The SS125A retailed at £174 19s in the UK during 1968.

The CB175 replaced the CB160 for the 1968 model year. Its 174.1cc (52 × 41mm) ohc engine produced 20bhp at 10,000rpm.

The CB175

The new CD175 (*see* Chapter 8) arrived in 1967, followed by its more sporting brother, the CB175, the next year. Both shared the same basic 174.1cc (52 × 41mm) engine, which was a new unit and not simply a larger version of the CB160, even though both the 175 and 160 had four speeds. The CB175 put out a healthy 20bhp at 10,000rpm, which assured sprightly performance. A major change between the 160 and 175 was the frame, which was now of the full cradle type. When tested by *Motorcycle Mechanics* in June 1971, the CB175 K4 reached a maximum speed of 86mph (138km/h). According to the tester: 'The price for a 175cc bike at £280 including tax may seem a bit steep, but when you take into consideration the performance, which is almost equal to the 500 singles of just a few years ago, plus all the accessories such as flashing indicators, electric start, etc., the price begins to make some sense.'

Generally, the finish of the CB175 was considered 'excellent', although Charles Deane commented that 'some of the welding on the frame could be better'. He also said:'The toolbox location and construction is also tatty in that not only does water easily find its way into the toolbox, but the tools have to be carefully arranged in the wallet before they may be inserted in the box.' There was also criticism that: 'the CB175 is far happier as a solo machine, for although it will transport two people, and is equipped to do so, the rear suspension bottoms over bumps and the small size of the bike makes for cramped riding for all but two of the smallest people'. But in fairness, these last comments could equally apply to most of the machines covered in this chapter.

There were now separate, circular speedometer and rev counter 'clocks', which were similar to other Hondas of the late 1960s and early 1970s. Generally, the CB175 was a sound, reliable design which stood the test of time well, before being superseded by the CB200 from 1973. Several versions of the 175 series were offered by Honda – the CB, CD, plus the CL, SL and GL variants.

The CB200

Honda replaced the CB175 with the CB200 – much the same as it did with the CD series (*see* Chapter 8 – although in the latter case the CD185 came before the CD200). The 200 displaced 198.4cc (55.5 × 41mm), which, as with the 175, had been achieved with an increase in bore size (by 5.5mm over the 175). Although the compression ratio was reduced slightly (from 9.1 to 9:1) and the carburettor size had been reduced from 22 to 20 – there were still twin Keihin instruments. But the 12V 9-amp hour battery remained, as did the electric starter.

Some of the later 175s had five-speed gearboxes, a feature which was retained for the CB200. Cycle parts of the 175 and 200 CB series were closely related, although the fuel-tank, seat and side panels were different. However, the 200 retained the 175's chrome-plated (and rust-prone) mudguards. The 18in wheel

CL175 (not imported into the UK) at the Tokyo Show in October 1969. This was a Street Scrambler version of the popular 175 ohc twin, which was also sold in CD, CB, GL and SL guises.

1968 CB 175 Specifications

Engine	Air-cooled sohc parallel twin, alloy head and barrel, chain-driven camshaft, unit construction, 360-degree, pressed-up crankshaft, horizontally split aluminium crankcases	Front suspension	Oil-damped telescopic forks
		Rear suspension	Swinging arm, twin shock absorbers
		Front brake	2LS full-width alloy drum
		Rear brake	SLS full-width alloy drum
		Tyres	Front 2.75 × 18, rear 3.00 × 18
Bore	52mm		
Stroke	41mm		
Displacement	174.1cc	**General Specifications**	
Compression ratio	9.1:1	Wheelbase	50.3in (1,278mm)
Lubrication	Plunger pump, wet sump	Ground clearance	6in (152mm)
Ignition	12V; battery/coil	Seat height	30in (762mm)
Carburettor	21 × Keihin 22mm	Fuel tank capacity	N/A
Primary drive	Gears	Dry weight	264lb (120kg)
Final drive	Chain	Maximum power	20bhp @ 10,000rpm
Gearbox	Four speeds; foot-change	Top speed	86mph (138km/h)
Frame	Full cradle		

size and 2.75 (front) and 3.00 (rear) section tyres were also the same.

Most CB200s, at least those imported into the UK, had a single disc front brake; this was unusual in being cable-operated. The disc brake version arrived in mid-1975 and was known as the CB200B; the full-width alloy drum was retained at the rear. There is no dis-

The CB200 (198.4cc – 55.5 × 41mm) arrived in 1973 and was built with either a drum (shown) or disc front brake. Although no quicker than the 175, it proved popular in the mid to late 1970s.

47

The Juno Scooter

Although best known for its lightweight sports and touring motorcycles – plus of course the bestselling Super Cub 'step-thru' – in its formative years Honda also built and sold a number of different scooters. These included the K (1955–199cc) and the massively faired 219cc (70 × 57mm), both with ohv single-cylinder engines and three-speed gearboxes. Then in 1960 came the M80 powered by a 124.9cc (43 × 43mm) ohv horizontally opposed twin-cylinder engine featuring variable transmission. This latter machine was the forerunner of the little-known luxury scooter coded M85, but more commonly known as the Juno. This used the same basic engine as the M80 and debuted in 1962.

So what exactly was the Juno? Briefly described, it was something of a technical masterpiece, featuring a flat-twin engine of 168.9cc (50 × 43mm), which, running on a compression ratio of 8.5:1, produced 12bhp at 7,600rpm. Other details of this impressive machine included 12V electrics, push-button starting and a truly de luxe specification. But, like the earlier M80 model, what really set it apart was the transmission – a hydraulic device incorporating a swashplate pump and motor, providing infinitely variable gearing (controlled by the nearside twistgrip) between limits of 21.75 and 6.25:1.

Although an example was displayed at the London Earls Court Show in November 1962, no Junos were ever officially imported into Britain. But one did reach the UK, when the Lucas electrical concern, based in Birmingham, imported an example. This may come as a surprise to readers, but Lucas often imported foreign motorcycles (and cars) to examine technical progress abroad. From Lucas the Juno was transferred to the Ferguson tractor concern – who were interested in hydraulics. It then passed to one of that company's engineers, who subsequently sold it to Bicester dealer, Eric Trindor.

The origin of the hydraulic transmission was not Japanese but Italian, having been originally devised by the Rome-based Cambi Idraulici Baldini SpA. It was first exhibited on a 175 MV Agusta at the 1954 Milan Show. I fully described this system in my 1987 Osprey book, *MV Agusta – All Production Road & Racing Motorcycles*, but briefly it operated as follows.

Imagine a shaft on which a disc is set at an angle.

Next, surround the shaft with a number of cylinders in the same plane; each cylinder has a piston, the end of which is in contact with the inclined disc. As the shaft rotates, the disc revolves with a wobbly motion and, in doing so, causes the pistons to move up and down in the stationary ring of cylinders. If the cylinders are filled with oil, we have a kind of pump.

The second part of the transmission is more or less similar, except that the ring of the cylinders is attached to and rotates with the shaft, whilst the disc (technically called a swashplate) is stationary. If each cylinder of the pump is coupled to the corresponding cylinder in the motor unit, then the pump shaft rotates, oil pressure causes the piston in the motor cylinder to bear against the stationary swashplate and since the swashplate can't rotate, the ring of the cylinders, and with it the shaft, is driven around. It is also important to realize that, although the swashplate of the motor is stationary, its angle of inclination can be altered (in the Juno, this was done by the twistgrip), hence the speed of the motor shaft can be varied relative to that of the pump shaft. In other words, a hydraulic gearbox.

The Juno had no clutch in the normal manner. Instead, the conventional lever on the handlebar operated a bypass valve, allowing the pump to rotate without transmitting oil pressure to the motor (but, for most purposes, the lever could be totally ignored).

This might all appear rather complex, but actually riding the Juno was simplicity itself. A touch of the starter button brought the Juno to life – and the only precaution necessary before moving off was to check that the nearside grip was wound forward to the 'low' position. From then it was merely a matter of opening the throttle and the scooter took up its drive. As one tester of the period said: 'There is a fascination in holding the throttle position steady and varying the scooter's speed with the gear grip. And I've never ridden anything so uncannily smooth.'

Weighing in at 345lb (157kg), the Juno was capable of almost 60mph (98km/h), but it was such a nicely balanced machine that the weight was hardly noticed once under way.

Most Junos were sold on the domestic Japanese market, but a few were exported to North America. Today it is one of the rarest of all 'classic' Hondas.

1975 CB200 Specifications

Engine	Air-cooled sohc parallel twin, alloy head and barrel, chain-driven camshaft, unit construction, 360-degree crankshaft, horizontally split crankcases	Front suspension	Oil-damped telescopic forks
		Rear suspension	Swinging arm, twin shock-absorbers
Bore	55.5mm	Front brake	Drum or cable-operated disc
Stroke	41mm	Rear brake	SLS drum
Displacement	198.4cc	Tyres	Front 2.75 × 18, rear 3.00 × 18
Compression ratio	9:1		
Lubrication	Pump, wet sump	**General Specifications**	
Ignition	12V battery/coil	Wheelbase	50.78in (1,290mm)
Carburettor	2 × Keihin 20mm	Ground clearance	6.10in (155mm)
Primary drive	Gears	Seat height	30.70in (780mm)
Final drive	Chain	Fuel tank capacity	1.98gal (9ltr)
Gearbox	Five speeds; foot-change	Dry weight	291lb (132kg)
Frame	Full cradle	Maximum power	18bhp
		Top speed	81mph (130km/h)

puting that the 1975 CB200B looked like a real motorcycle.

Power-wise, the 200 was no different from the 175 version. However, the CB200 owner could expect far superior bottom-end and mid-range punch. As Dave Minton said in a 1975 test: 'This, to my mind, is a worthy sacrifice in view of the pleasanter and uncomplicated high average speeds possible.' He continued: 'Even when punching into a headwind on a motorway at 70mph, I found no necessity to drop down into fourth cog; not bad at all for a little twin like this, eh? And all done on 2-star petrol.'

There is no doubt that the Honda engineering team had made the CB200 much more civilized than the earlier small twin sportsters. Dave Minton, concluding his 1975

test, stated: 'All in all, the Honda CB200 is a super little machine. Powerful enough for long journeys, economical enough to satisfy Scrooge himself. A luxuriously equipped "utility" without the need for a new owner to spend a penny on further equipment to complete it.'

The CB200 was also to be the last of the small (under 250cc Honda) twins, except for the 125, which was to continue, in updated form, into the 1980s. Certainly in Britain at least, once new learner laws were introduced at the dawn of the 1980s restricting novice riders to a maximum of 125cc, the market for 150–200cc machines effectively died. A great pity really, because machines such as the CB92, CB160, CB175 and CB200 were some of Honda's best lower-capacity motorcycles.

4 C/CB72/77 Series

The very first Honda twin, the C70, was launched in September 1957. It had come from Soichiro Honda's drawing board, but was quite heavily influenced by his European visit of 1954 (*see* Chapter 1). Of all the companies Soichiro had visited, it had been the German NSU marque that had impressed him most. And with the new C70, the NSU – and other German influence – was clear to see.

The C70 Described

Although Honda's brand-new twin was influenced by Germanic engineering practices, the actual design was of Soichiro Honda's own pen. It was extremely modern, featuring an all-aluminium single overhead camshaft engine constructed in unit with the gearbox and clutch. The aluminium crankcases were split horizontally, which helped in making the engine extremely oil-tight.

The cylinders were inclined forward by some 30 degrees. With square bore and stroke dimensions of 54 × 54mm, the engine displaced 247cc, which, running on a compression ratio of 8.2:1, produced a maximum power output of 18bhp at 7,400rpm. Top speed was in the region of 75mph (120km/h); which in itself was a considerable achievement in the late 1950s.

In adopting the 360-degree crankshaft, which meant the pistons rose and fell in unison, Honda was following the format used by the British vertical twins such as Triumph, BSA, Norton and others. And like the British

machine, the C70 (and other early Honda 250 and 305 twins) used a dry-sump lubrication system.

A chain-drive camshaft system was employed. This saw a simplex chain connecting the camshaft in the cylinder head to the centre of the crankshaft, passing up through tunnels in the cylinder block and head under the control of guide rollers and tensioners.

A Pressed-Up Crankshaft

The C70 twin featured a pressed-up crankshaft, which was supported by four (two ball-race and two roller) main bearings (the British designs employed either two or three mains). Whilst the big ends were rollers, with the small ends carrying three-ring cast aluminium pistons, the camshaft itself ran directly in the head, the rockers operating 2- valves-per-cylinder, supported by coil springs. An ignition cam, together with an advance and retard mechanism, was to be found on the nearside of the camshaft end. Outboard of these was a distributor to fire a high-tension current to the appropriate spark plug.

Engine-Speed Clutch

An engine-speed clutch was a feature of Honda's first twin. This sat on the nearside (left) end of the crankshaft, which together with the alternator being located on the off-side (right), made for a reasonably wide engine. However, due to clever design, it wasn't over-wide. Another feature was gear primary drive, whilst the mainshaft of the gearbox was extended to the left to carry a centrifugal oil filter (this being simply a hollow drum through which the oil passed). As for the clutch itself, this was a wet, multi-plate device.

A Four-Speed Gearbox

A foot-operated four-speed gearbox was of the crossover design, featuring an output sprocket mounted on a sleeve gear on the off-side which was concentric with the mainshaft. This meant that the gearbox was not all-indirect and its layshaft was located at the rear of the mainshaft.

Gear selection was controlled by a barrel cam with the positive stop mechanism on the nearside, as was the foot-change pedal. This latter feature is particularly notable, as at that time the European industry had standardized on the offside. Today, at the beginning of the twenty-first century, the gear change is on the left – Honda and the rest of Japan long since having won the argument!

Final drive was by chain on the offside. It was fully enclosed with an all-enveloping case; the kick-starter was positioned on the same side of the machine.

The Chassis and Suspension

The chassis and suspension were very much designed for comfort rather than roadholding abilities. It must be remembered that when Soichiro Honda first laid down the C70 design in 1956, the main sales were to those needing everyday, reliable, comfortable transport – not an out-and-out sports bike. Even so, the combination of a pressed-steel, spine-type frame, leading link front forks and non-adjustable rear shock absorbers caused problems, unless a gentle throttle hand was applied – certainly over poorly surfaced roads. One tester commented: 'The suspension, which is unusually soft by European standards, provided armchair comfort at touring speeds. On the open road, however, the lack of adequate damping caused severe pitching over undulations; a turn of the steering damper was needed to steady the navigation on fast, bumpy bends.'

The front forks were very similar in general layout to those already used on the company's ohc singles, with short leading links and the spring unit hidden away behind the pressed-metal legs. Like the frame, the forks were built up from a series of metal pressings

The main difference between the 247cc C70, which was launched in September 1957 and the C71 (right, immaculately restored by the late David Livesey), was that the latter featured an electric start. A feature of these, the earliest of Honda's 250 twins, was an engine speed clutch (note the different engine cover compared to the later versions).

welded together and featured an unconventional rectangular section (as did the deeply valanced mudguards). The rear shocks were also of squared-section design, as was the headlamp shell, and, to a lesser degree, the fuel tank and side panels.

The Wheels

Both wheels carried 3.25 × 16 tyres. Again, compared with European machines this was quite unusual, but did have the advantage of providing a lower seat height. However, it didn't do much for ground clearance, with the result that the C70 was very prone to grounding (stand, silencers).

There were superbly cast (and polished) full-width light-alloy hubs, both featuring single leading-shoe operation; the front back plate was floating and was retained by a torque arm stay. Strangely, the rear brake was much more effective than the front stopper.

A Comprehensive Specification

Where the new Honda really shone was its comprehensive specification and attention to detail. For example, the handlebars were shrouded (by painted steel pressings), thus concealing the control cables and wiring which would otherwise have been left exposed. This was continued in the area to the rear of the cylinders with a cast-aluminium cover on each side of the frame (half enclosing the single Keihin carburettor). The speedometer (again in square section) was set in the top of the headlamp shell. The standard of the electrical equipment and its controls was probably the most outstanding feature of the entire motorcycle; quite simply, these were outstanding. There were even small turn signals. Another feature was the fitment of a rider's mirror (again, almost unheard of as standard equipment at the time).

A cantilever rider's saddle was provided, together with a carrier with grab handle, bolted to the rear mudguard. A pillion pad could be mounted to the carrier and passenger footrests were attached to the swinging arm (again, this latter component was manufactured from angular steering pressings).

The exhaust system, tank sides, suspension covers, front mudguard stay, headlamp rim and wheel rims were chrome-plated.

An Electric Start

In May 1958 the C70 became the C71. The main difference was the addition of an electric starter. The motor for this was mounted on the front of the crankcases. It drove the crankshaft by way of a short chain connected to a sprocket and roller clutch fitted inboard of the alternator. Except for the advantage of push-button starting, the C70 and C71 were essentially the same machines.

At the same time, two other models made their bow, the CS71 and RC70f. The first was essentially the C71, but with dual seat, raised exhaust (with perforated heat shields for the silencers) and a more highly tuned engine (9:1 compression pistons giving 20bhp at 8,400rpm).

The other newcomer was the RC70f. This was a pukka scrambler, not simply a lightly modified version of the touring model. For starters, the electric starter had been omitted and its dual exhaust pipes curled around either side of the motorcycle with open ends. A small heat shield was provided on each side to protect the rider's legs.

As for the frame, this was entirely new and of all-tubular construction, with a cradle running beneath the engine, which served the dual purpose of protecting it and at the same time providing increased support for the bike's off-road role. The front forks were no longer of the leading link type; instead, they were of the Earles variety and were built from tubing in which the link fork was formed from a single tube, constructed, as one commentator described it, as 'a hairpin'. At the other end of

1958 C71 Specifications			
Engine	Air-cooled sohc parallel twin, alloy head and barrel, chain-driven camshaft, 360-degree crankshaft, horizontally split aluminium crankcases	Frame	Spine-type, built from steel pressings, engine as stressed member
		Front suspension	Leading link forks
		Rear suspension	Swinging arm, twin shock absorbers
Bore	54mm	Front brake	SLS full-width alloy drum
Stroke	54mm	Rear brake	SLS full-width alloy drum
Displacement	247.3cc	Tyres	3.25 × 16 front and rear
Compression ratio	8.2:1		
Lubrication	Plunger pump, dry sump, centrifugal filter	**General Specifications**	
		Wheelbase	51.6in (1,310mm)
Ignition	12V, battery/coil, electric starter	Ground clearance	5.5in (140mm)
Carburettor	22mm	Seat height	29.5in (749mm)
Primary drive	Gears	Fuel tank capacity	N/A
Final drive	Chain	Dry weight	348lb (158kg)
Gearbox	Four speeds; foot-change; engine speed clutch	Maximum power	18bhp @ 7,400rpm
		Top speed	69mph (111km/h)

the machine, the swinging arm had been totally redesigned and its twin suspension units were now located further forward and laid down to a degree. This was done to improve wheel movement and control – similar to the latest Continental European practice.

In line with its off-road racing duties, the RC70f's handlebars were of the motocross type and braced for additional strength. Components such as the seat and mudguards were much smaller and lighter, whilst tyre sizes had changed (a 19in on the front and 18in rear) and knobbly scrambles tyres fitted. The engine output was said to be identical to the CS71, in other words 20bhp at 8,400rpm. Dry weight was down to 319lb (145kg).

A Larger Engine Size

In mid-1958 Honda gave a debut to two larger engined twins, the C75 (tourer) and CS76 (street scrambler). These two bikes displaced 305.4cc (60 × 54mm). This was achieved by increasing the bore size by 6mm. As with their 250cc brothers, the tourer put out 21bhp at 7,000rpm, the street scrambler 24bhp at 8,000rpm. This was largely achieved via compression ratio (8.2:1 and 8.5:1 respectively).

In the December 1958 issue of *The Motor Cycle*, columnist 'Nitor' brought readers the following story entitled *Dream Model on the Road*:

Japanese design is brimful of interest. Hence I am particularly intrigued to receive from Hong Kong a few impressions of the Honda Dream 300 from Lt Cdr PC Burfield, RN, who is stationed in those parts. The model is as modern as the day and even features electric starting. The overhead camshaft, parallel-twin engine has inclined cylinders with overall finning on the head and cambox. Pressings are used extensively – for the spine frame, stanchions of the leading link front forks, arms of the pivoted rear fork, and so on. The design, in its way, is quite space age, although in fact the machine has been in production for about three years [sic]. As with most modern Japanese models the gear change mechanism incorporates fully rotary ratchet and cam plates. The result is that a downward movement of the pedal after top gear has been engaged gives neutral, the next depression bottom

53

gear and so on up the scale. Conversely, top can be obtained by an upward movement of the pedal from neutral. The advantages are obvious: one can readily coast downhill, or find neutral from top without running down through the gears. The Japs didn't copy that feature from anyone! My correspondent found the arrangement delightful, and especially so since the Dream is fitted with a rocking gear pedal. The handling, says the Commander, is good and the model displayed no vices. The suspension, which is very soft on impact and has powerful damping, earned high praise. A point that impressed, too, was the complete absence of oil leaks, a feature for which the model is becoming renowned. Minor points of interest are a wind horn, twin mirrors and flashing light indicators fore and aft. All in all, very intriguing.

Exports to Europe

Although the 250 C70/71 and C75/76 series had been exported to Asian countries during 1958, it was not until 1959 that supplies reached Europe, with 144 C71s finding their way to Holland and 205 examples reaching Britain. Honda made its European debut at the Amsterdam show in late February 1959. Exact numbers to be exported to the USA are not fully recorded (figures range from some 200 C71s down to sixty-nine), but what is clear about the States is that the American Honda Motor Corporation was founded in June 1959, at the very same time as the first Honda racing team participated in the Isle of Man Ultra-Lightweight TT (125cc), winning the manufacturers' team prize. The first company to be officially appointed by Honda for Great Britain was Maico (GB) Ltd of London.

Wet-Sump Lubrication

The 1960 model year brought a redesign of the two-fifty twin in late 1959, this going on sale in February 1960. Essentially it was a revised C71, coded predictably C72. Its

appearance was little changed, with the same rectangular lines, but the engine had switched from dry to wet-sump lubrication – as virtually every Honda was to use thereafter.

As before, there was an electric start and single carburettor. But another major change was to be transmission, which saw the clutch moving from the crankshaft to the gearbox mainshaft and by primary chain on the nearside (left) of the engine; final drive (again by chain) continued on the offside (right).

To accommodate the change from dry to wet sump, the base of the horizontally split crankcases was extended – for the dual purpose of not only accommodating the lubricating oil, but also to provide additional cooling by way of quite extensive finning of the crankcase moulding.

The gear oil pump was assembled to a casting which was bolted to the underside of the crankcase and this held its drive in mesh with one cut on the crankshaft centre.

The existing centrifugal oil filter was retained, but space now prevented it being fitted to the crankshaft. Instead, it was mounted

The 1960 model year brought a redesign of the C71 into the C72 – this saw a change from dry-sump to wet-sump lubrication and moving the clutch from the crankshaft to the gearbox mainshaft.

1960 C72/1963 C77 Specifications (C77 in brackets where different)			
Engine	Air-cooled sohc parallel twin, alloy head and barrel, chain-driven camshaft, 360-degree crankshaft, horizontally split, aluminium crankcases	Front suspension	Leading link forks
		Rear suspension	Swinging arm, twin shock absorbers
		Front brake	SLS full-width alloy drum
		Rear brake	SLS full-width alloy drum
Bore	54mm (C77: 60mm)	Tyres	3.25 × 16 front and rear
Stroke	54mm		
Displacement	247.3cc (C77: 305.4cc)	**General Specifications**	
Compression ratio	8.3:1 (C77: 8.2:1)	Wheelbase	51.6in (1,310mm)
Lubrication	Plunger pump, wet sump	Ground clearance	5.5in (139mm)
Ignition	12V, battery/coil, electric starter	Seat height	30in (762mm)
Carburettor	Keihin 22mm	Fuel tank capacity	N/A
Primary drive	Gears	Dry weight	356lb (162kg) (C77: 372lb (169kg))
Final drive	Chain	Maximum power	20bhp @ 8,000rpm (C77: 23bhp @ 7,500rpm)
Gearbox	Four speeds		
Frame	Spine-type, built from steel pressings, engine as stressed member	Top speed	70mph (113km/h) (C77: 82mph (132km/h))

ahead of this in the primary chaincase and was driven from a sprocket at the very end of the crankshaft, via a short chain. There were now no fewer than five chains on the twin-cylinder Honda, these being for starter motor, camshaft, primary, oil filter and final drive.

Testing the C72 Tourer

The Motor Cycle, in a test of the C72 two-fifty twin in the 29 March 1962 issue, began by saying: 'Push-button starting has undeniable attractions. Add to this a totally enclosed rear chain, comprehensive mudguarding, winking turn indicators, high-class finish and mile-a-minute cruising – and you have the Honda Dream.' It continued: 'From the front mudguard to the rear number plate, the model is designed as a unit. Unusual to European eyes, the knife-edge styling appears ultra-modern and exceptionally smart.'

As for performance, the tester had this to say:

Conforming to orthodox practice, the standard Dream has 360-degree crankshaft throws. Low-

speed pulling power proved better than expected from a two-fifty. The model would accelerate briskly in top gear from 20mph (32km/h) and most main-road gradients seldom caused the speed to drop below 40mph (64km/h). Twisting the grip provided instantaneous crisp response. The revs soared cleanly right up the scale without hesitation and with a mounting drone from the air filter as the only audible sound. At peak rpm there was a very slight trace of vibration; otherwise the unit was exceptionally smooth.

As already noted earlier in this chapter, the C70/71/72 series were comfortable tourers rather than out-and-out racers. John Young, sharing his experiences of owning a C72 in the July 1984 issue of *Motorcycle Enthusiast*, could 'still vividly remember my worst experience of the Honda's suspension when, due to some amazing French road works, I discovered that the front and rear suspension could work in unison, and that's an experience I wouldn't wish upon anyone'. Another enthusiast described the handling on rough roads as 'riding a two wheel pogo-stick!'

John Young ended by saying:

Given that this was one of Honda's first European ventures, it wasn't at all bad. I must admit that if my bike was anything, it sure was reliable. Not once did it ever fail to start up or give any running problems, and that's surely worth ten out of ten. Another interesting thing about the Dream was its oil consumption; there wasn't any! It didn't seem to use or waste any, a very unusual phenomenon in those days.

In its test, *The Motor Cycle* recorded a top speed of 79mph (127km/h). This was achieved in a 'moderate three-quarter wind; 13½-stone rider wearing two-piece suit and over-boots'. Besides the poor suspension damping, the only other disappointment concerned poor braking performance: 'the front brake, especially, required heavy pressure, and excessive reach was needed between right grip and lever. Although the rear brake provided more bite it too required heavy pressure with resultant loss of sensitivity.'

Again, it was the attention to detail which impressed, including a 'most effective horn', both mudguards 'which deflected road filth very efficiently from the rider and machine' and a host of features including 'spindle-alignment marks on the rear fork ends, quickly adjustable timing chain, detachable silencer baffles (for cleaning) and lubrication nipples on control cables'.

Sophistication

Perhaps the Honda two-fifty (and 305cc) model's greatest asset was its sheer sophistication. This is how one commentator saw things: 'With their very full specification and equipment, excellent finish and attention to detail, they quickly made an impact which was augmented by keen pricing.' And continuing:

> In the showroom Honda brought a new image to motorcycling and the good electrics, silence and lack of oil leaks all went a long way to selling the machines to the general public. Even if the traditional rider frowned on the handling, he had to

admire the engines. They ran at speeds only used in road racing, seemed unburstable and kept their oil inside. It took a long time for even the press, let alone the public, to become used to running at the high speeds needed to keep the little twins on the boil. Those that learned this found a whole new world of riding opening up before them.

The CB72 Arrives

The famous CB72 Super Sport model was officially put on the market in February 1960. An earlier sportster, the CB71 had run from mid-1959, but was little known outside Japan. And so it was the CB72 which took all the glory – and sales – for its manufacturer.

The CB72 (and to much the same extent, the CB71, at least in its external appearance) was much changed from the touring C70/71 series. Although, externally, it appeared to be simply a twin-carb version of the touring model, inside it was notably different. Gone was the 360-degree crank, to be replaced by a 180-degree crankshaft. Although this change helped to inhibit vibes, it also made for uneven running lower down the rev range. There were twin contact breakers – still controlled by a single cam on the offside end of the camshaft. As before, the camshaft itself was of two-piece construction, with each half carrying two cam lobes and splining for the central drive chain sprocket.

Carburation was taken care of by a pair of 22mm Biliath instruments, with 9.5:1 compression pistons (some sources say bikes also appeared with 10:1 cr).

An Entirely New Frame

Even though the engine was not drastically different, the frame certainly was, being an entirely new design. Gone was the former pressed-steel affair, and in its place an extremely neat tubular assembly. Although it was still of the spine variety, the steering head area resembled that of a Featherbed Norton. There was, of

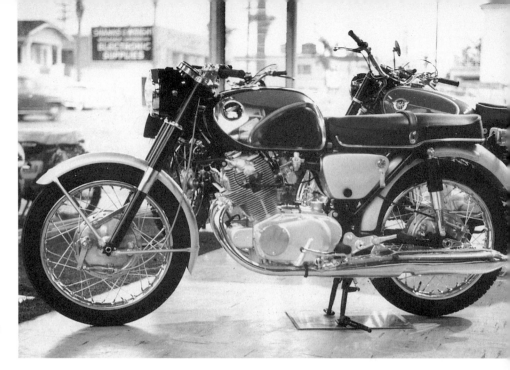

The famous CB72 Super Sport model was put onto the market at the beginning of 1960. One of the very first machines is seen here in an American dealer's showroom that year.

course, no front downtubes, with the engine being supported from the front of the cylinder head and the rear of the crankcase. Actually, this new frame didn't just help to transform the roadholding and handling abilities – it also makes for the likelihood of a simpler restoration job for today's restorers than the pressed-steel assembly found on the touring version. This is because the latter is rust-prone. With the rear mudguard section where the top of the suspension support can actually rust through! Although new complete rear sections can be found and welded on, it's not a simple job.

Back to the CB72 frame. A trio of tubes ran back from the steering head to a braced junction, through which the top tube ran before curving downwards to the rear swinging arm pivot point. Tubes also ran backwards and upwards to the rear shock absorbers, whilst bracing plates welded them all together and replaced the forged lug system and its brazing used on the pressed-steel frame of the tourer.

Front and Rear Suspension
Like the frame, the front and rear suspension were entirely new. Although it is generally

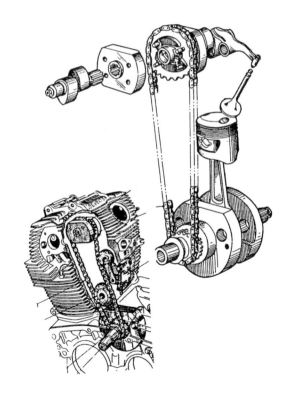

Drawing showing the CB72/77 centrally located cam and how the split camshaft and its driving sprocket were retained.

The CB72 247.3cc (54 × 54mm) sohc with twin carbs, 180-degree crank, electric start (12V) and four-speed gearbox.

Outstanding Brakes

Another feature of the CB72 that was a massive improvement over the touring model was the brakes. Although they were still full-width aluminium hubs, this is where the similarity ended. Those on the sportster were larger – 7.87in (200mm) against 7in (180mm), but they were now 2LS operation rather than SLS on the C72. Actually, if anything, the rear anchor was too powerful and could catch out an unwary novice rider, particularly in the wet. When one realizes that new British laws restricted learner riders to a maximum of 250cc, this was something of a problem. As was the fact that the CB72 was actually as fast as most British 500s and certainly virtually all the 350s!

The Motor Cycle recorded a top speed of 91mph (146km/h) in its road test published on 7 December 1961.

Ease of Starting

Another area where the CB72 excelled when compared to other sports models was starting. *The Motor Cycle* again:

> Still regarded as revolutionary in this country, electric starters are now taken for granted on Japanese machines. That on the Dream turned over the engine rapidly. The air control operates chokes on both carburettors and is accessibly located on the left. With the air closed, throttle set barely open, petrol and ignition switched on, the starter button – close to the twistgrip – was pressed. Even after a frosty night in the open, the engine usually fired within seconds. The air control was then opened slightly to prevent over-richness. It was advisable to let the engine warm up on half choke for half a minute or so before moving off, then the air control could be fully opened.

All of the above was conditional on the need to free the clutch by operation of the forward-acting kick-starter (located on the offside of the machine) prior to the first start of the day. This was needed on all early Honda twins to

agreed that this was considerably softer than usual for a sports mount at the time, it not only provided *The Motor Cycle* with 'an exceptional degree of comfort over pretty well all manner of going', but also 'taut and positive' steering at high speeds.

This could be improved still further by the substitution of British Girling rear shocks. But in truth these were only really necessary for racing events. The front forks were now of the fully enclosed oil-damped telescopic type, whilst the original equipment shocks were also fully enclosed, but now of conventional circular shape. Unlike the tourer, these had three-position adjustment for load.

There was also a wide range of settings for both the footrests and the rear brake and gear change pedals.

prevent a noisy first-gear engagement when first setting off. Once warm, this was not a problem.

Needing Five Ratios

If the CB72 had a fault, it was that it really could have done with a fifth ratio. But this step did not come until Royal Enfield and Ducati put another ratio into their two-fifty singles a few years later. As it was, the Honda Super Sport called for frequent use of third on undulating main roads if its ability to cruise at 70–75mph (113–120km/h) was to be maintained.

Even without five gears the CB72 had still emerged as the 250cc class winner of the 1961 Thruxton 500-mile (800km) endurance race for standard roadsters. The winning CB72 was piloted by professional racer, John Hartle, and dealer/rider, Bill Smith. The pairing completed 209 laps in 7hr 27min, 7.2sec at an average speed of 63.4mph (102km/h). This compared well to the overall winners, Tony Godfrey/ John Holder, on a 649cc Triumph Bonneville, who managed 220 laps in 7hr 26min 18.8sec at an average speed of 67.29mph (108.27km/h). The race had been staged in a mixture of driving rain and later a drying track as conditions improved later in the day. Another Honda, ridden by privateers, J Dunn and C Peak, finished fifth in class. There were no Honda retirements.

In the following year, 1962, a CB72 was at both Thruxton and the Silverstone 1,000km race. In the USA at the Vineland Four-Hour Production Race in California four Honda Hawks came 1–2–3–4, with their closest competition 3½ laps behind!

18in Wheels

In creating the CB72, the Honda engineering team had sensibly given the sports model 18in instead of 16in wheels, with a 2.75 section at the front and a 3.00 at the rear. This also helped when riders wanted to race their model, as racing tyres in those days were usually restricted to either 18in or 19in sizes.

The mudguards were narrow and much more sporting than the deeply valanced type found on the touring C72, the rear being

Barry Lawton with the CB72 that he shared with P Bugden during the 1962 Thruxton 500-mile endurance race.

deeper than the front and the latter having stays at both the front and rear extremities.

Combined Speedo and Tacho

A feature of the CB72 (and the later CB77 three-hundred) was the combined speedometer and tachometer assembly.

Although a neat-looking assembly, the idea didn't catch on, only being found on the CB160 and CB450 and a few other early Hondas. After this, a switch was made to separate instruments. This was probably on cost grounds – if one instrument failed, the whole assembly had to be replaced. The assembly, an elongated circular shape, was incorporated as part of the headlamp shell. Another facet of the combined unit was its vertical mileage recorder. Like other Hondas of the period, a manually operated friction steering damper was part of the standard equipment, as were twin mirrors and 12V electrics. But unlike the C72, flashing indicators were only supplied as an option at additional cost.

The Dream Becomes the Hawk

In the States the CB72 was known as the Hawk. When testing an example in its May 1962 issue, *Cycle World* said:

Rider position on the Hawk is of necessity, because of the low, flat handlebars, very 'Mike Hailwood', and although it looks ferociously uncomfortable for touring, the controls and the seat are positioned in such a way that it is, in fact, quite good. In any case, the combination makes the rider feel as though he is very much a part of the machine – and it is fun to drop into a crouch and bare your teeth as other riders go by.

With a power output of 24bhp at 9,000rpm (*Cycle World* gave figures of 25bhp at 9,200rpm) and a dry weight of 337lb (152kg), the CB72 could sprint the standing quarter-mile in some 17sec. But, like the C72, this was achieved without causing offence to others. *The Motor Cycle* said: 'No sporting mount is quieter than the Super Sport Dream. On full throttle, the exhaust and air intakes combined to provide a distinctive and pleasant high-pitched growl, which could not offend even the most crotchety layman.'

The CBM72 and CL72

For 1962 Honda increased its choice for prospective 250cc buyers by increasing its range to four separate models. These comprised the existing C72 (tourer) and CB72

The 1963 Singapore Grand Prix, 250cc class. Nobby Wales with his race-kitted CB72 (104) leads Ducati-mounted Doug Curran (40).

A feature of the CB72 (and its bigger 305cc brother, the CB77) was the combined speedometer and tachometer mounted above the headlamp.

(super sports), plus the CBM72 and CL72.

The CBM72 was essentially the stock CB72, but with high 'bars and flashing indicators, whereas the CL72 was a street scrambler, rather on the lines of the RC70/CS72. Except for the gearing, the engine was the same as the CB72 – even to the point of having the twin 22mm carbs. Instead, it was the running gear and chassis which separated the two machines.

Although the frame bore a strong resemblance, there were changes to make it more suitable for rough going. The biggest was that there was now a substantial front downtube, which then branched into two and ran under the crankcase. There was also a stout 'bash plate', which, as *Cycle World* said, permitted 'a lot of banging over rocks without breaking the sump'.

The front forks and rear shocks had been modified to provide more travel, whilst the former was equipped with a hydraulic steering damper – in place of the manually operated friction discs used on other Hondas. The front forks were equipped with rubber gaiters.

Large Wheels and Small Brakes

Another feature of the CL72 was its use of large wheels and small brakes. Actually, both were necessary in Honda's attempt at a street scrambler conversion. The wheels were 19in front and rear, with a 3.00 section tyre at the front and a wider 3.50 assembly at the rear; both were of the knobbly off-road pattern.

As *Cycle World* commented: 'out on the dirt, big brakes are just so much excess weight to carry around; the wheels don't get enough grip to enable the rider to brake very hard in any case. And, too, the CL72's brakes did seem to be adequate during the road riding we did with the bikes.' Again, in typical Honda fashion, these were of the full-width aluminium drum type, with a massive torque arm at the rear and a slotted retainer device for the brake plate at the front. Both were single leading-shoe operation. Diameter was in the region of 160mm (6.3in).

A Siamesed Exhaust

Yet another distinctive feature of the CL72 Street Scrambler was the high-level siamesed exhaust system. *Cycle World* described the CL's exhaust system thus:

The CB72 on display at the Earls Court Show in London in 1964.

1960 CB72/1963 CB77 Specifications (CB77 in brackets where different)

Engine	Air-cooled sohc parallel twin, alloy head and barrel, chain-driven camshaft, 180-degree crankshaft, horizontally split, aluminium crankcases	Rear suspension	Swinging arm, twin shock absorbers
		Front brake	2LS full-width alloy hub
		Rear brake	SLS full-width alloy hub
		Tyres	Front 2.75 × 18, rear 3.00 × 18
Bore	54mm (CB77: 60mm)		
Stroke	54mm		
Displacement	247.3cc (CB77: 305.4cc)	**General Specifications**	
Compression ratio	9.5:1	Wheelbase	51in (1,295mm)
Lubrication	Plunger pump, wet sump	Ground clearance	6in (152mm)
Ignition	2 × Keihin	Seat height	29.7in (754mm)
Carburettor	2 × Keihin 22mm (CB77: 26mm)	Fuel tank capacity	N/A
Primary drive	Gears	Dry weight	337lb (152kg) (CB77: 350lb (159kg))
Final drive	Chain		
Gearbox	Four speeds	Maximum power	24bhp @ 9,000rpm
Frame	Tubular, spine-type	Top speed	CB72: 85mph (137km/h) (CB77: 95mph (153km/h))
Front suspension	Oil-damped telescopic fork		

It is not a very complicated array of plumbing; it consists of a pair of straight pipes that curl back, high on the left side, and while a set of baffles are provided (and they do a surprisingly good job of silencing the exhaust) the carburation settings are tailored to straight-pipe running and the bike's performance is a trifle 'fluffly' with the baffles in place.

No Electric Starter

A feature of the CL72 was that no electric starter was provided, this mainly being dispensed with to save weight. There was a mass of features to reduce the pounds. Another was the use of aluminium wheel rims in place of the usual chromed-steel components. *Cycle World* quoted a 'curb weight' of 315lb (143kg), which included fuel and oil.

Although it had a dual seat, this and the fuel link were considerably smaller and narrower than the stock CB72 articles. This had the disadvantage of offering only enough room for the rider, whilst the tank was OK for short journeys, but not serious touring.

The more one studied the CL, the more dif-

ferences there appeared to the CB72. For example, there was now only a speedometer, with a conventional trip mileage meter, the handlebars were high, wide and braced; the side panels had been dispensed with in favour of two air filters with much smaller side covers; and the rider's footrests and controls were

The CS72 Street Scrambler version was a curious mixture of the touring C72 with its massive mudguards and a high-level (dual) exhaust system.

new, as was the final drive chain guard, mud-guards and many more minor components.

Purely as an off-road machine, the CL72 had its limitations. Compared with the lighter European two-strokes it was too heavy for serious competition use. In addition, its handling, although fine on good surfaces (firm dirt or clay) was not entirely suitable, due to its ultra-quick steering.

The CL72 cost US$690 in 1962; this compared with US$640 for the CB72 and US$665 for the newly released CB77 305cc model. And remember the CL didn't have an electric start or tachometer. But if one wanted the dirt-bike look there were very few suitable four-strokes, except for Italian models from the likes of Ducati or Parilla, plus the Harley-Davidson Sprint TT (which was also built in Italy). Even with a bigger price tag, the CL72 became a massive sales success in the States, often outselling the C72 and CB72 versions. However, it was never officially sold on the British market.

The Super Hawk Arrives

In the May 1962 issue of *Cycle World* Americans got what they called the Super Hawk. This was the new CB77. This was, as the title hinted, essentially a CB72 Hawk, but using the 305.4cc (60 × 54mm) engine size previously fitted to the earlier C72, CS76 and C76 models. But, like the CB72, the CB77 employed a 180-degree crank.

Compared to the original '305' models (like the later 250s), there were considerable changes to the engine unit besides the 180 instead of 360 crank. On the 'new' 305 the dry-sump oil system had gone, as had the engine speed clutch.

As on the two-fifty, the crankshaft ran no fewer than four main bearings: ball-races between the cylinders; caged rollers on the outboard ends of the crankshaft. Roller bearings were also (again on the two-fifties) employed at the connecting-rod big-end journals, running directly against the crankpin and the hardened eye of the rod. The con rods were manufactured

in one piece, without a removal cap. The crankshaft itself was manufactured in pieces, with crankpins integral with one crank flywheel and pressed into a matching hole in the other. The only disadvantage to this system was that fairly extensive special tooling was required to do a proper job of getting the crank assembly apart and back together. To start with, at least in the US, Honda had stocks of spare crank components spread around its dealer network. However, unfortunately the crankshaft rebuilds in the field did not always fare too well. This resulted in crankshaft repairs being confined to the replacement of the entire crankshaft assembly – an expensive option.

Crankshaft life could be extended quite drastically by never exceeding the safe maximum rpm limit and regular oil changes. Oil changes were absolutely vital – and Honda's otherwise effective oil-filtration device needed clean, fresh oil to be able to do its job. And do not forget that we are talking about engine and transmission oil. As on the 250 twin, the 305 had a centrifugal fil-

The CL72 was a very popular street scrambler version of the CB72. But unlike the earlier CS72, the newcomer, which debuted in mid-1962, was a comprehensively different motorcycle, with many changes that are detailed in the main text.

A 1962 CL72; note the siamesed exhaust, hydraulic steering damper, knobbly tyres, fork gaiters, new full-loop frame and much more.

tration system. This worked in the following manner: all oil, before being fed to the engine unit, passed through an engine-driven centrifugal oil filter. Vanes inside the filter spun the oil, and centrifugal force separated metal or hard-carbon from the oil and deposited them around the inside of the filter casing – from which they had to be removed at each oil change.

Three Variants on Offer

For the Stateside market from 1963 onwards Honda offered three models of its 305 series, the CB77 Super Hawk (super sports), the C77/78 (tourer) (the C77 having encased handlebar control cables and wiring, the C78 having higher handlebars with 'naked' cables and wiring) and finally the CL77 (scrambler).

When *Cycle* did a 'Three Honda 305s' giant test in its December 1966 issue it asked the question: 'What of the Honda 305 from a rider's standpoint?' The answer it gave was 'We think so. Provided of course that one makes proper allowance for the fact that each one is made to satisfy a rather wide segment of the total motorcycle spectrum.'

The only model which *Cycle* had 'any real

reservations' about concerned the Dream (a C78 was on test), which *Cycle* said: 'feels a lot like 1958 to us'. Going on: 'Undeniably, it has its good points. One of these is a fine soft ride, which should delight the true-blue touring rider. True-blue will also appreciate the Dream's easy starting (just flip up the choke-lever and poke the little button with your thumb) and exceptionally smooth and tractable running characteristics.' Whereas the Super Hawk and Scrambler models had twin carburettors, the Dream had only a single 22mm instrument.

In addition, the hotter Super Hawk and Scrambler motor had their crankpins spaced 180 degrees apart, whereas, as *Cycle* pointed out, 'Some of the low-speed smoothness is given by the Dream's crankshaft, which has crankpins circulating together like any decent, Anglo-Saxon crankpins do (i.e., 360 degrees).' But, again to quote *Cycle* (in pointing out that the Super Hawk and Scrambler had 180-degree cranks), 'That spacing gives an uneven firing order, and some rather strange rocking-couple vibrations at low-speeds, but up around 8,000rpm it improves the engine balance.'

What *Cycle* didn't really like was that: 'The Dream has what was once a typically Japanese frame and suspension.' However, as the magazine went on to voice quite strongly: '*Our way, whatever that is, is all wrapped up in one nice package called Super Hawk.' Cycle* then went on to point out the advantages, including a 'tubular frame', 'well damped telescopic forks', 'brakes' and a 'high-compression engine with a pair of 26mm carburettors, and a camshaft that does a lot for the engine when the revs are high.'

The 305 Scrambler

Cycle described the 305 Scrambler 'as a real charmer', going on to explain why: 'Something, probably the longer exhaust pipes or perhaps a small difference in valve timing, makes the engine less fussy and it works like a (you should pardon the expression) dream.'

Distance Runners

Honda Touring bikes go the distance. The long distance. They're made for people who like to travel in comfort and style. Winners of International Design Awards, Honda Touring bikes are quiet, vibration-free and smooth to ride. You can go a long way on any of the Hondas pictured here. When you're on a long trip it's nice to know the Honda four-stroke engine is famous for dependability. But, on the outside chance that help should be needed, you know where you can go for genuine Honda parts and service. Honda has more than 1700 dealers from coast to coast. Relieves your mind. Leaves you free to enjoy the trip and your Honda. These bikes are just part of the big picture from Honda. There are ten more to choose from. Whatever your motorcycling needs, Honda has the bike to meet them.

HONDA
World's Biggest Seller!

Send postcard for free brochure. American Honda Motor Co., Inc., Dept. KM, Box 50, Gardena, Calif. See Yellow Pages for nearest dealer. © 1966, AHM.

An American Honda Motors advertisement dating from 1966, showing the final 305 touring model, the C78 introduced, together with its 250 brother the C111 72, in 1963, the main difference being a new handlebar layout and revised fuel tank styling.

As for the cycle parts, in the main these were identical to the CL72 already described, as the CB77 was to the CB72. But, as with the two-fifty, *Cycle* felt:

> it is because of the tires as much as anything else that the Honda Scrambler misses being a 'real' scrambles motorcycle. The tires will grip on hard-packed dirt; they are all but useless in soft dirt, mud or sand. Anyone who wants to get far away from the beaten path will need something with a coarse tread.

But *Cycle* also pointed out just why it still thought so highly of the CL:

> The Honda Scrambler's real charm is that it serves so well as an all-round 'play' motorcycle. It handles

well, on the street or in the rough, and now that it has inherited the 450's big front brake [from the recently introduced CB450 – *see* Chapter 5], it stops with the best of them. You can cruise at higher speeds than most states will permit without straining anything, and yet the gearing is such that off-the-road riding is taken in its stride. The transmission ratios are, incidentally, staged differently than those of the Hawk or Dream. The same gears are used, but placed on the shafts to get a different combination.

Cycle also explained something about the American market as it was in the mid-1960s:

> At present, the 305 Scrambler is the most popular of the three medium-sized Hondas, nationwide, and the Dream trails well behind the Super Hawk. This is not so much because one is better than the other as it is a reflection of the American motorcyclist's tastes. More people like to go where the whim of the moment leads them, like to stick to the pavement and ride fast or slow. The same vote-with-dollars poll shows that there are also more riders who like to be fast and sporty than the people who favor the slow and comfortable. We will go with the two majority groups.

European Trends

So what of European trends? During the same period, the main '305' seller was the CB77 Super Sport (Super Hawk in the USA). Charles Deane, writing in the October 1965 issue of *Motorcyclist Illustrated*, set out to explain 'how the CB77 differs from the 250 it closely resembles'.

The natural questions were: What was the point of building two machines so much alike that they only varied in cylinder bore dimension and slightly in the ratios provided by the four-speed gearbox? Where did the extra 58cc count on the CB77?

To answer these questions Charles Deane said: 'One has only to compare the specification of the two Hondas.' The fact was that the

247.3cc CB72 produced 24bhp at 9,000rpm, whereas the 305.4cc CB77 put out an additional 4.5bhp (at, it was claimed, an identical 9,000rpm). In pure speed terms this meant a 5mph (8km/h) additional top speed. But, as Deane continued, 'It is also interesting to note that the power band is wider on the 305, with maximum torque of 18ft/lb at 7,000rpm, compared with 15ft/lb at 7,500rpm from the 250.'

This meant that the CB77 was more flexible than its 250cc counterpart, and with more urge lower down, acceleration was also improved. However, otherwise the bikes were the same in both character and features.

Tuning the Hawk

The Americans in particular were soon tuning the CB72 and CB77 models – both for the street and for competition. One of the most popular means of gaining additional performance was to increase the engine size. The Forgetrue company, specialist manufacturers of aftermarket pistons, began offering a '350' kit for the 305 Honda in 1963. As Honda itself had done, the bore was increased, this time to 64mm, raising

displacement to 347.4cc (a gain of just over 12 per cent). For US$135 the kit comprised:

• forged aluminium pistons with rings, pins and clips
• centrifugally cast-iron liners
• special valve springs with damper-type retainer cups
• an eight-page set of instructions, plus decals.

If readers are wondering why valve springs were included in the kit, this was because the stock Honda components had an unfortunate tendency to settle and lose tension. The replacement springs were claimed to be manufactured of superior steels, which offered a longer effective life.

Forgetrue 350 conversion kits were available from Webco. Webco also distributed Harman and Collins camshafts, which, together with H & C number 7164 camshaft and racing valve springs, allowed even greater performance capabilities than the Forgetrue springs. The 350 Honda conversion gave around 31bhp (at the rear wheel) – compared with 23.5bhp (again at the rear wheel) for the stock 305 Super Hawk.

Supercharged Hawk

If there is a substitute for cubic inches, it would definitely be manifold pressure and that was the thinking behind the supercharged Honda Hawk-based drag bike, developed by owner/builder/rider, Dennis Manning, which was featured in *Cycle World*'s October 1965 issue. Manning employed a Marshall-Nordic rootes-type blower to put air into the engine at 17psi, and feed the fuel (alcohol and nitro) through a Hilborn injection system.

The plenum chamber between supercharger and inlet ports had been the subject of much experimentation, but by the time of *Cycle World*'s story had flat sides and a volume of 1530cc. Dennis Manning discovered that it was necessary to mount the chamber so that its floor

Reads of Leytonstone, East London, built a small number of CB77 Titan models with various tuning and cosmetic components.

was level with the bottom of the ports. Otherwise, as *Cycle World* said, 'puddles of fuel collect'.

The supercharger was driven by a chain, with drive taken from a sprocket on the generator end of the crankshaft. The generator (alternator) had been removed and ignition current provided by a battery.

Displacement had been upped to 350cc, using a Webco big bore kit (already described), whilst the bottom half of the engine had been strengthened to take all the added pressure by welding between the support webs in the crankcases. Manning also produced special gudgeon pins, but the con rods and crank were stock Honda components. Webco valve springs and super-light steel retainers were used in conjunction with a one-off Dempsey Wilson camshaft. Manning claimed the engine would 'run up to 15,000rpm', but *Cycle World* queried this as the bike was not fitted with a tachometer.

Frame Modifications

Modifications to the frame consisted mainly of removing unwanted bracketry, whilst the whole bike had been lowered and the fork rake increased by the simple expedient of removing the rear suspension units and adding a couple of very short struts in their place. A lengthened version of the standard Honda swinging arm was retained, but now served only to support the rear wheel. There was no rear suspension. The combination of a longer wheelbase and increased fork rake made the handling 'very much to Manning's liking'. The whole Manning Supercharged 350 Hawk weighed in at 215lb (98kg) with the tiny tank full of fuel and oil in the engine (he preferred Valvoline).

Of course, there were many other racing conversions of the CB72/77 models on both sides of the Atlantic with varying degrees of success, including a 500cc four using two 250cc engines built by sidecar racer, Alan Young, of Purley, Surrey. Honda even offered works CR72 and CR77 versions (*see* Chapter 9), but these were double overhead cam engines with six-speed

transmissions and, except for bore and stroke dimensions, shared little in common with their series production counterparts.

Production Ends

Production of the C77 Dream ceased in January 1966, and its close brother, the C78 Dream, ceased in January 1968. This was at the same time as the CB77 sportster and the CL77 Street Scrambler. The story was similar for the two-fifty versions.

All had contributed in their own way to Honda's rise outside Japan and had bridged the period from the very early export drive to a time when Honda had become world-renowned and a huge sales success. To many, the two-fifty and three hundred sohc twins of the late 1950s, until they were superseded by the new CB250/350 models (plus CL and SL variants) in 1968, were the definitive Honda motorcycles of that era. And as such they command a very special place in the Japanese marque's history.

American Dennis Manning built this supercharged Honda CB77 Hawk-based drag bike, using a Marshall-Nordic rootes-type blower. Displacement was increased to 350cc using a Webco big-bore kit.

5 CB450 and CB500T

First news of an impending Japanese onslaught on that bastion of the British motorcycle industry, the large four-stroke twin, came in 1964, when a visiting journalist discovered an entirely new 500-class vertical twin. This motorcycle, clearly styled on British lines, was seen undergoing 'secret' tests on Honda's test track.

At that time everyone – at least outside Japan – believed that the Japanese had left the design and production of larger capacity machines to other countries, notably Great Britain, and would limit their efforts to a total concentration of the lightweight market. How wrong those pundits were proved to have been!

Enter the Black Bomber

The newcomer, later to be identified as the Honda CB450 'Black Bomber' (also at various times referred to as the 'Black Hawk' and 'The Dragon'), sent a cold shiver down the very spine of the industry. The British manufacturers in

particular had thought, hoped and prayed that the Japanese would never introduce such a bike. And as subsequent events were to prove, it was this machine which heralded the era of what was, in retrospect, the final push for supremacy by the industrial warriors of Nippon, culminating a few years later with the really big guns, headed by Honda's CB750 four.

Firms such as BSA, Triumph and AMC (which included AJS, Matchless and Norton) had hoped that the 305cc CB77 signalled the limit of how far the Japanese intended advancing. But the CB77 (*see* Chapter 4) was in reality little more than an overbored CB72 two-fifty, and although fast, with a maximum speed approaching 100mph (160km/h), it was no match for the performance of the British 650cc twins.

The Need for a Flagship

However, Honda, having successfully attacked the lightweight sector, then set its sights high-

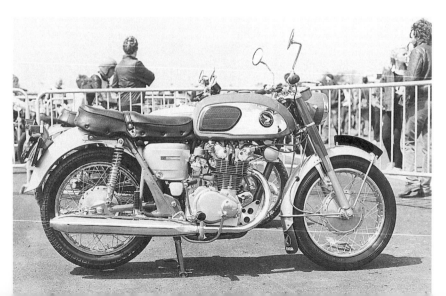

The CB450 came as a very nasty shock to the British motorcycle industry, which had previously hoped (and prayed!) that the CB77 305cc twin would be Honda's limit.

er and, needing a flagship model, saw the CB450 as just such a machine. Something that could provide a true performance potential against the opposition on both motorways and back roads, the dreaded Black Bomber was just that – at least on paper.

The first of the new breed appeared on British roads in early 1965, when Honda UK's first example arrived. After being uncrated and assembled, it was eagerly sought out by the British press. This bike, registered FYN 444 C ('444' being the exact cubic capacity of the 450's engine) soon proved that it was a sports tourer – rather than an out-and-out sportster as predicted by many observers.

Having said that, it proved to have a genuine 100mph-plus potential coupled with a particularly modern engine design, outstanding brakes and a high standard of build and reliability. The only real fly in the ointment was in the handling department, where there was still plenty of room for improvement.

Engineering Wizardry

For most engineers working in the 1960s, tradition was something to be followed – but not at the Honda Motor Company. Earlier designs had already shown that Honda was far too enterprising to follow tradition. And with the engine of the CB450 this love of technical innovation was taken a stage further, in the shape of several features which departed quite drastically from the engineering norm.

Most obvious for a roadster of the era were its twin overhead camshafts – the British relied on pushrod-operated valves. Next came the method of drive, namely by a long chain from a sixteen-tooth sprocket set in the middle of the crankshaft. Then there were the unusual torsion bar valve springs, a 180-degree crank throw and, on such a large engine, a mind-blowing (for the time) peak engine rpm figure of 8,500.

Torsion Bar Springs

The most novel of these features was the employment of torsion bar valve springs. What were they? Well, torsion means twist. Each torsion bar was a short, stiff length of spring steel, splined at both ends. One end was anchored in a retainer bolted to the cylinder head; the other end was splined into a tubular guide, which itself was splined into the pivot end of a forked arm, that in turn closed the valve.

During engine assembly the bar was given a slight twist by a tool engaged with the retainer, before this was clamped to the head. This ensured that the forked arm exerted a firm pressure on the valve collar. When the valve was opened by the cam follower, the arm was pivoted downwards, turning the guide with it, and in doing so imparting a further twist to the bar. As the cam relaxed its pressure, the wire untwisted, turning the guide and arm back again to close the valve.

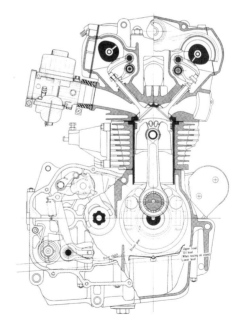

An official Honda technical drawing from the offside (right) showing the layout of the CB450 engine assembly.

In reality, there was nothing really unusual in twisting a length of rod to provide a spring effect. This was, after all, the very principle of the conventional coil valve spring – which is simply a long, thin torsion bar coiled up for compact installation.

Other Engine Features

One extremely lengthy chain drove both overhead cams direct from the centre of the camshaft, with no fewer than seven guide and jockey wheels, made of synthetic rubber. Three, including the adjustable tensioner in the slack run, were toothed and supported on needle bearings, the others having a plain periphery and plain spindle.

Largest of the rollers was a plain one, spanning the two vertical runs in the crankcase mouth. The pivoted cam-chain tensioner was normally locked by a bolt nipping the stem. Slackening this bolt allowed the spring to take up excess chain play automatically.

The cam boxes were cast integrally with one-piece, sand-cast aluminium cylinder heads (featuring cast-iron skulls with part-spherical combustion chambers), whilst each camshaft

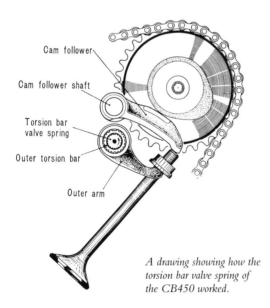

Cam follower

Cam follower shaft

Torsion bar
valve spring

Outer torsion bar

Outer arm

A drawing showing how the torsion bar valve spring of the CB450 worked.

was supported at both ends in plain, light-alloy bearings spigoted into the sides of the head.

There were four caged roller main bearings in total, with caged roller big ends. A small sprocket for the cam chain was formed integrally with the middle portion of the crankshaft and this was pressed into the inner discs of the two pairs of flywheels.

These discs featured integral crankpins, diametrically opposed to one another and supporting the one-piece steel connecting rods. Pressed onto the crankpins, the outer flywheel discs were integral with the crankshaft ends. This whole assembly was clamped to eight studs in the upper half of the horizontally split pressure-die-cast aluminium crankcases, thus relieving the crankcase joint of stress.

The crankshaft and float were governed by bronze thrust washers on both sides of the extreme offside (right) main bearing. One was behind the twenty-three-tooth primary drive gear splined to the crankshaft; the other was outboard of the end flywheel disc.

Shallow-Dome Pistons

The gudgeon pins ran directly in the rods, whilst the pistons (8.5:1 compression ratio) featured shallow-dome crowns recessed for valve clearance, full skirts and three rings (two compression, one slotted oil scraper). Bore and stroke were 70 × 57.8mm, giving a displacement of 444cc. Another aluminium die-casting, the cylinder barrel had flanged, austentic-iron liners.

Ignition

Ignition was by 12V battery and twin coils, with double contact breakers (some early engines used a single points set-up) on the nearside (left) end of the exhaust camshaft. The rotor of the 70W alternator was tapered and keyed on the end of the crankshaft, as on the nearside, whilst the stator was housed in a crankcase side cover.

The starter motor was bolted across the front of the crankcase mouth; its thirteen-tooth sprocket drove a bronze-bushed, thirty-seven-

The 444.9cc (70 × 57.8mm) dohc CB450 power unit was certainly an impressive piece of engineering for the mid-1960s.

tooth sprocket supported on the engine shaft inboard of the rotor. Projecting from the outer cover face of the large sprocket was a boss which drove a free-wheel-type (sprag) clutch in the rotor. A kick-starter was provided in addition to the electric motor. Carburation was by way of two Keihin CVB 32mm instruments.

Transmission

Besides an in-unit four-speed gearbox, there was also a wet multi-plate clutch. Primary drive reduction was well over 3:1. A seventy-six-tooth clutch gear was riveted to an eight-rubber shock absorber vane, in a light alloy drum which had a dual bronze bush to carry it on the gearbox input shaft.

The seven driving plates were also in light alloy, with bonded friction rings. Steel was employed for driven plates, whilst the clutch centre was splined to the input shaft.

Lubrication was particularly comprehensive, with oil force-fed to the gearbox as well as the engine. A wet-sump system was used, with the 5pt (2.8ltr) oil compartment in the lower crankcase half – this was partitioned off from the crankshaft flywheel chamber by two steel pressings located by a long, transverse pin. An eccentric on the rear of the clutch gear drove a 16mm diameter, aluminium plunger pump.

Oil was sucked through a gauze screen and forced into a centrifugal filter splined to the crankshaft outboard of the primary drive gear.

On leaving the filter, the oil divided into two circuits. In the upper circuit, it passed up the two offside (right) cylinder retaining studs to lubricate the camshaft bearings, cam lobes and levers, before spilling onto the valve stems and into troughs serving the torsion bar sleeves. Troughs were also formed to lubricate the spindles of the four chain rollers carried in the brackets attached to the cylinder head.

The lower oil circuit fed the main and big-end bearings (with splash to the barrels and pistons) and also the gearbox input shaft via the coppered bush. From the bore of this shaft, oil found its way to the free gears and clutch drum bushes. The bores of the free gears on the output shaft received their oil from the other coppered bush, which had a trough to collect splash.

There was no scavenge pump; all oil returned to the sump by gravity. At peak-power revolutions, circulation rate, according to Honda, was 'about a gallon a minute'.

Out on the Road

So what was the newcomer like out on the road? The cycle parts closely resembled those of the existing CB72/77 series, except for the frame design, which instead of the spin type now employed a full cradle design, with a single front downtube, branching into two underneath the power unit. As with the existing smaller twins, the suspension and in particular the Japanese original equipment tyres were best described as abysmal. The rear suspension and, to a lesser extent, the front forks provided a pogo-stick effect, which didn't go down too well with the British press. *Motor Cycle*, in a special Honda Supplement published in March 1966, went as far as a comment about 'instability in the wet'.

With a tankful of petrol, the CB450 tipped the scales at almost 450lb (204kg), some 75lb (34kg) heavier than the Triumph T100SS, its nearest British competitor. So although offering a list of notable technical features it was also considerably heavier – heavier, in fact, than the 649cc Triumph Bonneville!

But the biggest difference between the Japanese invader and the traditional British big twin was engine torque. To extract its full performance potential the Honda had to be revved. Up to 6,000rpm the performance was nothing special, but from this figure onwards up the rev range the CB450 showed its true colours, with all previous vibration disappearing as the bike screamed towards the horizon. In fact, in the vibe stakes the CB450 was just the reverse of the British vertical twins, the latter vibrating ever more as the revs rose. The 180-degree crank throw no doubt helped here, compared with the British machines' usual 360 throws.

However, all those high revolutions caused many pundits to voice their concerns that the CB450's engine wouldn't last long. But, in truth, providing the engine oil was changed religiously at 1,000-mile (1,600km) intervals, the engine was remarkably free of major hassles.

Another 'do not' involved not revving the engine hard when still cold. This was because the oilways were very small and the main engine power was developed at the top end of the scale. The CB450's Owner's Handbook actually stated quite clearly (almost like a present-day Government Health Warning!): 'Leave the bike ticking over for about 2 minutes before riding off.' Tickover problems (even with the choke off) were quite a source of problems on early model CB450s, to such an extent that Honda went as far as issuing a special kit to dealers in an attempt to overcome this.

British Sales

Then there was the matter of purchase price – at some £360, the CB450 was more expensive than virtually any British bike at the time of its UK launch. For example, it was possible to buy the brand-new BSA 650 Lightning from London dealers, Comerfords, for only £308 at the time. Yet initial press reaction was enthusiastic, and nowhere more than Great Britain.

Because of this, Honda made a commercial error, by allocating more bikes than could be sold, including diverting a complete shipment of American-bound CB450s. These US-spec-

---

1965 CB450 Specifications

Engine	Air-cooled dohc parallel twin, alloy head and barrel, chain-driven camshafts, valve closure by torsion bars, 180-degree crankshaft, horizontally split, aluminium crankcases	Frame	Tubular semi-duplex
		Front suspension	Oil-damped telescopic forks
		Rear suspension	Swinging arm, twin shock absorbers
		Front brake	2LS full-width alloy drum
Bore	70mm	Rear brake	SLS full-width alloy drum
Stroke	57.8mm	Tyres	Front 3.25 × 18, rear 3.50 × 18
Displacement	444.9		
Compression ratio	8.5:1		
Lubrication	16mm diameter aluminium plunger pump	**General Specifications**	
		Wheelbase	53.1in (1,349mm)
Ignition	12V, double contact breakers, battery/coil, 70W alternator	Ground clearance	5.8in (147.32mm)
		Seat height	30in (762mm)
Carburettor	2 × Keihin 32mm	Fuel tank capacity	3.5gal (16ltr)
Primary drive	Gears	Dry weight	411lb (186kg)
Final drive	Chain	Maximum power	43bhp @ 8,500rpm
Gearbox	Four speeds	Top speed	106mph (172km/h)

ification bikes had small turn signals and a different wiring loom, which did not match any of the diagrams in the official Honda Workshop Manual for the model.

Unfortunately for both the company and its UK dealer network, 1966 was to witness a sudden fall in British motorcycle sales (hence the heavily discounted BSA twins), leaving Honda with a relatively large number of unsold machines.

The Ken Ives 'Specials'

These bikes took some time to be cleared and resulted in Leicester dealer Ken Ives, then one of the major Honda UK outlets, purchasing a large number of CB450s at a heavily discounted price. But instead of marketing them simply as discounted machines to the public, Ives offered them in café racer guise at some £15 below list price. The specification included clip-ons, chrome-plated mudguards and headlamp, fork gaiters – the customer could even specify his own choice of colour for the tank and side panels. This stylish package sold strongly, turning what had been a relatively poor seller into a dream machine which attracted many riders moving up from their smaller CB92 and CB72 machines.

A Controversial Advertising Campaign

Another interesting aspect of the early CB450 story, at least on the British market, centred around Honda UK's marketing campaign for the new model. Honda's advertising agency ran a whole string of adverts depicting a CB450 compared with certain British bikes – including an ancient early 1950s BSA A7 plunger-framed twin – and, worse still to many a British bike enthusiast, a Vincent V-twin (production of which had ceased a decade previously in 1955). Comparing the cheeky Japanese invader to a BSA was bad enough, but a Vincent – this was just sacrilege! Not only did the letters pages of the specialist magazines carry words of criticism, but the phone lines were soon buzzing at Honda's London headquarters.

Model Development

But the real home of the CB450 (and the later CB500T) was the USA; it was also here where the design was most respected.

A popular variant (not sold in Britain) was the CL450, which was introduced in the States during 1967. This reflected the street scrambler craze that was at the time sweeping the North American continent. The CL had a higher 9:1 compression ratio, even though maximum power (at the crankshaft) remained unchanged at 43bhp. But an advantage was that the CL kicked out torque lower down the scale. Combined with lower gearing, this meant a far more flexible engine response.

Besides a smaller, rounded tank, braced motocross-type handlebars, hi-level twin exhaust (both on the nearside), chrome exhaust with heat shields, separate instruments, 19in front wheel (instead of the stock 18in), which was retained at the rear, and smaller dimension mudguard (chrome-plated) together with a new colour scheme, the CL450 was pretty much as its touring mainstream older brother.

The 450 'Mark 2'

Late 1967 saw a new, revised 450 (still available in CB and CL variants). This featured a revised chassis, with the wheelbase extended from 53in (1,346mm) to 54in (1,372mm). There were also changes made to the engine unit as well, the most notable being to the gearbox, which was now a five-speeder. Maximum power had also risen to 45bhp at 9,000rpm, whilst on the roadster the fuel tank had been restyled, as were the side panels (the CL already having different assemblies to either the original or the new CB). The instrument layout followed that already adopted by the street scrambler, but was two separate clocks, mounted above the top fork yoke (triple clamp in the States).

The first British enthusiasts saw of the new model (coded CB450K1) was on Stand 141 at the London Earls Court Show in September 1967. Gone was the old silver/black finish and 'Black Bomber' image, because the new five-speed model sported a bright red colour scheme. It carried a price tag of £365. The following year, 1968, was the year that the parent company produced its ten-millionth machine, and Soichiro Honda himself rode the garlanded bike off the production line in a blaze of publicity. It was fitting that this was a CB450.

Racing Successes

Although largely aimed at the sports touring market in Britain, the CB450 gained some notable successes in production machine racing later in its life. Strangely, at first the ACU (Auto Cycle Union) banned the model on the grounds that it had double overhead cams and torsion bar valve springs. It was this that prevented Mike Hailwood from riding an example in the Brands Hatch 500-mile endurance race in 1966, after Mike had signed to race Hondas that year in Grand Prix events. It was not until much later that the rule makers finally relented and allowed the Honda twin to compete.

The most notable successes racked up by the CB450 came in the 500cc class of the newly introduced Isle of Man Production TT during 1969 and 1971. In the first year a Le Mans-type start was held for the three-lap, 112.11 mile (180.38km) race, with CB450 rider Graham Penny firing up the Honda on the electric button while rest of the field were getting ready to kick-start their bikes into life.

The Honda's instantaneous starting gave Penny an initial advantage, but Tony Dunnell soon used the extra speed of his Kawasaki Mach III triple to head the 500cc class and record the fastest lap of the race. From a standing start, Dunnell averaged 90.84mph (146.16km/h) but crashed on Lap 2, leaving Penny's CB450 in the lead. The Honda rider then went on to win at an average speed of 88.18mph (141.88km/h) finishing just under 29sec ahead of Ray Knight's Triumph Daytona. The following year, Frank Whiteway won the event on a Crooks Suzuki T500.

In 1971 the record books show a Honda 1–2. John Williams led the race from start to finish, but for three of the four laps he was chased by the Triumph of Roger Bowler and the Suzuki of Welshman Gordon Pantall. But both dropped out on the last lap and the 1969 winner, Graham Penny, took over the runners-up spot. John Williams averaged 91.04mph (146.48km/h) for the 150.92-mile (242.83km) race, with a fastest lap was 24min 45.4sec.

But by now the 450 was a machine of the past, with the CB500 four arriving in 1971 in the wake of the huge success garnered by the CB750. The final CB450 was sold in the US as the model K7 in early 1974, with a disc-braked front end. Everyone thought that for anything above a 350, Honda would in future be offering their customers fours, but they were wrong.

The CL450 Street Scrambler. This was very popular in America, but not imported into Britain.

Enter the CB500T

As *Cycle* said in its February 1975 issue: 'The CB450 landed in America in 1965; it has endured, earning its ten-year campaign pin. That's hard to do, because time clocks in Japan run full-speed ahead. Motorcycles like the CB450 quickly get upstaged by newer products with more brio – like the 4-cylinder CB500/550 series.'

But this time Honda had decided to refine rather than design an all-new motorcycle. Unfortunately, as *Cycle* was to point out, it 'inevitably become more civil and more appliance-like'. Continuing: 'Hard core, fast-riding enthusiasts will snicker at the CB500T, which has been so patently styled and so thoroughly processed into the cult of appliqué.'

However, *Cycle* also had to admit that 'riders who are not consumed by the sport of motorcycling will find the CB500T a pleasant, reliable, and generally fulfilling motorcycle'.

Technically Speaking

Honda increased the engine displacement from 444cc to 498cc, not by increasing the bore but by lengthening the stroke. The 450's bore and stroke measured 70 × 57.8mm, the 500T's stroke was pushed up to 64.8mm. Interestingly, the 450 had sufficiently thick liners to offer Honda the simple expedient of opening the bores to 74mm – this would have created a 496cc twin, something American and European tuners had already become used to doing in building a full-size five-hundred. And one must ask why Honda hadn't done so originally?

According to sources at the Japanese Honda works, its engineering team had rejected this path of 'boring for placement'. Larger pistons would increase crankshaft loads, so Honda technicians concluded that the CB450 crankshaft would have to be modified to absolutely guarantee Honda-like reliability. Clearly, if larger pistons would mean crankshaft modifications, then a simpler route was the preferred option.

For the 1968 model year the CB450 was revised, becoming the CB450K1. The update included a five-speed gearbox, revised styling and new colours.

To increase the stroke by 7mm, Honda repositioned the crankpins, moving them farther away from the crankshaft's centre line. That kind of modification usually entails a lengthening of the cylinders, but there's no need to change the cylinder head. And indeed, the 500T's head was exactly the same component from the outgoing CB450 K7.

CB450 owners had no way of using the new 500T crankshaft. The CB450 series employed roller bearings to support the crank, but the 500T had large ball race bearings. This, Honda stated at the time, was because ball bearings 'were much more tolerant of crankshaft flexing than roller bearings'. So this assumed (correctly!) that the 500T's crank flexed considerably more than the old short-stroke 450 assembly.

Another 'detuning' move was to reduce the compression. The CL450 and the final CB450s had 9:1 ratios, the 500T 8.5:1 (exactly the same as the original mid-1960s 450!).

Environmental Concerns

Honda's concern to be a 'good citizen', and thus to ensure cleaner air, had led to what the company termed a 'Blow-By Gas Circulator' system on the 500T. The cylinder head contained breathers which connected to a breather box via tubes. This breather box was located between the air filter units: inside the box, the gases from the cylinder head got separated. This gas was channelled back into the pleated paper air filters, where it joined incoming fresh air on the way to the pair of 32mm Keihin CV carburettors, whilst the oil wound up in the basement of the breather element, where it trickled down a small tube and thence back into the crankcase. As Honda said: 'The breather system contains the blow-by-gases from the combustion process: without the system these gases would vent directly into the atmosphere.'

No Change in Carb Size

The vacuum-controlled carburettors had not increased in diameter on the 500T, but the instruments had been further refined by the addition of an 'Air-Cut Valve' first seen in 1973 on the XL350 (*see* Chapter 7). The idea behind this development was to cut down the chance of misfiring in the combustion chambers when the twistgrip was snapped shut quickly. The Air-Cut Valve prevented this.

Honda had also made the outgoing plumbing more complex, with the exhaust header pipes now having an interconnector which incorporated a resonator.

Restricted Performance

But these moves, although making for a more civilized approach, also led to reduced performance. To illustrate this is to recall that when *Cycle* tested the final version of the CB450, the K7, in its April 1974 issue, it went through the standing-start quarter-mile in 14.35sec, with a terminal speed of 89.28mph (143.65km/h), whereas the CB500T tested in February 1975 could only manage 14.83sec and 85.55mph (137.65km/h). This was almost 5 per cent less with an extra 56cc!

When the respected Dave Minton tested a CB500T for *Motorcyclist Illustrated* in the February 1976 issue, he slated the general instability of

The CB500T, with Honda giving the newcomer something of a British styling job, which was not altogether successful.

the machine, even relating the story of a certain owner, R.A. Killelay of Doncaster, who was in hospital after crashing his 500T. Discovering 'it weaved and wobbled at high speed', Mr Killelay had returned the motorcycle to his dealer for investigation. Dave Minton again: 'the dealer, whoever he may be, found everything in good order and returned it to the unsuspecting Killelay with the maniacal instruction to accelerate through the trouble should it arise again! It did and Killelay, following the advice of his dealer, ended up in hospital.' It should be pointed out that Killelay had a pair of panniers fitted.

But the stability of the CB500T was called into question – even though the wheelbase had been increased by some 38mm (1.5in) over that of the CB450. The only explanation as to why the 500T was more unstable than its forebear was an increase in weight by some 30lb (14kg), which Minton said had the effect that the newer bike 'can no longer discipline it'. He continued: 'I hate to give what is, or should be, a good bike a critical bashing, but much as I admire some of Honda's new progressive attitudes, I'm blessed if I can condone the sick non-development of this model's frame and steering.'

It has to be stressed that overall Dave Minton didn't dislike the CB500T, ending the test with this statement: 'Asked to mark the 500T out of 100 as an all rounder for the majority of people

1974 CB500T Specifications

Engine	Air-cooled dohc parallel twin, alloy head and barrel, chain-driven cams, built-up crankshaft, 180-degree crank throws, valve closure by torsion bar, chain-driven camshafts, horizontally split, aluminium crankcases	Gearbox	Five speeds
		Frame	Tubular semi-duplex
		Front suspension	Oil-damped telescopic forks
		Rear suspension	Swinging arm, twin shock absorbers
Bore	70mm	Front brake	Single hydraulically operated disc
Stroke	64.8mm	Rear brake	SLS full-width alloy drum
Displacement	498.8cc	Tyres	Front 3.25 × 19, rear 3.75 × 18
Compression ratio	8.5:1		
Lubrication	Gear pump, with replaceable filter element	**General Specifications**	
		Wheelbase	55.5in (1,409mm)
Ignition	12V, twin coil/contact breaker; 144W alternator	Ground clearance	6in (152mm)
		Seat height	30in (762mm)
Carburettor	2 × 32mm Keihin CV	Fuel tank capacity	3.5gal (16ltr)
Primary drive	Gears	Dry weight	453lb (206kg)
Final drive	Chain	Maximum power	42bhp @ 8,000rpm
		Top speed	102mph (164km/h)

interested in everything but high speed riding, I'd rate it around 90.'

But, in truth, the day of the larger vertical twin was coming to an end, and as Roy Bacon says in his 1985 book *Honda: The Early Classic Motorcycles*: 'The machine itself tended to be overshadowed by the fours on the market and like other firms, Honda found out the hard way that public taste had moved away from big vertical twins.'

For once, Honda had misjudged the market, which in itself was to be a rare occurrence in its rise to the number one position in the industry.

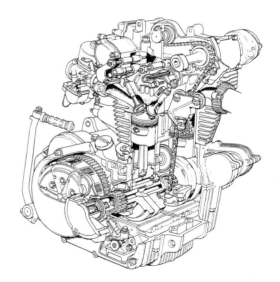

ABOVE: *The power unit of the CB500T (and CB450) was certainly innovative for a series production unit with double overhead cams, torsion bar valve springs and a 180-degree crank.*

LEFT: *Clearly based on the outgoing CB450, the CB500T displaced 498.8cc, achieved by lengthening the stroke by 7mm to 64.8mm. The large object between the two exhaust header pipes is a balance box.*

6 CB250, 350, 360 and 400

To British enthusiasts, Honda in the early days meant 250cc twins, the touring C72 with its square styling and the more highly tuned CB72 Super Sport (*see* Chapter 4). The latter sold much better, at least in the UK, where buyers preferred the extra performance and better handling, rather than the standard model. Both bikes proved pretty reliable and there were few modifications over the years.

The CB250 Arrives

But in 1967 the basic model (C72) was discontinued and the CB72 was replaced by the CB250 Super Sport. Although this seemed at

first glance to be a development of the earlier model, it was in fact a completely different machine, incorporating many lessons learnt over previous years, both on series production bikes and GP racing.

The Engine Design

Compared to the CB72, the engine of the CB250 appeared quite different, with a new appearance, including cylinders which were now vertical rather than inclined as before. The crankshaft was set at 180 degrees for superior balance. The four main bearings, centrally placed chain drive to the single overhead camshaft, alternator on the nearside (left), gear

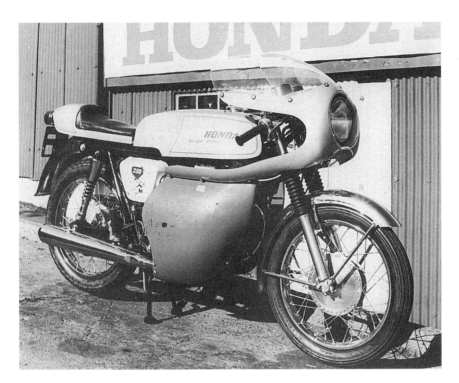

primary drive on the offside (right), ignition cam at the end of the camshaft and electric start motor at the front of the crankcase were all standard Honda practice. The new engine also had new bore and stroke dimensions of 56 × 50.6mm, giving a displacement of 249.3cc (compared to 54 × 54mm and 247.3cc).

The top end of the new CB250 differed from the outgoing engine design in that the cambox was separate from the cylinder head, the camshaft sprocket being bolted to the shaft, whilst the rockers were mounted on eccentrics which rotated to set the valve clearance. The bottom half was essentially the same except for five instead of four gears.

OPPOSITE: *The new CB250 replaced the CB72 for the 1968 model year. This CB250KO was originally sold by London dealers, Pride & Clarke, and was first registered on 1 September 1968.*

A New Frame

Although of different design, both the C72/CB72 models employed a frame with no front downtube, but the CB250 introduced a full/open tubular cradle frame, with not only a single front downtube, but twin tubes under the crankcases; there were also some pressings used in the area behind the engine.

The CB72 had featured twin leading shoe brakes front and rear, but on the CB250 the latter had been replaced by a single leading shoe – both, however, remained of the full-width aluminium type with cast-iron liners. The reason for this change had been that although the CB72's rear unit was powerful, it had proved rather too efficient, particularly in the wet, especially for novice riders.

Separate Speedo and Tacho

Another major change between the CB72 and CB250 was that the original combined speedo and tacho assembly had been discarded in favour of two separate units. This not only looked more sporting, but kept replacement costs down should one instrument prove faulty or become damaged.

Another major change was the design and efficiency of the silencers. And as Charles Deane reported when he tested one of the new CB250s in the July 1968 issue of *Motorcycle Mechanics*: 'Silence is golden so far as most people are concerned and it's a great pity that the CB250 hasn't inherited the golden qualities of the CB72. This was one of the few complaints against the machine and although the megaphone-type silencers look sporty, I personally would like to see them made more efficient.' And 'the exhaust noise was such that many a man, woman, child and beast showed signs of discomfort'.

Mechanically Quiet

In contrast to the over-noisy exhaust, mechanically, the engine and gearbox of the CB250 was,

Tommy Robb rode this CB250 in the Production TT for Worcester dealer, John Skellern, circa early 1970s.

said Charles Deane, 'quiet' with 'the large air cleaner filter taking away any induction roar'.

Another feature Charles Deane praised was the flexibility of the engine, saying 'one could waffle along happily at 30mph in fifth gear and the flexibility of the engine was such that a minimum non-snatch speed of 16mph could be achieved in top just below 2000rpm'.

Other features which got the thumbs up from Charles Deane were 'the lightest of clutches and the sweetest gear change', the 'comfortable dual seat happily accommodated two' and acceleration which was described as 'vivid'.

But he didn't approve of: 'a sharp cut-off beam for the headlamp', whilst 'the Japanese tyres are not up to British standards in the wet', which was a common complaint on all early Hondas. Also:

It is virtually impossible to see the acid level for topping up below the (lockable) dual seat. I seem to remember earlier Hondas with the battery on the side of the bike and very easy to maintain. The tool roll was also carried in the battery cover, but now it's tucked away in a non-lockable, tiny tin box just above the gearbox housing. It seems a shame that in these detail points the design had made retrograde steps.

Performance

The CB72 put out 24bhp at 9,000rpm, giving a maximum speed of 86mph (138km/h), whereas the new CB250 gave an extra 6bhp at a higher 1,500rpm, equating to a top whack of 90mph (145km/h). Handling was also adjudged to have improved. But it was in more than just the performance stakes that these early Honda two-fifties scored over their European rivals. Not only did the Honda boast decent 12V electrics, but it was such an easy bike to live with, as this road test extract from the period reveals.

Starting the CB250 was never any problem with the electric starter fitted as standard equipment.

This happy couple got married on their 1971 CB250K2. The K2 embodied various engine modifications over the earlier CB250. A new single colour of Candy Gold was adopted.

The procedure was simply to turn on the fuel, fully close the choke, switch on the ignition and, without touching the throttle, press the starter button. As the engine burbled to life, it was picked up on the throttle and in a matter of seconds the choke was fully opened. A couple of minutes at fast idling to warm the engine and one could drive off without further fuss.

The CB350

Although the CB250 was the big seller in Great Britain, it was its bigger brother, the CB350, which fitted this role in North America, where it was known as the Hawk. Both models were introduced in 1968. To illustrate just how important the 350 Honda twin was to Stateside sales is to record that 21.6 per cent of the 650,000 units sold by Honda in 1971 were 350 twins. This comprised 64,350 CB350 roadsters, 42,900 CL350 street scramblers and 33,150 SL350 trail bikes. And at that time, the Honda 350 twin was the best-selling motorcycle in the world.

Tecnhically, the CB350 was almost identical to its smaller brother, sharing the same stroke of 50.6mm, but bored out from 56 to 64mm, giving a true capacity of 325.6cc and not the quoted 350 as the name would imply. Power was raised to 36bhp at 10,500rpm.

In practically all other aspects the machines were identical, except in colour schemes. Gearbox ratios were the same, although the final drive ratio of the 350 was higher, using a 2.250 as the final reduction in comparison with 2.375:1 on the CB250. This provided a very slightly higher top speed without detracting anything from the acceleration. Most commentators still considered the CB350 to be undergeared – and even sitting up, the engine could spin into the red area in top gear at just over 90mph (145km/h), with the top speed being just under 95mph (153km/h).

But the biggest advantage in choosing a CB350 instead of its smaller brother was its ability to cope more easily with a pillion passenger. However, a complaint in this area was that these pillion passengers noticed a buzzing

1968 CB250/350 Specifications (CB350 in brackets where different)			
Engine	Air-cooled sohc parallel twin, alloy head and barrel, chain-driven camshaft, 180-degree crankshaft, unit construction, horizontally split aluminium crankcases	Rear suspension	Swinging arm, twin shock absorbers
		Front brake	2LS full-width alloy drum
		Rear brake	SLS full-width alloy drum
		Tyres	Front 3.00 × 18, rear 3.25 × 18 (CB350: 3.00 × 18)
Bore	56mm (CB350: 64mm)		
Stroke	50.6mm		
Displacement	249.3cc (CB350: 325.6cc)	**General Specifications**	
Compression ratio	9.5:1	Wheelbase	52in (1,321mm)
Lubrication	Wet sump	Ground clearance	5.5in (140mm)
Ignition	12V, battery/coil, electric start	Seat height	29.5in (749mm)
Carburettor	2 × Keihin	Fuel tank capacity	N/A
Primary drive	Gear	Dry weight	328lb (149kg) (CB350: 330lb (150kg))
Final drive	Chain		
Gearbox	Five speeds; foot-change	Maximum power	30bhp @ 10,500rpm (CB350: 36bhp @ 10,500rpm)
Frame	Full loop, tubular single front downtube		
		Top speed	90mph (km/h) (CB350: 94mph (151km/h))
Front suspension	Oil-damped telescopic fork		

vibration via the footrests when the full performance was used, plus ground clearance was a problem when two-up, even with the suspension on the hardest setting. Another problem (also found on the two-fifty) was marginal brakes with the heavier load.

The SL350 (not sold in the UK) was tested by the American *Cycle World* in December 1969. It achieved a maximum speed of 86mph (138km/h). The magazine considered it a 'reliable, stylish play bike' but not 'a true dirt bike', even though it had greater potential off-road than earlier Honda twins. Power was a claimed 33bhp at 9,500rpm.

By the 1973 model year the CB350 had reached its K4 series. And, as with the CB250, Honda thought it was time to move on, even though it was estimated that some one-fifth of all motorcycles in the world were 250/350 Honda twins.

Enter the 360

As *Motorcycle World* reported in its October 1974 issue, 'They're [the 350] being replaced with a 360. So for Honda's sake, the new machine had better be good. It isn't.' But

A 1971 CL350 Street Scrambler, based on the CB350 roadster.

A best-seller in the States, the CB350K4 of 1973. The 325.6cc (64 × 50.6mm) sohc, five-speed engine put out a claimed 36bhp at 10,500rpm.

For 1974 the CB350 was replaced by the new CB360. But although continuing to sell in millions, the new machine was generally not liked as much as the older bike.

It is a bureaucrat's dream, quiet and unobtrusive as a Swiss watch, reliable as Big Ben, clean and tidy enough to be parked in the lobby of the Dorchester, comfortable as an easy chair and a willing starter. It never begs to be ridden fast. That's just as well as the handling on the open road left plenty to be desired. As a result the CB360 is about as characterless as a real motorcycle can get. True, it performs all the tasks the everyday motorcyclist will demand of it, but there's a somewhat bitter aftertaste at the end of each ride.

Meanwhile, the American journal *Cycle Illustrated* described the CB360 thus: 'Ladies and Gentlemen, the Rolling Stone. Honda's motorcycle for the common man is mediocrity with a dash of class.' This final statement really highlights just why the CB360 (and the later CX500 V-twin) were successes even though purely in terms of performance, power and style they left much to be desired. Like the 360, the CX wasn't particularly fast, certainly didn't handle, but still sold like hot cakes. To illustrate this, in its first production year no fewer than 2,132,902 360s were built and sold – this figure includes the smaller quarter-litre CB250G model. This latter machine retained the same 56 × 50.6mm bore and stroke dimensions as its predecessor, but strangely was only offered with a disc front brake, hence the G prefix.

although the CB360 was an unexciting bike, it was nonetheless a spectacular sales success.

The CB360 (with disc brake coded G), together with the smaller engined CB250, was launched at the Paris Show in October 1973. On paper, the newcomers were a considerable advance, with six speeds and the choice of a 2LS drum or disc front brake. But as *Motor Cyclist Illustrated* noted, it was very much a case of 'Potential rather than actual.'

Honda had set out to make a 'motorcycle for everyone', but by doing so had managed to fall between two stools. By adding a sixth ratio, a disc brake (some bikes had drum brakes, but not in Britain), together with totally new styling, Honda was successful in its aims. But the engineering team had also created a highly civilized motorcycle which was also totally soulless. *Motor Cycle* commented:

> When legislators have finally hounded the motorcyclist to the brink of extinction, he will probably be riding something like the Honda CB360 twin.

Engine Details

Actual engine capacities were 356.8cc (67 × 50.6mm) for the 360 and 249.3cc for the smaller bike. This meant that although the 250 remained the same as its forerunner, the 360 was considerably larger than the mere 10cc suggested by its designation; in fact, it had an additional 31.2cc.

By 1974 all Honda twins featured 360-degree crankshafts and because of this went through a vibration patch between 5–6,000rpm. It was nothing too serious, just enough to be felt and get annoying after a while, particularly because this represented the lowest figure at which the motor was happy and therefore the ideal speed for gear changing and gentle cruising. Above and beyond this rough patch the engine smoothed out. Maximum power was 34bhp at 9,000rpm (2bhp down on the smaller capacity CR350!), with maximum torque being produced in typical Honda fashion at a fairly high 7,500rpm.

British Debut
Both the 360 and 250 made their British debuts at the Racing and Sporting Show in early 1974. From a spectator's viewpoint there was nothing externally, except colours and side panel badges, to tell them apart. But from the prospective owner's seat, there was not only the asking-price difference, but also power output and insurance figures; also, only the smaller model could be used by a novice on British roads.

The new CB250, in fact, felt quite gutless until the motor was screaming near the red line. Sixth gear was very much an overdrive – with the machine capable of just over 80mph

The CB360 engine size was actually 356.8cc (67 × 50.6mm). Another feature was an additional gear ratio over the CB350, making six in total.

(130km/h) whether in top or fifth. To hold a high speed, the smaller unit needed frequent gearbox use – using fifth or even fourth to hold station against headwinds or steep inclines and for overtaking.

More Torque with the 360
By comparison, the 360 had more torque and therefore urge, particularly in the mid-range. For any given throttle opening it would pull away that much better and could hold a 70–80mph (113–130km/h) cruising speed. Maximum speed was now 90mph (145km/h), in spite of what Honda sources claimed in their press releases. But as with the 250, the 360 suffered from being overgeared. The official factory line was 'this is to provide comfortable cruising without stretching the engine and to improve fuel consumption by keeping the revs down'. Unfortunately, in this author's opinion, this only works where there is a much larger displacement engine and far more torque available than with the 360 twin.

In reality, the new middleweight was no performance machine. Instead, its attraction lay in being quiet, smooth and easy to live with. An unseen advantage of its relatively mild performance was that consumables like chains, brakes and tyres lasted longer; even the oil level stayed constant. All the rider had to do was add petrol, get on and go.

A Large Seat and Soft Suspension
The large dual seat and soft suspension provided a luxurious ride, but the downside was roadholding, which could only be described as poor to average. The CB360 (and the new CB250G) had a rather negative, sloppy feel which didn't inspire any attempts at hard cornering, whilst the performance of the original equipment rear shocks meant a sales bonanza for aftermarket suppliers during the mid- to late 1970s.

Fuel consumption when ridden hard averaged around 50mpg (5.7/100km), and *Motor-*

	1974 CB250G/360G Specifications (CB360G in brackets where different)			
Engine	Air-cooled sohc parallel twin, alloy head and barrel, chain-driven camshaft, 360-degree crankshaft, unit construction, horizontally split aluminium crankcases	Front brake	Single hydraulically operated 260mm disc★	
		Rear brake	SLS full-width alloy drum	
		Tyres	Front 3.00 × 18, rear 3.50 × 18	
Bore	56mm (CB360G: 67mm)			
Stroke	50.6mm	**General Specifications**		
Displacement	249.3cc (CB360G: 356.8cc)	Wheelbase	53in (1,346mm)	
Compression ratio	9.5:1 (CB360G: 9.3:1)	Ground clearance	5in (127mm)	
Lubrication	Wet sump	Seat height	30.5in (775mm)	
Ignition	12V, battery/coil, electric start	Fuel tank capacity	2.3gal (11ltr)	
Carburettor	2 × Keihin	Dry weight	364lb (165kg)	
Primary drive	Gears	Maximum power	28bhp @ 10,000rpm (CB360G: 34bhp @ 9,000rpm)	
Final drive	Chain			
Gearbox	Six speeds; foot-change	Top speed	82mph (132km/h) (CB360G: 87mph (140km/h))	
Frame	Full loop, tubular, single front downtube			
Front suspension	Oil-damped telescopic fork			
Rear suspension	Swinging arm, twin shock absorbers	★ Some machines sold with front brake drum.		

cycle Mechanics stated that: 'It is easy to improve these figures by about 10mpg but it would be so much nicer to be able to quote 80 or 90mpg [3.54 or 3.14100/km] like the B31, Model 50 and Viper [British 350s built by BSA, Norton and Velocette in the 1950s and 1960s] owners.' To many observers, the twin 30mm CV (Constant Velocity) Keihin carburettors were too large and complicated, with *Motorcycle Mechanics* continuing 'on friendly little machines like these I'd rather see something simple with a maximum of two adjustments'.

An Outstanding Front Stopper

One area on the CB250G/360 which received almost universal praise was the outstandingly effective front brake. Although it might have lacked the all-out stopping power of a racing unit, the single 260mm hydraulically operated disc was not only extremely progressive, but was a genuine improvement on the old 2LS drum which had begun service with the CB72 at the beginning of the 1960s.

Another well-received feature was the efficient 12V electrics and push-button starter, though a kick-starter was retained as a back-up. 12V also meant a 50W headlamp, which was more than adequate for the 250/360 series performance. This was in stark contrast to many other under 400cc bikes of the early 1970s, which still retained 6V systems that were hard-pressed to produce more than a yellow glow from the headlamp.

Problem Areas

Problem areas included the upswept, rot-prone silencers and the small 2.3gal (11ltr) fuel tank. Another dislike was the side-stand. But Honda had tackled one existing problem which had displayed itself on the earlier CB350. Several, mainly American, owners, who tended to leave their bikes ticking over on the side-stand for some time, had experienced seizures of the offside (right) camshaft bearing due to lack of lubrication. The oil would drain to the nearside whilst the other end would become starved. To alleviate this, Honda had on the 360 and latest 250 used an entirely different stand. They made it longer so that the bike stood more upright, although this had the drawback that even a slight gust of wind could knock the bike over!

So how does one sum up the mid-1970s' CB250G and CB360? By direct comparison with other models (and certainly the models it replaced in the Honda line), it simply didn't measure up. Performance was lacking, vibration was there and its roadholding far from perfect. However, it still managed to outsell almost everything on the market at the time. Why? The answer I'm sure lay in its easy-to-live-with nature, its reliability and the fact that it had the Honda badge.

The CJ250T/360T

The next development in the 250/360 story came at the end of 1976 with the arrival of the much-revised CJ250T and CJ360T models. A major technical change was a switch back to a five-speed gearbox.

Colin Mayo, the then editor of *Motorcycle Mechanics*, had this to say in the January 1977 issue:

> One can only speculate on why it has taken Honda such a very long time to sort out the horrible handling of their 250 [also read 360] twin. Whatever the reason it must have been a very good one for it probably cost them a fortune in sales lost to the taut handling two-stroke competition in the ultra competitive quarter-litre market.

Motorcycle Mechanics continued:

> Standard procedure for those of a cowardly disposition and a friendly bank manager was to throw the original equipment dampers away and replace them with Girlings or Konis. So the bad news for the damper manufacturers is good news for all Honda fans, for the new 250T handles outstandingly well and in many respects is better than the

The CJ360T replaced the G in 1976. The 'Euro-style' attempted to replicate the CB400F, but without the same measure of success. Note 2-into-1 exhaust.

1976 CJ250T/360T Specifications (CJ360T in brackets where different)

Engine	Air-cooled sohc parallel twin, alloy head and barrel, chain-driven camshaft, 360-degree crankshaft, unit construction, horizontally split aluminium crankcases, siamesed exhaust header pipe with single silencer	Front suspension	Oil-damped telescopic fork
		Rear suspension	Swinging arm, twin shock absorbers
		Front brake	Single hydraulically operated 260mm disc
		Rear brake	SLS full-width alloy drum
		Tyres	3.00 × 18 front, rear 3.150 × 18
Bore	56mm (CJ360T: 67mm)		
Stroke	50.6mm	**General Specifications**	
Displacement	249.3cc (CJ360T: 356.8cc)	Wheelbase	54.1in (1,374mm)
Compression ratio	9.5:1 (CJ360T: 9.3:1)	Ground clearance	6in (152mm)
Lubrication	Wet sump	Seat height	30in (762mm)
Ignition	12V battery/coil, electric start	Fuel tank capacity	3gal (14ltr)
Carburettor	2 × Keihin	Dry weight	357lb (162kg) (CJ360T: 359lb (163kg))
Primary drive	Gear		
Final drive	Chain	Maximum power	26bhp @ 9,500rpm (CJ360T: 34bhp @ 9,000rpm)
Gearbox	Five speeds		
Frame	Full loop, tubular, single front downtube	Top speed	80mph (130km/h) (CJ360T: 86mph (138km/h))

rival two-strokes for it can be stuffed into a bumpy corner on the overrun or on a progressively opening throttle and come out the other side with the rider in complete control.

The new CJ250T/350T had a 'Euro-style' not dissimilar to other Hondas of the late 1970s, including the CB400F and CB750F. This included not only the style of components such as the fuel tank and side panels, but also the use of a siamesed exhaust system – the single silencer running down low on the offside (right) of the motorcycle. This silencer was of truly massive proportions and, as Colin Mayo said, 'does an excellent job of keeping the exhaust note, even at 9,500rpm'. However, he continued: 'But the price of the Honda's silence is a high one so far as mid-range torque goes and this motor takes a long time to spin

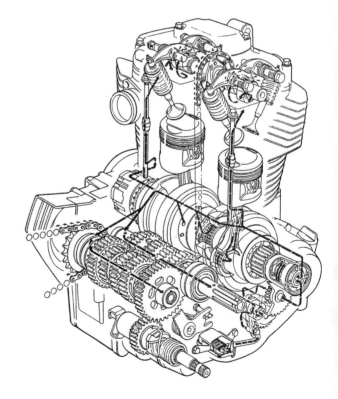

An X-ray view of CJ360T/250T lubrication details. It also shows features such as valve gear, pistons, crankshaft and gearbox, the latter having moved back to five ratios.

up to the 8,000rpm mark where it starts to really respond, as it should, to the demands of the throttle.'

As before, the 360 offered a more flexible torquey power output than the 250 version.

The New Dream

In truth, the 360T (and its smaller brother, the 250T) were destined to have a very short production life – of only a single year. This was because in the late summer of 1977, Honda produced a new series of middleweight twins – the CB250T Dream, the CB400T and a two-speed automatic based on the latter model, catalogued as the Hondamatic 400.

The big seller worldwide was expected to be the CB400T and at the same time Honda sources confirmed what many suspected, that this newcomer would effectively replace the 400 four (*see* Chapter 11). The problem was that the four, although popular in Europe, was not so in America and at that time in the late 1970s, America still called the tune so far as Honda was concerned.

Three Valves and Two Balancer Shafts

The newcomers featured not only new ultra short-stroke engine dimensions, but also 3-valves-per-cylinder (two inlet, one exhaust) and twin balance shafts. The 3-valve layout had been adapted, said Honda, 'to give improved mid-range torque without loss of power higher up the rev range'. Valve sizes were 26mm inlet and 32mm exhaust.

The new '400' twin was actually 395cc (70.5 × 50.6mm) and produced a claimed 40bhp at 9,500rpm, whilst the equally new 249cc (62 × 41.4mm) put out a claimed 27bhp at 10,000rpm. The 400 Hondamatic (*see* box) gave a 'detuned 35bhp'.

Performance of the 400T was, as *Motorcycle Mechanics* said in its September 1977 issue, 'particularly lively, with 95mph coming up quickly and effortlessly'. However, as Colin Mayo pointed out, 'the engine is nowhere near as smooth as the four, in spite of the use of twin balance shafts on the crankshaft'. Maximum speed was almost 100mph (162km/h). At cruising speeds ranging from 50–70mph (80–113km/h), the 400T produced mild

In the late summer of 1977, Honda introduced its new CB400T Dream (shown) – plus a smaller-engined version, the CB250T and the Hondamatic 400.

400 Hondamatic

In the autumn of 1977 Honda launched the new CB400T twin – and gave riders the choice of manual or automatic transmission. The latter machine was marketed as the Hondamatic. However, in truth it was not an automatic gearbox motorcycle at all – the gearbox being quite conventional in that it had a mechanical foot-change, but only incorporated two speeds. What made it worthy of the 'Hondamatic' tag was a fluid flywheel coupling the engine to the gearbox; something BSA had produced in prototype form as long ago as the 1930s!

Like any other motorcycle the engine was started in neutral and the rider 'lifted' the pedal to obtain either of the two gears. The left hand clutch lever was a parking brake and was fitted with a lock-out device so that you couldn't pull it on when riding. And pulling away for the first time was a strange experience; using the first, low, ratio initial take-off was pretty rapid, if only because all one needed to do was snap the throttle open. However, this initial progress was blunted as the flywheel slipped for quite a time. Although it was possible to scream the engine up to 55/60mph (90/100km/h) in first, this was totally unnecessary, and it was much better to change up around 30mph (50km/h) – the higher ratio could be retained well below this figure. And in truth the Hondamatic 400 twin was really most suited to city use, rather than open road sports mode. As *Motorcycle Mechanics* said in the October 1980 issue: 'performance isn't exactly shattering'. The magazine recorded a top speed of 90.75mph (146km/h) – compared with a genuine 100mph (162km/h) for the conventional six-speed 400T.

The 400A had the same basic 395cc engine as the 400T, but it had been detuned by using smaller valves. Maximum power was cut to 30bhp at 8,000rpm.

One disconcerting feature of the Hondamatic system was the freewheeling effect the torque converter gave on the overrun. On a dry road this wasn't so much of a problem as on wet surfaces – and as for ice…

Although technically interesting, the 400A didn't prove popular, going the same way as Honda's own seven-fifty four auto and the Moto Guzzi V1000. Quite simply, unlike the four-wheel world, motorcyclists were not interested in the automatic route.

The CB400A, marketed as the Hondamatic, was not in truth an automatic gearbox motorcycle at all – it was in fact quite conventional, with a mechanical foot-change but only two speeds.

vibes, but over 7,500rpm these increased quite considerably.

FVQ Dampers

Motorcycle Mechanics were impressed with the newcomer's handling, pointing out that this had been 'helped' by the introduction of new FVQ rear shocks, which featured a switch to a secondary damping system when suspension movement reached a certain level. These new dampers were fitted to all new Hondas for the 1978 model year of 125cc or above, except the CG125.

Another feature of the new 250 and 400 twins was the use of a Tri-pulsar capacitor discharge ignition system (CDI), which was maintenance-free. This CDI system was magneto-energized and therefore generated its own spark.

Comstar Wheels

Another new feature Honda that introduced for several of its models for the 1978 season were Comstar wheels. Effectively, these were an aluminium rim, riveted to five spokes and a central hub. Braking on both the 250T and

400T (plus the Hondamatic) was by way of a single disc up front and a drum at the rear. Once again, this was an area which testers and owners generally agreed could have been improved, certainly when two-up. Quite simply, the front brake was not powerful enough. *Cycle* magazine saying: 'The rear drum brake, carrying less of the load, performs just fine; braking is progressive with good feel. The front disc, however, will fade with constant hard use.'

Compared to the outgoing CB250T/360T, the new 250/400 models had a totally new styling – much more rounded, dumpy even, than the outgoing machines. *Motorcycle Mechanics* commented: 'Fairly ordinary, quite neatly styled but with no great flair.' And instead of the siamesed exhaust, the new models sported separate exhausts, with two dumpy megaphone silencers – and a massive rustprone collector box connecting these latter components.

Comfort – The Bike's Best Feature

It was generally agreed that comfort was probably the 250T/400T series' best feature, helped by a large dual seat and for once decent suspension on a middleweight Honda twin.

However, this latest attempt at mass sales was largely to fail, resulting in yet another revamp within a few months.

The CB250N/400N Super Dream

The Super Dream models didn't totally replace the 250/400T models; instead, the two series ran alongside each other, at least during the late 1970s. The Super Dream duo (no Hondamatic version was offered) debuted in the spring of 1978. As *Motorcyclist Illustrated* commented: 'Nobody could fail to be impressed. The stocky, stubby look [of the T series] had been replaced by new styling specially for the European market.'

The motor cycle press liked the new styling, the dealers fell over one another to place orders for both the 250 and 400cc variants, and the only murmur of discontent came from those riders who had just forked out for what they thought was a new motorcycle in the shape of a 250 or 400T!

OK, the CB400N cost an extra £80 more than the T version, at £949, including VAT in Great Britain (summer 1978). But besides the brand-new, much-loved style, buyers got a number of detail improvements, most notably dual discs on the front wheel (400 only). Honda claimed 43bhp at 9,500rpm and a maximum speed of 108mph (174km/h). Mechanically, the T and N power units were virtually identical, except for state of tune.

Modifications for 1980

Honda introduced some modifications for the 1980 model year 250/400N machines. Tighter air pollution standards in the States prompted

Besides the CB250/400T series, there were also the CB250N and CB400N Super Dream models which appeared at the end of the 1970s and ran into the early 1980s. A 250N is shown here in the Wisbech dealership of Mick Walker Motorcycles in 1980.

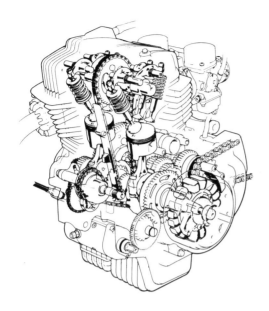

The Super Dream models featured a large bore, ultra-short stroke configuration, providing high rpm and power within a safe piston speed.

two Keihins so as to maintain sharp throttle response despite the leanish slow speed and mid-range circuitry. The smaller carbs meant a drop in horsepower, but this was offset against the introduction of a new six-speed, close-ratio gearbox that allowed the 1980 engine to work higher in its power band and to maintain performance better. The smaller carburettors also had improved fuel-consumption figures by some ten per cent.

It is also worth noting that in North America many 400s were sold with a five-speed gearbox, these models being coded CM400T and CM400E. In Great Britain the CB250N Super Dream was the top-selling bike in 1980 regardless of capacity. Together with other sales successes, including the CB900F and CX500, this cemented Honda's number one position in the market as the 1980s began.

The CB250N and CB400N were also destined to be the last of a line, the middleweight 250/400 sohc twin-cylinder Hondas with twin rear shocks and a relatively low purchase price, as the new decade was not only to witness rapid technical changes, with different engine formats, but a move away from the mass market motorcycle-for-basic-transport era.

the company to reduce carburettor size on the 400, switching from the original 32mm CV Keihin to 30mm instruments. Honda also added a common accelerator pump for the

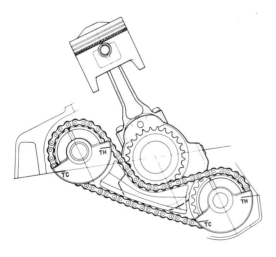

A pair of chain-driven counterbalancers helped to eliminate most of the vibration associated with a 360-degree crankshaft.

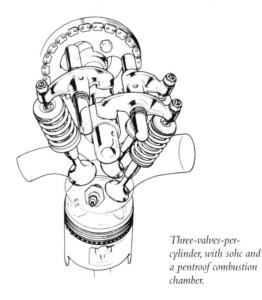

Three-valves-per-cylinder, with sohc and a pentroof combustion chamber.

7 XL Trail and TL Trial

The American market was largely responsible for one of Honda's most technically interesting single-cylinder motorcycles. At last, the Stateside arm of the Honda Motor Company responded to countless calls for the market leaders to offer a genuine green lanes four-stroke single.

An All-Time Great

As 1972 dawned, the company was finally in a position to come up with one of its all-time great bikes, the all-new XL250 (known in some markets as the SL250S).

At the conclusion of Honda America's week-long 4,000-member dealer convention, the press were at last given the lowdown, where at the giant Las Vegas Convention Centre, some eighty or so of the world's journalists were briefed on the 1972 range. According to *Motorcyclist*: 'The star of the show was the all-new lightweight 4-valve XL250 single that Honda has created to take dead aim at the two-stroke off-road market.' ('Off-road' in reality meant what we now call trail riding.)

Honda America had originally been set-up in 1959; the Japanese and their carefully selected American lieutenants were not only aggressive salesmen, but were also innovative, dedicated and extremely sensitive to the mood of their new land. They had, in fact, not only done a Pearl Harbor on the motorcycle industry, but this time almost won the war too!

Skirting the tactics which had brought them fame in Europe, Honda had shied away from a GP-type race programme. Instead, it set out to look after the needs of the average rider, both on- and off-road. This policy worked in the States, with Honda America having seen off the European competition thanks to machines such as the C50, 350 Hawk and CB750 four. However, its dirt bikes had never quite made the grade.

Originally success in this area had called for large capacity four-stroke singles, which the British had filled with bikes such as the BSA Gold Star and Matchless G80 until the early 1960s, when the lightweight two strokes had begun to take over, including Honda's rivals Suzuki and Yamaha.

This spurred Honda into action – after all, pride was at stake. But at that time Honda meant four-stroke and this gave its engineers back in Japan a challenge – to come up with a competitive four-stroke 250 dirt-oriented bike in a sea of two-strokes.

And so, late in 1971, had come the first rumours that Honda had designed a 'suitable' bike.

A 4-Valve Single

The result was the XL250, Honda's first 4-valve *production* engine, and because of this it is worth examining its technical features in detail. Taking it from the beginning, the XL250 Motor Sport (the official Honda title for the newcomer) employed four valves because this had been shown by the Honda GP racing team as the necessary requirement der for equal cooling. The very short camshaft had only two lobes since each rocker was forked on the valve side to accommodate two valves rather than one. In the head, the top half of the camshaft was secured by the rocker box when in place, whilst the rocker arms were fully contained in the rocker box above and adjusted by means of conventional threaded adjuster screws and lock nuts, which were accessible through cover plates front and rear. The nearside (left) end of the camshaft carried the contact breaker ignition; the camshaft ran direct in the aluminium – a feature which Honda had employed in some of its other engines over the years, including the CB500 four. Combustion pressure sealing was assured with a six-bolt head pattern, with the bolts' wide spacing from the centre of the head hinting at a larger bore to come.

The Advantages of 4-Valve technology

What were the advantages of a 4-valve head? The answer was many. Although a few more moving parts were involved – two additional valves and their springs – its use triggered a landslide of advantages, as both manufacturers and tuners had known since the vintage days. Most beneficial was the greatly increased valve area permissible; more than 20 per cent on the XL250. This additional breathing capacity meant it was possible to achieve shorter cam timing or duration of time during which it was necessary to leave the valves open to obtain maximum filling of the cylinder.

Compare this short cam timing advantage to a conventional 2-valve head for just a moment; if higher engine revolution performance is expected from a 2-valver, it becomes necessary to open the inlet valve early and close it late to achieve adequate cylinder filling at high rpm. This was all right for high speed but permitted leakage, even spit-back, at the lower end of the rev scale needed in a dirt bike

Honda went on to dominate the World Trials Championship as the 1970s gave way to the 1980s. Here, works rider, Eddy Lejeune, shows how to remain 'feet up' on a difficult section in the Scottish Six Day Trials event.

in achieving ultimate performance in a four-stroke power plant.

But unlike its 2-, 4-, 5- and 6-cylinder tarmac racing brothers, the new production bike used a single-cylinder, single overhead cam engine, with chain-drive camshaft. This was taken directly off an internal sprocket on the left side of the crankshaft and was contained within a special tower cast in the cylinder head and barrel. This tower stood free of the cylinder through most of its length, allowing ample air flow around the nearside (left) of the cylin-

The 1972 XL250 'Motor Sport' featured a short-stroke 248.6cc (74 × 57.8mm) engine with five speeds and Keihin 28mm carb. Maximum power of 22bhp at 8,000rpm produced healthy on- and off-road performance.

engine. Consequently, the 2-valve head tuner had to decide where he wanted his best power spread – at high or low revs – but not both! This was where the 4-valve design offered its biggest advantage outside Grand Prix racing. Because of their superior area, the dual–inlet valves, for example, could be lifted later and because of their individually lighter weight, not only was the top end improved, but the excellent sealing at low rpm provided superior bottom end characteristics. In addition, the valves in a 4-valve head could be considerably smaller, which meant extra torque. Smaller valves also meant less reciprocating weight per valve, permitting smaller springs and superior spring control. Although valve lift, rate and time of opening are determined by flow meter, the multitude of advantages offered by the 4-valve design gave Honda engineers a wide latitude of movement in several directions in achieving the ideal.

Narrow Valve Angle
Another feature was the narrow angle between the inlet and exhaust valves in the XL250 engine. Putting them more vertically contributed to shorter and therefore reciprocating rocker weight, less possibility of the valves tangling on overlap and less valve head restriction of air flow with the inlet valves in the open position.

Central Spark Plug Placement
Yet another advantage was central spark plug placement invited by the 4-valve layout. This encouraged even flame propagation, with the flame spreading evenly and equally from the centre in all directions. Additionally, the layout

lent itself to the pent-roof head configuration, which left space for a squish area at the outer perimeters of the head, giving the flame room to spread out as it expanded into the small flat cavities between the outer extremities of the head and piston. This squish area was extremely difficult to achieve in a 2-valve head without choking off the combustion area and limiting compression ratio. In the production XL250, Honda did really make much use of this latter point, running only a 9.1:1 compression ratio, even though it would have been possible to go as high as 12:1.

Individual Ports

On the XL250, the port behind each of the four valves was individual, with a wall separating the two respective ports of the inlet and exhaust systems rather than opening out into a common plenum chamber arrangement immediately behind the valves. This thin wall extended from between each of the respective valves most of the distance to the outside of the head in the interests of optimum flow direction and velocity. In addition, the inlet port was offset to the offside (right) of the centre, which positioned the carburettor outside the chassis framework, allowing a straight shot from air filter to carb mouth to assist breathing at higher rpm.

Moving the carb towards the outside of the frame also aided adjustment and eliminated much of the usual interference between throttle cables, tank and top frame tube. There were, as on some early Honda fours, two throttle cables; one pulled the throttle open while the other pulled it closed. The piston slide-type carburettor was a 28mm Keihin.

Short-Stroke Dimensions

The XL250 had short-stroke 74 × 57.8mm bore and stroke dimensions, giving a displacement of 248.6cc. Even so, the motor produced excellent torque, a point I well remember from my own 1973 XL250 Motorsport machine.

Sliding down the bore we'll now take a look

at the bottom end. The crankshaft was pressed together and ran in roller bearings, with a combination flywheel and magneto on the nearside (left) end, with access being gained by the removal of the outer engine casing. Incidentally, both outer covers (left and right) were manufactured in magnesium – a material normally reserved for pure competition engines.

The offside (right) side of the crankshaft was splined to accept two straight cut gears and a centrifugal oil filter. The larger of the two gears served as a primary drive to the clutch basket, whilst the smaller pinion's sole purpose was to drive the tachometer. If the tacho was removed (for serious dirt use, for example), this gear could be dispensed with – slipped off its shaft and removed to save further weight and friction. But its shaft should not be taken out since its hollow centre carried pressurized oil to the overhead camshaft components. The connecting-rod bearings consisted of a plain bearing small end and a caged roller big end.

Horizontally Split Crankcases

Split horizontally, the crankcases were very much in the traditional Japanese mould, with the bottom section serving as a wet sump for both engine and gearbox. The oil pump was of the Trochoid type – which Honda claimed to be 'extremely efficient, practically frictionless and utterly simple'. Well, they would, wouldn't they? Also known as the Eaton type, this design of pump featured an off-centre driven inner vane which rotated within a free outer ring having a matching inner profile. But since there was one fewer tooth on the vane than on the ring, the ring had to run faster than the vane in making one complete revolution, and the resulting opening and closing between the teeth meant that a positive amount of oil was induced and discharged every revolution.

The Oil Supply

Oil from the pump was split – part was directed to the gearbox shafts nearby, while the rest

1972 XL250 Motorsport Specifications			
Engine	Air-cooled sohc 4-valve single-cylinder inclined 15 degrees, chain-driven camshaft, unit construction, vertically split crankcases, magnesium outer covers, vertically split aluminium crankcases	Frame	Full loop, tubular; single front downtube
		Front suspension	Oil-damped telescopic fork
		Rear suspension	Swinging arm, twin shock absorbers
		Front brake	SLS conical drum
		Rear brake	SLS conical drum
Bore	74mm	Tyres	Front 2.75 × 21, rear 4.00 × 18
Stroke	57.8mm		
Displacement	248.6cc		
Compression ratio	9.1:1	**General Specifications**	
Lubrication	Trochoid pump, wet sump	Wheelbase	56.5in (1,435mm)
Ignition	Flywheel magneto/contact breakers	Ground clearance	6.12in (156mm)
		Seat height	32in (813mm)
Carburettor	Keihin 28mm	Fuel tank capacity	1.76gal (8ltr)
Primary drive	Gears	Dry weight	279lb (127kg)
Final drive	Chain	Maximum power	22bhp @ 8,000rpm
Gearbox	Five speeds	Top speed	77mph (124km/h)

was routed out through the magnesium outer crankcase cover and then back to the crankcase proper via two aligning orifices at the crankshaft and aforementioned tachometer drive shaft levels. One line, of course, went to the crank, while the other was routed through an oversize cylinder stud tunnel to the overhead cam mechanism. Oil return, from overhead to sump, spilled over and down the cam-chain passage. Interposed between the end of the crankshaft and the oil passage emanating from the magnesium outer cover was the centrifugal oil filter, which purified the oil before it sent it to the main bearings and crank journals. One other filter, a screen mesh, was located in the system, in the lower right side of the crankcase outer cover, which, like the main filter compartment, could be cleaned periodically.

Last in a Four-Gear Train

The small gear which operated the Trochoid oil pump was the last gear in a four-gear train. This originated from another small gear on the rear of the clutch hub; the clutch gear, which was

mounted on the gearbox mainshaft, drove an idler off the end of the countershaft. This meshed with the kick-starter gear, which, in turn, drove the oil pump gear. This design allowed the five-speed gearbox to be started in any gear simply by pulling in the clutch prior to kick-starting it through. Called primary kick-starting, this feature was to become an almost universal feature of later Japanese trail bikes; the 1972 XL250 was a pioneer in this respect.

Ball and Needle Bearings

The gearbox shafts ran in ball and needle bearings and were so close-coupled with the engine that one flywheel flange had to be notched to clear a gear. The sweet operating box was complicated by an efficient seven-plate, rubber-damped clutch.

Ownership

If the engine had a weakness it was that the offside (right) outer crankcase cover carried the main oil passages to the crankshaft and cam

Why Honda Won The World Grand Prix

What makes a motorcycle great? How did Honda set new records in the Dutch Tourist Trophy and the Belgium Grand Prix, and then go on to win the World Grand Prix? The answer to both of these questions is precision engineering!

No other motorcycles . . . and few machines of any kind . . . are built with greater care and precision than the Honda. Every one of the 85,000 Honda motorcycles produced each month is custom engineered with the accuracy of a watchmaker to insure perfection; then carefully tested for durability . . . to bring you the finest machine in the world. Buy a Honda . . . it is your assurance of precision engineering.

HONDA 250 Super Sport

Engine: O.H.C. Twin cylinder, 4-stroke
Cylinder capacity: 247cc
Max. HP: 24PS/9,000rpm
Max. speed: 93mph
Fuel consumption: 109mpg

HONDA 250

Engine: O.H.C. Twin cylinder, 4-stroke
Cylinder capacity: 247cc
Max. HP: 20PS/8,000rpm
Max. speed: 84mph
Fuel consumption: 106mpg

HONDA 50

Engine: O.H.V. Single cylinder, 4-stroke
Cylinder capacity: 49cc
Max. HP: 4.5PS/9,500rpm
Max. speed: 45mph
Fuel consumption: 221mpg

Please write inquiries to:
MAICO (GREAT BRITAIN) LTD.
81A Gloucester Road, London, S.W. 7,
England

ARTIE BELL
454, Woodstock Road, Belfast,
Northern Ireland

REG. ARMSTRONG MOTOR CYCLES LTD.
South Dock Work Ringsend Road, Dublin,
Republic of Ireland

HONDA MOTOR CO., LTD.

No. 5, 5-chome, Yaesu, Chuo-ku, Tokyo, Japan Tel: (281) 2921

ABOVE: A Honda advertisement dated August 1961 using the Japanese marque's GP success to promote its series production roadsters; riders shown as Tom Phillis (26) and Mike Hailwood (22).

ABOVE: Honda's — and the world's — best-seller, the legendary Super Cub. Production began in 1958. To date, over thirty million have been sold worldwide.

BELOW: The legendary jewel-like CB92 arrived in 1959. Its 124.7cc (44 × 41mm) sohc parallel twin engine put out 15bhp at 10,500rpm, giving a maximum speed of 81mph (130km/h).

ABOVE: *Called the Super Hawk in the States, the 305cc CB77 twin (together with its smaller 247cc brother, the CB72) had a 180-degree crankshaft, 12V electrics and push-button starting.*

BELOW: *Later versions of the square-style, C92 (125) and C95 (154) touring twins had higher 'bars with exposed control and electrical cables; a 1964 C95 is shown.*

LEFT: The Honda stand at the London Earls Court Show, November 1964, with a 154cc C95 twin in the foreground.

BELOW: For the 1963 season Honda produced the CR110 (50cc) and CR93 (125cc) dohc production racing machines. One of the smaller bikes is pictured here at the 50cc Enduro, Snetterton summer 1964.

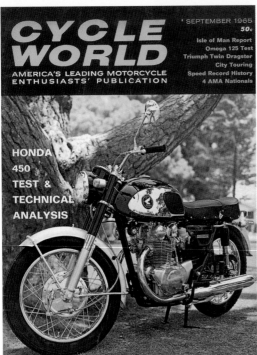

CYCLE WORLD

AMERICA'S LEADING MOTORCYCLE ENTHUSIASTS' PUBLICATION

SEPTEMBER 1965
50¢

Isle of Man Report
Omega 125 Test
Triumph Twin Dragster
City Touring
Speed Record History
4 AMA Nationals

HONDA 450 TEST & TECHNICAL ANALYSIS

The 444cc CB450 dohc twin debuted in 1965 and caused shock waves for the once-dominant British industry, particularly in the USA.

ABOVE: The American, Bob Hansen, was responsible for putting Honda on the Stateside racing map, entering a team of 450 twins at Daytona during February 1967.

BELOW: Leading privateer Ron Pladdys with his specially converted 182cc CR93 during the 1965 250cc Isle of Man Manx Grand Prix; he finished sixth at an average speed of 84.60mph (136km/h).

ABOVE: In 1969 Honda launched the across-the-frame 4-cylinder CB750; quite simply, it changed the face of motorcycling.

BELOW: A 1976 CD175, with aftermarket screen and leg shields. This model proved very popular with the ride-to-work brigade, because of its rugged reliability and excellent performance.

Your move. 1972.

Scrambler
CL-70K3
CL-100K2
CL-175K6
CL-350K4
CL-450K5

Motosport™
SL-70
SL-125K1
XL-250

SL-100K2
SL-175K1
SL-350K2

Mini Bike
QA-50
Z-50AK3

Super Sport
CB-100K2
CB-175K6
CB-350K4
CB-450K5

Trail
CT-70K1
CT-90K4

CT-70 HK1
ATC 90

The Fours
CB-350 Four*
CB-500 Four
CB-750K2 Four

*Available later in 1972

ABOVE: *Displacing 1047cc (64.5 × 53.4mm), the CBX engine had no fewer than seven main bearings, 24-valves, dohc and could reach 140mph (225km/h).*

LEFT: *During the 1970s, America was Honda's biggest market; many of its 1972 Stateside range were exclusively built for the USA.*

BELOW: *The 999cc (72 × 61.4mm) liquid-cooled flat-four GL1000 arrived in the mid-1970s. It was the first of the Gold Wing series. Its 6-cylinder successor is still a best-seller today.*

THE HONDA GL1000 GOLD WING

ABOVE: The CBX1000 aped Honda's amazing 250/297cc
6-cylinder GP racers of the 1960s. It went on sale in 1978
as the company's top-of-the-range sports bike.

BELOW: The 1978 CX500 V-twin, with pushrod-operated
valves and shaft final drive, was a big departure for Honda,
but it still proved a massive sales success.

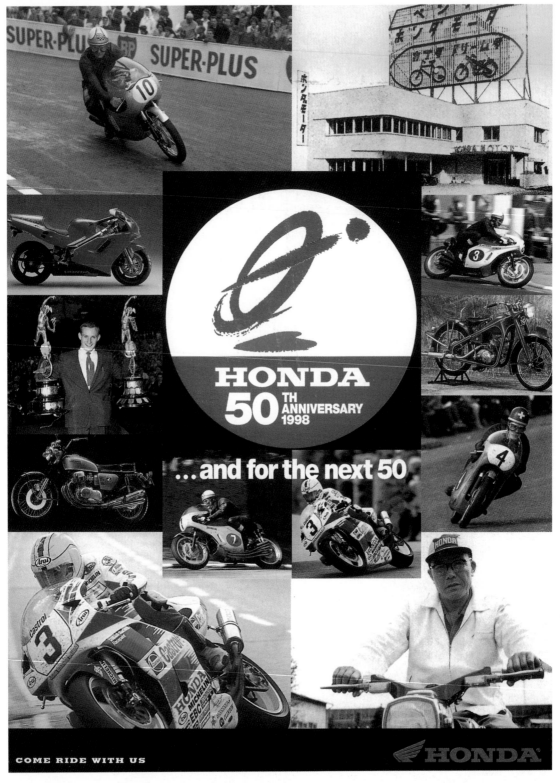

Honda celebrated its fiftieth anniversary in 1998 (even though it had begun back in 1946!). Here are the images that the company thought represented its history. Founder Soichiro Honda is bottom right.

gear, this case being more vulnerable than usual. If it was damaged or cracked (which could easily occur with magnesium), the rider had to ascertain immediately that he still had full oil pressure to both the bottom end and camshaft.

Otherwise, the XL250 power unit was a real honey – and I should know as the one I owned covered many pleasurable miles, both on- and off-road, before making way for something else.

It was also a very comfortable bike, both from a good riding position and because of its smooth, torquey motor and excellent transmission. My only real complaint was with its on-road handling, which never inspired much confidence. Off-road, at least for the green lane stuff which I undertook, it was more than adequate, as were the small conical drum brakes.

There were quickly detachable wiring plugs front and rear to allow the lights to be removed easily, but even so this was a trail bike, rather than a pukka fire-breathing dirt racer. The mudguards (at least at the front) were manufactured in plastic, as was the chainguard. Alloy wheel rims (without water-retaining wells, thank goodness) helped to reduce weight, but even so the Motorsport couldn't be called light, being 279lb (127kg) dry. The dualseat hinged sideways to give instant access to the battery, tools and electrics.

The 1973 Honda TL125 trials (known as the 'Bials' in Japan). This was built as a serious trials bike; the road equipment shown here was normally stripped off for competition use. Wheel sizes: 21in front; 18in rear.

Other Important Features

Besides the 4-valve head and primary kick-start, the XL250 also acted as a pioneer – certainly as regards Japanese motorcycles – in two other important areas: torque and the use of a four-stroke single-cylinder engine for a quarter-litre on-/off-road model.

First, the matter of torque. This was the keystone of the original XL250's character and appeal. The Honda engine gushed over with superb low-end pulling power; it could pull itself out of almost any situation – and it made off-road riding so much more fun than constantly stamping on the gear pedal as one was forced to do with an early 1970s two-stroke.

And the same torque hung in there too, right up to the 8,000rpm red line, pulling strongly all the way through fifth gear.

The XL250 Shows the Way

The other facet of the XL250 was that its success was responsible for not only Honda, but also Suzuki, Yamaha and Kawasaki all eventually taking the four-stroke path when it came to designing a new generation of trail bikes – often of larger capacity. *Motorcyclist* back in 1972 came up with a very accurate prediction:

> But possibly more important than the model itself is the promise it offers; I got the distinct impression that if this first bona fide (real Japanese!) off-road four-stroke hits the mark and achieves rewarding acceptance, Honda will be encouraged to follow it with similar four-stroke singles of increasing displacement and exotica verging on 500cc.

How right they were! Of course, today the off-road sector has seen a huge increase in four-strokes – including Honda's own XR series.

Future Development

Testers and buyers were generally pleased with the original XL250, but Honda, being Honda, improved things. For a start the XL250 grew into a 350 (348cc – 79 × 71mm), which arrived in 1974. Stateside the 350 proved a big seller – and had a direct bearing on Yamaha arriving in the mid-1970s with its classic XT500 single.

So for the 1976 season, Honda decided to rehash the two-fifty. Formerly, the cradle sections of the frame joined together behind the engine, forming a single tube which butted up

Close-up of the TL125 engine and frame. The 121.9cc sohc engine produced 8bhp at 8,000rpm. The gearbox was a five-speeder.

ABOVE: The SL125 used the same basic 121.9cc engine as the TL125, but was intended mainly for public highway usage. It ran from the end of 1972 through to mid-1978.

BELOW: The TL125 (and the larger TL250 seen here) was developed by Honda in conjunction with the legendary trials ace, Sammy Miller. Arriving for the 1975 model year, the TL250 had its 248.6cc engine based on the existing XL unit.

to the main backbone. To accommodate this simple, inexpensive design, Honda originally cast the XL's cylinder head with an offset inlet tract. But for 1976, since the frame was going to be restructured to accommodate a new exhaust system, Honda didn't mate the engine cradles until way up top of the rear of the backbone, thereby allowing utilization of a new centre-port head. This new head fed both inlet ports more evenly, resulting in a power increase to offset slightly the power losses caused by the new, more restrictive inlet and exhaust systems.

Repositioned Rear Shocks

Apart from the redesigned frame section behind the cylinder head, Honda engineers moved the upper rear shock mounts slightly forward. This gave what can be best described as a mild cantilever effect, which *Cycle World* described as making 'trail riding very pleasur-

able'. Up front, the steering rake had been kicked out to 32 degrees with 5.5in of trail. These figures were very close to the CR250 Elsinore's 32 degrees and 5.8in and helped to account for the XL's improved steering over the original version.

The engine of the 1976 XL250 was very much unchanged over previous years, save for the already mentioned new cylinder head.

So why, you may ask, did Honda bother with the XL250 when it had the XL350? Plus the latter cost a mere US$76 dollars extra at the time. *Cycle World* dated August 1976 carried the answer:

For some, a 250cc motorcycle is just the right size. It may not matter that it weighs within five pounds of its larger brother. Compared to the 350, the 250 yields slightly better gas mileage, much less engine vibration, easier kick-through when starting, and a generally milder manner. In addition, it handles

The TL250 engine and frame details. The crankcases were magnesium, whilst the chassis was of a particularly neat design; note the comprehensive sump bash guard.

1975 TL250 Specifications

Engine	Air-cooled sohc single with vertical cylinder alloy head and barrel, unit construction, vertically split aluminium crankcases	Front suspension	Oil-damped telescopic forks
		Rear suspension	Swinging arm, twin shock absorbers
Bore	74mm	Front brake	SLS drum
Stroke	57.8mm	Rear brake	SLS drum
Displacement	248.6cc	Tyres	Front 2.75 × 21, rear 4.00 × 18
Compression ratio	9:1		
Lubrication	Trochoid pump, wet sump		
Ignition	Flywheel magneto and ignition coil	**General Specifications**	
		Wheelbase	52.2in (1326mm)
Carburettor	N/A	Ground clearance	7in (178mm)
Primary drive	Gear	Seat height	32in (813mm)
Final drive	Chain	Fuel tank capacity	0.8gal (3.6ltr)
Gearbox	Five speeds	Dry weight	218lb (99kg)
Frame	Full loop type, with single front downtube, extending to two under the engine	Maximum power	16.5bhp @ 7,000rpm
		Top speed	70mph (113km/h)

better than the 350 because the larger machine's greater speeds can more easily overtax the suspension and chassis.

But in the final analysis, the XL series was a green laner, a trail bike – not a serious enduro mount.

Besides the 250 and 350 version, Honda also offered, at various times, the XL70 (47cc – 41.4 × 71.8mm); XL100 (99.3cc – 53 × 45mm); XL125 (124.1cc – 0 56.5 × 49.5mm) and XL175 (173.7cc – 64 × 54mm).

TL – Trials

At the Tokyo show late in 1972 Honda launched 'the Bials', more commonly known as the TL125 – Honda's first attempt to build a pukka feet-up trials iron. This employed the 121.9cc (54 × 49.5mm) 2-valve sohc engine from the existing SL125 model, with the compression lowered from 9.5 to 8:1. It was a particularly neat little bike. Then in 1975 it was joined by the TL250, using a detuned version of the existing XL250 power unit. Honda sources claimed 16.5bhp at 7,000rpm (compared with the XL250s, 22bhp at 8,000rpm). But whereas the XL weighed in at 279lb (127kg), the TL250 tipped the scales at 218lb (99kg). Other details included a 9:1 compression ratio, 2.75 × 21 front and 4.00 × 18 trials universal tyres and a wheelbase of 52.2in (1,326mm).

Later, of course, Honda built more serious dirt bikes, both for trail and trials, but the models described here set them on the path to off-road success in future years.

8   CD Touring Twins

The CD series of touring twin-cylinder models was one of Honda's unsung successes, being produced in vast numbers and giving its owners years of reliable service, virtually unmatched before or since, except by the C50 itself.

CD125

The first CD twin-cylinder model arrived in 1966 and was powered by a 124.7cc (44 × 41mm) sohc engine featuring inclined cylin-

ders and a four-speed gearbox. In fact, Honda introduced three new 125s – the CB125 (sports), CL125 (street scrambler) and the CD125 (tourer). Although the first two sported a tubular frame and narrow mudguards, the CD125 had been provided with the pressed-steel frame which had been a feature of more sedate Hondas in the past, but updated by way of what the company described as a T-form, which was already in use on a number of single-cylinder models.

The wheels were also smaller, being 16in diameter whilst the touring theme continued by deeply valanced mudguards, a totally enclosed final drive-chain case, comprehensive silencing and a separate seat for both the rider and pillion passenger (the latter being mounted to the rear carrier). Although telescopic forks were employed, the full-width brakes were restricted to single leading shoe front and rear. For the 1967 season the model became the CD125A, but with little changed except the additional prefix.

CD175

Next came one of Honda's most popular bikes, certainly at the budget end of motorcycling – the CD175. Fellow author, Roy Bacon, had this to say of the model: 'This was to become a minor classic and the motorcycle for

The original 1967 CD175A touring model, with 174.1cc (52 × 41mm), four speeds and open-type pressed-steel frame; no electric start.

1967 CD175 Specifications

Engine	Air-cooled sohc parallel twin, chain-driven camshaft, cylinder inclined forward by 30 degrees, 360-degree crank, alloy head and barrel, horizontally split aluminium crankcase	Frame	Pressed-steel, spine-type
		Front suspension	Oil-damped telescopic forks
		Rear suspension	Swinging arm, twin shock absorbers
		Front brake	SLS full-width alloy drum
		Rear brake	SLS full-width alloy drum
Bore	52mm	Tyres	3.00 × 16 front and rear
Stroke	41mm		
Displacement	174.1cc		
Compression ratio	9:1	**General Specifications**	
Lubrcation	Plunger pump, wet sump	Wheelbase	49.2in (1,250mm)
Ignition	6V battery/coil with single contact breaker	Ground clearance	5.5in (140mm)
		Seat height	29.5in (749mm)
Carburettor	Keihin PN22	Fuel tank capacity	2.2gal (10ltr)
Primary drive	Gears	Dry weight	260lb (118kg)
Final drive	Chain	Maximum power	17bhp @ 10,500rpm
Gearbox	Four speeds	Top speed	75mph (121km/h)

commuting if a C50 was too small. I had one as a town bike for five years and for that job it was superb, slim and nimble in traffic, fast enough to keep ahead of the stream and dead reliable.'

This first variant, the CD175A, was a parts bin special, using a mixture of components from the CD125 and CB160. Displacing 174.1cc, the engine capacity came from boring out the cylinders to 52mm, whilst retaining the 41mm stroke from the 125. Maximum power, Honda claimed, was 17bhp at 10,500rpm. Engine design followed the familiar Honda layout with chain-driven sohc, single Keihin PN22 carburettor and a four-speed gearbox built in unit with the engine and primary transmission. Like the CD125, no electric start was provided (for reasons of economy), but there was the luxury of a fully enclosed final drive chain.

The Cycle Parts
Framewise, the T-spine layout was retained, with enclosed telescopic front forks, 16in rims with 3.00 section tyres, full-width alloy hubs,

valanced mudguards – plus direction indicators, twin mirrors and a one-piece (comfortable!) dual seat. The only real criticisms were weak 6V electrics and handling which had comfort as its priority and thus cornering abilities could only be described as 'adequate for purpose'. Well, the CD175 was a commuter, not a sportster! In fairness, the machine steered well, despite the softness of the suspension, except two-up.

Testing the CD175A

In October 1967 the people at *Motorcycle Mechanics* got their hands on an example of the newly introduced CD175A. And as they explained: 'These new Hondas have proved so popular since their introduction that it was impossible to get one for test in time for this issue. We were lucky, however, in that one of our readers, PC Dick Bedford [who worked at Scotland Yard] very kindly offered us his CD175 for test.'

The *Motorcycle Mechanics* test began: 'Are you looking for a quiet, safe, trouble-free machine which doesn't cost the earth and already sports several useful "extras"? If you are, then it's time you took a good long look at the new Honda CD175. For the price paid you will own a luxurious, pokey, yet safe little motorcycle that is ideal for commuting or weekend runs.'

The tester made a useful observation for prospective purchasers: 'Whilst on the subject of mudguards, these are made of plastic, as are the toolbox and battery covers, and the colour is very cleverly bonded. Unless it is pointed out to you, it is very difficult to pick out plastic from metal, so quite possible we may even have missed something ourselves!' In fact, the 1967 CD175A was one of the very first mass-produced motorcycles to use plastic for these components and thus did not suffer from the rotting mudguard problems associated with many early (including Honda) Japanese bikes.

Although, as already mentioned, there was no electric starter (to keep down price), the *Motorcycle Mechanics* tester found that the test

bike: 'started, first kick every time'. And that: 'It doesn't have to be a great lunging kick either, for a half-hearted prod is enough to set the engine burbling.' Starting procedure was pretty straightforward too: 'First start of the morning meant freeing off the clutch first [it being of the wet type], just in case the plates were sticking. Push the choke in, switch on the ignition, one prod and away. The choke had to be withdrawn about half-way and the motor run with the choke half in for about a mile to warm up.'

Motorcycle Mechanics also found: 'The engine is similar to most small capacity Hondas, virtually vibrationless with a liking for revs.' The transmission too, came in for praise: 'Like a good wine complementing a superb meal, the clutch is sweet and light and serves the engine well.' And 'The lever can be operated with only a couple of fingers, and the clutch feeds in smoothly without trace of jerking. The gearbox has a positive selector and it will be a really ham-fisted rider who misses gears on this bike.'

By 1976 when this photograph was taken, the CD175 had evolved into a much dumpier-looking machine with a full-loop cradle frame. But all versions were respected for their comfort, reliability and fuel economy.

Other features of the machine which came in for praise were the 'loud alpine-sounding horn' and that it was 'one of the quietest machines we have tested in a long time – BMW excepted!'

The standing quarter-mile was covered in 17.8sec and the 0–60mph in 14.3sec, whilst maximum speed was 83mph (134km/h).

It is worth noting that in 1968 a two-fifty version was offered. This shared the engine from the newly introduced 249.3cc (56 × 50.6mm) CB250, but with only four speeds.

Updating the Line

The three basic guises of the 125cc twin, the CB, CL and CD, received a redesigned power unit for 1969. Previously, the cylinders of both the 125 and 175 were canted forward by some 30 degrees, but now the cylinders were repositioned almost vertically as on the newly introduced CB250/350 series and a tubular frame was adapted (with the introduction of a front downtube). Shortly afterwards, the same changes were introduced to the CD175, which now became the A-1 rather than the A, with much heavier styling and with dry weight increasing from 249lb (113kg) to 269lb (122kg).

Although the engine configuration had changed, its basic specification, including compression ratio, carburettor type/size and ignition system, had remained the same, including the power output and maximum engine revolutions. However, the appearance of the machine had changed, with much larger side panels, a larger capacity fuel tank (now 2.2gal (10ltr)) and the use of 17in wheels (the 3.00 section tyre size remaining as before).

Reliability with a Capital R

From then on, the CD175 was to remain virtually unchanged and by 1977 it had reached its A5 series, being offered with a choice of

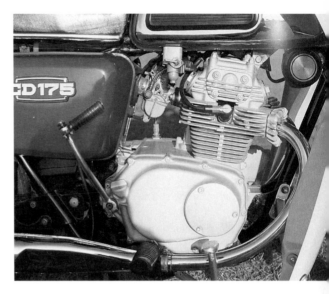

An offside view of the mid-1970s CD175; by now the cylinders were repositioned almost vertically.

Candy Red Metallic or Kingfisher Blue Metallic.

The April 1977 issue of *Motorcycle Mechanics* carried a Reader's Report – the following coming from Martin Vey who had used his CD175, purchased new in September 1975, to commute to London from Guildford, in the process clocking up almost 13,000 miles (20,917km) in fourteen months. Here are some of Martin's findings:

> It looks unfashionable. There is no electric start, rev counter, disc brake or adjustable rear dampers, and only four gears, one carburettor and six-volt electrics. But, if you had been in my position fourteen months ago, wanting a machine for a daily seventy-mile round trip to college and for weekend use, and yet not having enough money for a bike with all mod cons, you might seriously have considered Honda's ever-popular CD175.

The following is a list of ownership information which appeared in Martin Vey's report:

• *Running-in* 'gave up to 120mpg', with even 65mpg being obtainable two-up 'once run-in'.

• *Handling*: 'Mostly due to soggy non-adjustable rear dampers' wasn't 'the most reasonable, but when the original Jap rear cover ran out of rubber at 5,500 miles a £10 Continental helped traction.' And: 'The bike definitely doesn't like thick white lines, nor does it appreciate large bumps or Hampshire potholes.'

• *Centre stand* 'Grounds fairly easily on the left-hand side at low cornering speeds.'

• *Front brake* 'Lacking power.'

• *Rear brake* 'Lacks feel and locks up too easily (especially in the wet).' To overcome this, Martin Vey fitted Ferodo AM4 competition linings.

• *Lighting* 'Not the best in the world, being barely adequate for 45mph night riding.'

• *Performance* 'Top whack is about 75mph, with the needle flickering a few mph either way. Acceleration is good.'

• *Two-up* 'I was pleasantly surprised to find that the four-stroke's torque makes two-up journeys not that much slower than when riding solo.'

• *Phillips screws* (used on engine unit) 'So soft that they should be replaced with a good set of Allen screws at the first opportunity.'

CD185T

Towards the end of 1977, Honda introduced a replacement for the CD175, which by now was over ten years old, with the new CD185T. Although many of the features employed by the 175 were retained (sohc, single 22mm Keihin carburettor, four speeds, fully enclosed chain and drum brakes with 17in rims and 3.00 section tyres), there were some notable changes.

Obviously the first of these concerned the engine displacement. The bore and stroke dimensions of 52 × 41mm had been retained through the various changes to the 175 range. The engine had been given a bore job when the CB200 version (*see* Chapter 3) was intro-

The CD185T arrived as a replacement for the by now decade-old CD175 towards the end of 1977. The actual capacity was 180cc – achieved by reducing the bore size of the CB200 sports model from 55.5 to 53mm. The engine was also extensively restyled.

The CD200T (194cc – 53 × 44mm), which kept four speeds but was the first CD model with an electric start. The CD200 ran from 1981 to 1988.

duced, but now it had been contracted from 55.5mm to 53mm for the new '185', which was actually 180cc.

Though the engine looked completely different from the outside to the 175, the bottom end (except for outer covers) was essentially the same. But the top end had been considerably revised. Not only were the cylinders now inclined forward slightly, but there was also a one-piece rocker cover on the new engine which resembled the equally new CB250 and 400 Dream models. Additionally, the rocker housings had been redesigned and the overhead camshaft was linked to the crankshaft by a duplex rather than a single row chain. The cam-chain tensioner was also different and was adjusted from the rear of the engine rather than the front.

The contact breaker had been relocated from the overhead camshaft drive down to the crankshaft. The wasted spark system was still employed, but there was only one lobe instead of two on the points cam now that it spun at engine speed.

An East European Look

One tester of the period said 'that Honda have purposely made the four-stroke twin look Russian in appearance'. The April 1979 issue of *Motorcycle Mechanics* continued in a similar theme: 'If MZ and CZ can sell motorcycles to the thriftier end of the market, then so can Honda. That surely must be the Japanese giant's outlook on introducing the new CD185T.'

Motorcycle Mechanics also considered Honda had 'chickened out' when it came to the idea of 'turning completely "red"' by substituting a deeply valanced front mudguard with built-in mudflap for a sporty guard to suit British mar-

Last of the line, the CD250U arrived in 1989. The specification included 233cc (53 × 53mm), electric start, five speeds and a disc front brake.

ket tastes.' And it was soon discovered that: 'The engine becomes dirtied with front wheel spray.'

Another major problem for a commuter bike was a relatively high purchase price, which in early 1979 was a shade under £600 – more than twice what one would have paid at the time for similar commuter machines of similar performance, albeit powered by single-cylinder two-stroke engines.

Yet another was performance, or lack of it, with Honda quoting a maximum power out-put of 15.6bhp at 8,750rpm and a dry weight of 282lb (128km/h). The newcomer was therefore both less powerful and heavier than the machine it replaced.

CD200T

This lack of performance compared to the 175, together with a high price, transpired to curtail sales of the CD185T. This resulted in a relatively short production life and it was replaced in 1981 with the CD200T. The latter machine featured a new engine size of 194cc, achieved by lengthening the stroke from 41 to 44mm; the bore remained unchanged at 53mm. The main result was to improve torque figures rather than outright performance, which remained in the 75mph (120km/h) region. Also the compression ratio was dropped from 9:1 to 8.8:1. There had been yet another increase in weight, now up to 298lb (135kg). However, for the first time the new CD sported electric starting. Other changes were mainly cosmetic, including chrome-plated steel mudguards, exposed spring rear shocks and revised graphics and new colours.

CD250U

The CD200 was to give way to the much-revised 233cc (53 × 53mm) CD250U. Although strictly speaking this machine is outside the scope of this book, it is worth mentioning it if for no other reason than besides the basic engine design it was considerably updated with a five-speed gearbox, disc front brake and CDI ignition. The Honda brochure in describing the machine said: 'Traditionally styled for a variety of rugged uses, yet price-competitive in terms of insurance when compared with other middleweight models, the CD250U is the ideal, all-round economy motorcycle for getting there on time.'

But the CD250U was destined to be the last of the line, the age of the motorcycle as a cheap means of transport having effectively ended in West European markets, including Great Britain. But the fact remains that from its inception during the late 1960s until its replacement by the '185' just over a decade later, the CD175 twin had proved a showroom success for Honda. It was, as with all the best Honda designs, the right bike at the right time.

9 Racing

Although the vast majority of Honda's early production motorcycles were street bikes, there were more specialized (and expensive) racing models too. Soichiro Honda's interest in speed saw to this – and his factory's racing efforts did not stop at the exotic works specials. He realized that it was a good idea to provide machinery that could be termed 'customer racers'. Honda had seen that bikes such as the British Manx Norton, BSA Gold Star and Italian Gilera Saturno had managed to gain valuable publicity for their respective marques, even though they were production, rather than restricted to factory riders only.

The CR71

As early as 1959, there were a couple of Honda designs that could be offered as 'Super Sport' – the CB92 sports roadster and clubman racing CR71. The latter was based firmly on the series production CS71 roadster with its single overhead cam 247cc (54 × 54mm) engine and four-speed gearbox. In the CR71, the compression ratio was upped to 9.5:1 and the maximum power output increased to 24bhp at 8,800rpm, but it retained the crankshaft-mounted clutch with its characteristic cable entry and lift mechanism cover.

1959 CR71 Specifications

Engine	Air-cooled sohc parallel twin, four valves, 360-degree crankshaft, alloy head and barrel, chain-driven camshaft, pressed-up crank, unit construction, horizontally split crankcase		
Bore	54mm		
Stroke	54mm		
Displacement	247.3cc		
Compression ratio	9.5:1		
Lubrication	Plunger pump, wet sump		
Ignition	Magneto		
Carburettor	Keihin		
Primary drive	Gears		
Final drive	Chain		
Gearbox	Four speeds		
Frame	Steel, spine-type construction,	engine employed as a stressed-member	
		Front suspension	Leading link forks
		Rear suspension	Swinging arm, twin shock absorbers
		Front brake	2LS full-width drum
		Rear brake	SLS full-width drum
		Tyres	Front 2.75 × 18, rear 3.00 × 18

General Specifications

Wheelbase	51.2in (1,300mm)
Ground clearance	6in (152mm)
Seat height	30in (762mm)
Fuel tank capacity	N/A
Dry weight	297lb (135kg)
Maximum power	24bhp @ 8,800rpm
Top speed	108mph (174km/h)

The Cycle Parts

The CR71 cycle parts differed considerably from the roadster and closely followed those of the RC141 125cc works dohc twin of the same year, notably the use of a leading link front fork assembly and twin leading shoe front brake. The wheels were 18in, in place of the 16in type fitted to the CS71 tourer.

When delivered, the CR71 came complete with all necessary road-going equipment – including lights and silencers (in much the same way as the Italian Formula 2 and 3 racers of the same era). Top speed was 95mph (153km/h). However, by the simple expedient of removing the silencers and fitting a pair of optional open megaphones, the maximum velocity could be raised to a genuine 100mph (162km/h).

Originally, all CR71 production was intended for domestic use, plus certain Far Eastern markets, such as Hong Kong, Malaysia

OPPOSITE: *British serviceman Chris Profitt-White, winner of both the 250cc and 350cc event at Sambawang, Singapore, in autumn 1960 on a Honda CR71 production racer. The CR71 produced 24bhp at 8,800rpm.*

and Singapore. But at least one CR71 reached Great Britain in the early 1960s, when it was brought home from Singapore by British serviceman/racer, Chris Profitt-White.

The CB92

Compared with the small numbers of CR71 machines produced, the CB92 (*see* Chapter 3 for its full development history) could be labelled a series production machine, being mass-produced from 1959 until the end of 1964. I owned one of these superb little bikes when stationed with the Royal Air Force in Aden (now South Yemen) during 1963–4 and soon realized that it could match the vast majority of 350cc machines. In fact, my home-tuned CB92 actually saw off a Norton Dominator five-hundred with an engine size four times bigger than its own!

From personal experience, the only criticisms that I could find were a need for an extra gear (four were standard), a camshaft which ran directly in the cylinder head and a front end which could be skittish at very slow speeds on

Steve Murray screaming his CR93 to victory at Oulton Park, Cheshire, spring 1963.

tight bends; otherwise it was a splendid little bike.

Its 124.7cc (44 × 41mm) chain-driven sohc engine put out 15bhp at 10,500rpm in standard guise. With the factory race kit (including open exhausts), this rose to almost 20bhp. Needless to say, many CB92s were thus converted, several being successfully raced during the period 1959–62, even in international events. One particular example was taken by its owner, Londoner Tom Jackson, to compete in Soviet Russia, while another was mounted in a Cotton frame to create a very interesting and competitive special. In Australia, as early as February 1960, no fewer than eight race-kitted CB92s appeared in a field of twenty-one machines in the 125cc Victorian TT at Fisherman's Bend, Melbourne, with Alan Osbourne bringing one of the Japanese bikes home as runner-up, ahead of several more expensive bikes, including Len Tinkler's MV Agusta.

The CB72

By 1961, the CB92 had been joined by the CB72. This was a totally redesigned CS71,

with not only a much-improved engine (including a 180-degree crankshaft, twin carburettors and a five-speed gearbox), but also a new tubular frame, telescopic forks and full-width 2LS brakes at both the front and rear. It was, in fact, improved in virtually every single way over its predecessor. With an output of 24bhp, albeit at the higher engine speed of 9,000rpm, the CB72 matched that of the limited-run CR71 production racer. And, once again, Honda offered a speed kit.

In Great Britain, the CB72 (*see* Chapter 3 for its full technical details) was a class winner in both the Thruxton 500-miler and Silverstone 1,000km endurance races, two of the most demanding events in the sporting calendar.

A Totally New Breed of Honda

The first indication of a totally new breed of Honda came at the Tokyo Show in October 1961. It was here that the company, already Japan's largest two-wheel concern, displayed a prototype of what was to emerge later as the CR110, a 49cc (40.4 × 39mm) 'over-the-counter', pure-bred racer for paying customers. The original prototype CR110 put out 8.9bhp at the then amazing 14,000rpm and featured a five-speed gearbox. At the exhibition, Honda referred to the newcomer as the 'Cub Racer'.

Almost six months were to elapse before Honda introduced the larger CR93. This was manufactured in two forms and went on sale in Japan during May 1962. In its standard guise, the 124.8cc (43 × 43mm) dohc, five-speed twin was offered with full road-going equipment, including lighting equipment, horn, comprehensive silencers and even a rearview mirror. Thus fully equipped, the CR93 could reach 84mph (135km/h), Honda claimed. However, today, at least in Europe, the CR93 is remembered in its stripped-for-racing mode, with a performance of 96mph (155km/h) naked and 102 (164) with a dolphin fairing. The CR93 road racer (with open exhausts) produced 20bhp; the street version gave 16.5bhp.

Designed by Suzuki

The CR93 was designed by a Honda engineer with the name of Suzuki ... no relation to the rival bike builder. It shared the 4-valves-per-cylinder technology of the works racers. A conventional roller big end, 180-degree crankshaft drove the close-ration five-speed, unit-construction gearbox via helical spur gears. There was a surprisingly large primary reduction of 3.7:1. The standard Honda technique of wet-sump lubrication (with a scavenge pump) was employed.

Producing maximum power at 11,500rpm, the CR93 engine was still safe mechanically at 13,000rpm. Within these limits – and most importantly provided the oil was changed after every meeting – it would give long life with reliability. The CR93 would rev beyond its red line, but with a greatly increased likelihood of mechanical failure.

When the CR93 went on sale in Britain during early 1963, it cost £609, but was later reduced to £504 and remained available on the British market for only two seasons.

An Easy Bike to Ride

Generally, the CR93 was an easy bike to ride and was very easy to bump into life. There was absolutely no power below 5,800rpm. Then the engine surged into action – almost like a flick-switch. It was entirely free from vibration and would run straight up to the 'safe' 13,000rpm peak. A change at this speed brought revs down to the 9,500 mark. Therefore, it was a simple task to keep smack in the effective powerband, which was just as well because of the lack of urge and the severe 'megaphonitis' when out of it. The shallow-taper megaphones emitted a superb mellow howl, which, although not ultra sharp, carried over a long distance.

Other features of the design included a compression ratio of 10.2:1, 22mm Keihin carburettors, an energy transfer magneto ignition, spine-type frame (with the engine as a structural member), an aluminium fuel tank and a dry weight of 279lb (127kg).

Some forty CR93s found their way to the UK, where they were ridden by the likes of Bill Ivy, Rod Scivyer, Derek Chatterton and Chris Vincent. It is a fact that the CR93 ruled the British 125cc short circuit scene for many years – until the appearance of Austin Hockley and his Terry Beckett-tuned Granby Yamaha YAS1 twin in 1970.

Other notable achievements by the CR93 included capturing the British National speed record for the 125cc and 175cc categories in the standing-start quarter-mile and kilometre at Chelveston airfield, Bedfordshire, on 7 November 1965 in the hands of Jack Terry. Another was an overbored 182cc model used in 250cc races by Ron Pladdys and later Jim Curry. When this was outclassed by the ever-improving Yamahas, the Pladdys brothers built a 249.2cc (49.6 × 43mm) 3-cylinder machine. This unique bike achieved a number of victo-

Andrew French finishing runner-up at Little Rissington in 1964 on his CR93.

Close-up of the 124.9cc (43 × 43mm) CR93 power unit. Specification included twin Keihin 22mm, energy transfer magneto ignition and a compression ratio of 10.2:1.

Rod Scivyer at Snetterton, Norfolk, summer 1964; he was later to become British champion on the same machine.

1963 CR93 Specifications			
Engine	Air-cooled dohc parallel twin, alloy head and barrel, unit construction, horizontally split crank-cases, gear-driven cams, 180-degree crankshaft, caged roller big ends	Front suspension	Oil-damped, telescopic fork
		Rear suspension	Swinging arm, twin shock absorbers
		Front brake	SLS, full-width, drum
		Rear brake	SLS, full-width drum
Bore	43mm	Tyres	Front 2.50 × 18, rear 2.75 × 18
Stroke	43mm		
Displacement	224.9cc		
Compression ratio	10.2:1	**General Specifications**	
Lubrication	Plunger pump, wet sump	Wheelbase	50.2in (1,275mm)
Ignition	Magneto	Ground clearance	6in (152mm)
Carburettor	2 × Keihin	Seat height	29in (737mm)
Primary drive	Gear	Fuel tank capacity	2.5gal (11.4ltr)
Final drive	Chain	Dry weight	280lb (127kg)
Gearbox	Five speeds	Maximum power	16.5bhp @ 11,500rpm
Frame	Spine-type, with engine as a stressed member	Top speed	102mph (164km/h)

ries and proved its reliability by finishing in the gruelling Isle of Man TT.

The only real change during the CR93's production life concerned its front brake. Some examples were fitted with a production-based, single-sided 2LS type, whilst others came with the pukka works double-sided, single leading shoe front anchor.

There is little doubt in the author's mind that the CR93 was the most successful of all Honda's customer racers.

CR110 Technical Features

Next came the single-cylinder CR110 50cc model, which was officially announced in July 1962, some eight months after the previously described prototype had been displayed at the Tokyo Show. As with the CR93, the CR110 was offered with full road-going equipment for the Japanese home market or as a racer for export.

The most significant technical difference between the production version and the original prototype was that it now had eight instead of five gears. This had come as a direct result of Honda's own GP experiences, which had shown that at least eight ratios were required to extract maximum performance from the dohc 49cc (40.4 × 39mm) 4-valve engine. Like the CR93, the CR110 was the work of Honda engineer, Suzuki. And again, like its larger brother, the CR110 was introduced into Britain in time for the 1963 season. Relatively few were sold (twenty-one to be exact were imported that year), with a price tag of £330, but were even scarcer twelve months later, when production was discontinued.

Like the CR93, the CR110 was a high-revving engine, producing maximum power at 13,500rpm – and able to reach 15,000 for occasional drastic use. Running on a compression ratio of 10.3:1, the 'egg-cup' racer put out 8.5bhp and 3.55lb/ft of torque. Ball and needle-roller bearings were used in profusion, the gear train to the overhead camshaft mechanism being a case in point. Roller-bearing big end and mains were featured, the crankpin being formed integrally with the drive-side flywheel.

An Eight-Speed Gearbox

Using a crossover, all-indirect, eight-speed gearbox, the CR110 had its clutch on the off-side, gear-driven directly from the engine shaft. The multi-plate, dry clutch was on the offside (right) of the engine. There was, like the CR93, a wet sump, integrated with the transmission, the lubricating oil being circulated by a clutch-driven plunger pump.

A 26mm Keihin carburettor was operated by an unusual, but effective, twin-cable arrangement with the throttle wire wrapped round a pulley on the side of the instrument. A single 10mm spark plug was fired by a crankshaft-mounted magneto; however, several bikes were to be modified by their owners to battery/coil ignition to improve starting.

The cylinder was inclined 35 degrees forward, and, like the CR93, the engine unit was installed in a spine-type chassis with the motor functioning as a structural member. Besides ensuring that the engine itself was mechanically sound at all times, there were two other areas of special preparation. One was making

absolutely sure that the oil was changed between races and that on cold days it was pre-warmed before being put into the sump. The other was checking rear chain tension, which was critical. If too tight or loose gear-change quality would be impaired.

As for the gear ratios themselves, these were very close, as little as 800rpm apart on some changes. No power at all was produced below 8,000rpm and not much until 11,000. Above that, it flowed in with increasing gusto up to the recommended 13,500rpm red line. Once again, to exceed this figure would be to court the spectre of reduced mechanical reliability.

The first British customer to take delivery of a CR110 in 1963 was Val Knapp of Dorking, Surrey, but the list of riders to campaign one of the jewel-like Honda fifties reads like a 'Who's Who' of the class – Bill Ivy, Dave Simmonds, Brian Kettle, George Ashton, Charlie Mates and Jim Pink. Perhaps the bike's most noteworthy achievement was Chris Walpole's tremendous runner-up spot in the 1963 50cc TT.

Late 1962 and Honda started limited production of the CR110 – in both road and race versions as shown here. The 50cc dohc (40.4 × 39mm) engine had no fewer than eight gears.

The jewel-like CR110 dohc single-cylinder engine with steeply angled carburettor and cylinder, plus dry multi-plate clutch.

Like the CR93, Honda offered the CR110 on the home market in full road-going trim. In this guise its maximum speed was limited to 62mph (100km/h), whereas the full racing version could top 80mph (130km/h).

The CR72 and CR77

After the 125cc and 50cc models came the CR72 (two-fifty) and CR77 (three-zero-five) – or at least this was Honda's original idea.

1963 CR110 Specifications

Engine	Air-cooled dohc single, alloy head and barrel, unit construction, vertically split crankcases, gear-driven cams	Front suspension	Oil-damped, telescopic fork
		Rear suspension	Swinging arm, twin shock absorbers
Bore	40.4mm	Front brake	SLS, full-width drum
Stroke	39mm	Rear brake	SLS, full-width drum
Displacement	49.99cc	Tyres	Front 2.00 × 18, rear 2.25 × 18
Compression ratio	10.3:1		
Lubrication	Plunger pump, wet sump	**General Specifications**	
Ignition	Magneto	Wheelbase	45.5in (116mm)
Carburettor	Keihin	Ground clearance	5.5in (140mm)
Primary drive	Gear	Seat height	28in (711mm)
Final drive	Chain	Fuel tank capacity	2gal (9ltr)
Gearbox	Eight speeds	Dry weight	134lb (61kg)
Frame	Spine-type, with engine as a stressed member	Maximum power	8.5bhp @ 13,500rpm
		Top speed	80mph (129km/h)

Chester racer/dealer Bill Smith (second left) was an early Honda supporter in the UK. He is seen here with a mixture of machinery in early 1966, including a CR110 (extreme left) and a CR93 (30, in foreground). The bike on the extreme right is a new Thompson-Suzuki T20 twin.

However, even though several pre-production models were raced by various riders, including Tommy Robb (who debuted the CR77 in the 1963 West German GP at Hockenheim), Luigi Taveri, Bruce Beale, Ralph Bryans and Bill Smith, the machines were never officially offered for sale in the UK. The CR72 produced 41bhp at 12,500rpm, with the larger displacement CR77 47bhp at the same engine speed. Both bikes shared the same bore and stroke dimensions as their CB72/77 roadster brothers – even though the pukka racers employed double overhead cams and six-speed gearboxes.

The CR72/77 models had 4-valves-per-cylinder with the cylinder block in two pieces, bolted together on the centre line to allow the central timing gear train to be inserted before

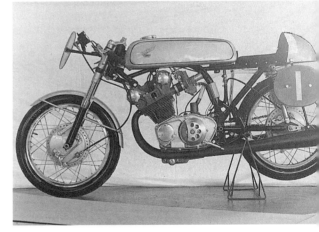

One of the then brand new CR72 two-fifty dohc twins, spring 1963.

the whole assembly was fitted. The cylinder head was a one-piece casting; with the power taken from the nearside (left) end of the crankshaft, which had the pins located at 180 degrees for better balance.

1963 CR72/77 Specifications (CR77 in brackets where different)

Engine	Air-cooled dohc parallel twin, eight valves, 180-degree crankshaft, gear-driven cams, alloy head and barrel, unit construction, horizontally split crankcases	Front suspension	Enclosed spring, telescopic fork
		Rear suspension	Swinging arm, twin shock absorber
		Front brake	Double-sided 2LS drum
		Rear brake	Single-sided 2LS drum
Bore	54mm (CR77: 60mm)	Tyres	Front 2.75 × 18, rear 3.00 × 18
Stroke	54mm		
Displacement	247.3cc (CR77: 305.4cc)		
Compression ratio	10.5:1	**General Specifications**	
Lubrication	Gear pump, wet sump	Wheelbase	50.4in (1,280mm)
Ignition	Magneto	Ground clearance	6in (152mm)
Carburettor	2 × Keihin	Seat height	29.5in (749mm)
Primary drive	Gears	Fuel tank capacity	3gal (14ltr)
Final drive	Chain	Dry weight	345lb (157kg)
Gearbox	Six speeds	Maximum power	41bhp @ 12,500rpm (CR77: 47bhp @ 12,500rpm)
Frame	Steel, spine-type construction; engine employed as a stressed-member	Top speed	129mph (208km/h) (CR77: 135mph (217km/h))

The 1963 TT

At the 1963 TT, the factory showed that it had been in some difficulty over the frame design, as there were no fewer than three versions, all based on their well-known spine-type construction in which the engine acted as a frame member.

The first model incorporated duplex downtubes, so relieving the engine of dynamic road loads. The second model retained these tubes and duplex tubes substituted for the vertical portion of the spine tube at the rear. This permitted a redesign of the rear fork (swinging arm), which was carried between gusset plates on the downtubes. While this set-up was the most rigid of the three, none of them was particularly neat or attractive to the eye.

Three of the new CR72s took part in the 1963 Lightweight (250cc) TT, ridden by Luigi Taveri, Kunimitsu Takahashi and Chester-based rider/dealer, Bill Smith. First to strike trouble was Takahashi, who retired with engine gremlins, then Taveri's machine was hit

Swiss Honda works rider Luigi Taveri screams his CR72 away from the start of the Lightweight (250cc) TT, 10 June 1963.

by serious misfiring problems, after which he too struck terminal engine failure. This left Smith, who eventually came through the field to finish an excellent third, averaging 91.12mph (146.61km/h).

There was only one of the new 305cc CR77s in the Junior event, ridden by Ulsterman Tommy Robb. This was timed at 134mph (216km/h), the second quickest bike in the race – only the Honda team captain, Jim Redman, was faster on a 4-cylinder works model. Perhaps most impressive of all was that the Honda twin was faster than Mike Hailwood's MV four and the Gilera fours of Phil Read and John Hartle. But unfortunately Robb was sidelined after crashing the machine.

Continued Development

Development continued throughout the remainder of 1963, with a number of good results being obtained both in the Grand Prix and short circuit meetings. Everyone fully expected, after what was generally seen to have been an outstanding year with the 250/305 prototypes, that Honda would offer them for sale in 1964. But this was not to be the case, and in January 1964 the company issued a statement saying that it had 'decided not to produce any twins that year' (meaning the CR72/77 series). It is thought a total of some seventy machines were built, two-thirds of them the two-fifty.

Particularly disappointed was Chester racer and dealer, Bill Smith, who in addition to having taken several orders for 250s and 305s, had already sold his G50 Matchless to a Swiss rider and was planning to organize a Honda team consisting of himself, John Hartle and the Australian, Jack Ahearn. Later, in a letter published in *Motor Cycling* dated 22 January 1966, Bill Smith had this to say on the saga of just why, in his opinion, Honda didn't put the twins into production:

The Honda [the CR72 two-fifty he rode in the 1963 TT] was factory-prepared and lent to me for the 1963 TT only. I knew I had a good chance of finishing quite well up, as this bike was as fast as any 350 I had ever ridden. Now, all the twin-cylinder 250cc production racers have been scrapped and only a few are maintained for Jim Redman and Luigi Taveri to ride in minor events. The bikes are considered obsolete by Honda, and no spare parts are being made. This, I feel, is detrimental to the sport. If Honda and the other Japanese factories do not make production racers, it can do racing a lot of harm. I am sticking my neck out, but Honda do not at present seem interested in the private runner. Despite numerous pleas from myself and other dealers, they seem to have no plans whatsoever to make production racers. The twins we rode in the TT were the forerunners of what were to be production racers for private owners. But the whole idea was abandoned – largely, I think, because of the very high cost of spare parts.

Dave Simmonds

But one man bucked the trend, when in October 1964, Londoner Dave Simmonds announced that he had in fact 'purchased a CR77'. This news created a big press interest, as these prototypes were supposed to have never been offered for general sale. Yet Simmonds had acquired one and had it shipped to London.

The story began when Dave had gone out to Japan to race Tohatsu's machine in the local Grand Prix at Suzuka in 1963. There he met an import–export agent who dealt with motorcycles, and Dave asked to be informed if he ever got hold of any works machines. Six months later, in the middle of the 1964 TT week, a letter arrived out of the blue, offering a 250cc, six-speed, dohc, ex-factory Honda twin. As the price was reasonable, Dave agreed to buy it. Then, when the bike was already on the ship, a cable came to say that a mistake had been made and the machine sent was actually one of the near-identical 305cc models.

What had happened was that the machine originally offered to Simmonds had been shipped to America. The Japanese exporter offered to send Dave a conversion kit – the motorcycles being the same except for components such as the cylinder barrels and pistons – or, alternatively, he said he could now supply a complete 250 as well. Eventually, after support from his father and brother, Dave got both bikes.

It was never established quite how this private exporter got the machines, but it is believed that they came from a small number sold to Japanese works riders at 'special' prices as part-payment for their services.

Dave Simmonds went on to race the CR72 and CR77 machines for some two and a half years before gaining a contract to race for Kawasaki in 1967 (he was later to win the 125cc World Championship in 1969).

Problems

Dave Simmonds' first outing on one of the Hondas came at Oulton Park in October 1964, when he rode the 305 (without a fairing) into fifth position – his first race on a motorcycle of more than 250cc. Then, during 1965 – his first full season with the 305 – it broke no fewer than six crankshafts! At first, Dave thought that this was due to the material not being strong enough. The team even had beefed-up replacements manufactured, but they kept breaking. Then it was realized that in fact the crankcase was distorted, so the bearings were out of alignment. This was putting stress on the crankshafts, thus causing them to fail.

After carrying out tests, it was decided that nothing could be done with the old cases, so the Japanese exporter was contacted in the hope that he could find a new crankcase set. To Dave's surprise, he said that not only did he have one, but that they could have it for nothing. The reason for this generosity was discovered when it

arrived – there being a large hole right through the bottom! It appeared that this had been caused by a broken con rod. Fortunately, this was able to be repaired, and as all the work was done by friends, costs were kept to a minimum.

Poor Handling

The other major problem with the 305 was poor handling. To remedy this, a Norton frame was fitted, which largely cured the trouble, even though it added extra weight. At long last, 1966 saw the 305 both reliable and with acceptable road manners.

On the 250, Dave Simmonds won the ACU Star (British Championship) in 1965, but in 1966 a trio of glitches appeared on the smaller Honda. These were a faulty magneto and broken clutch and cylinder head studs. To effect a cure, the magneto was ditched in favour of coil ignition, whilst clutch and cylinder studs of Simmonds' own design were fitted.

All of these modifications worked well, especially the coil ignition. In Dave's opinion 'it was better than the original magneto – it took no power to drive it, was no heavier and made starting very much easier'. A 12V system was employed, with a Japanese Yuasa battery and some Tohatsu bits and pieces, together with the original Honda contact breaker.

By the time Dave Simmonds signed to ride for Kawasaki, Honda had stopped its policy of letting existing works riders use the CR72 and CR77 machines at non-championship meetings, so the twins effectively disappeared from sight at the end of 1966.

The CYB350RSC

It came as somewhat of a surprise, therefore, when, at the Tokyo Show in October 1968, Honda displayed a brand-new 350cc production racer, the CYB350RSC. This, claimed Honda, produced 53bhp at 10,000rpm and was based around the CB350 roadster (*see* Chapter 6).

Instead of the specialized dohc and 4-valves-per-cylinder of the CR models, the newcomer only featured sohc and 2-valves-per-cylinder. However, whilst undergoing the test programme at Honda's Suzuka circuit, it had proved capable of well over 120mph (193km/h) and therefore offered a viable challenge to the British singles and the Italian Aermacchis that had been the mainstay of the class for so long.

The RSC was intended mainly as a conversion kit that could be fitted to the existing CB350 roadster, thus enabling the latter to be turned into a racer. Included in the kit were a modified cylinder head, with enlarged and polished ports, higher compression pistons and a polished and lightened crankshaft assembly. Carburation was by way of two butterfly-valve Keihin carburettors that were ignited by flywheel magneto.

The five-speed gearbox was given closer ratios, and there were five rear wheel sprockets included in the kit, from thirty to thirty-five teeth. The upgrade was completed by Ferodo racing brake linings, Dunlop racing tyres and alloy rims, a fibre-glass tank, seat and fairing, clip-on handlebars, rearset foot controls, a 19,000rpm rev counter and a pair of long, tapered, matt-black megaphones.

The 450

The arrival of the dohc torsion-bar CB450 Black Bomber roadster (*see* Chapter 5) had given rise to a number of interesting racing versions, on both sides of the Atlantic. The first of these debuted at Daytona in March 1967, when Zenya Nakajima, service director of American Honda, and Bob Hansen, of Wisconsin, got together to encourage the parent

Bob Hansen (right) and team manager, Terry Naughtin, De Land, Florida, 1 March 2002. The machine is the CR450 of the type used by Team Hansen at Daytona in 1967.

Hansen CR450 frame and engine details; note the oil cooler underneath the headstock.

company to develop a number of special components for the CB450. Early in 1967, Honda had agreed to this proposal, in time to enter a trio of Hansen 450s at Daytona. Ridden in the 200-miler by Swede Savage and Harry Schaffer, the 450s came home tenth and twelfth, an extremely good result considering it was their first race. Then in the Amateur 100-miler, Jim Odom broke the existing class lap record by over 5mph (8km/h) before crashing.

Meanwhile, in Europe three men took the 450 route: Marly Drixl, Fritz Egli and Colin Lyster. Swiss special-builder Drixl's first effort appeared in 1969, but for 1970 he enlarged the engine from 450 to 500cc. With a one-off crankshaft, con rods, pistons, camshafts and 38mm Dell'Orto carbs, the engine revved round to 9,800rpm and drove through a five-speed, close-ratio gearbox. The complete Drixl-Honda weighed in at 286lb (130kg) dry.

The most successful Drixl-Honda rider was the Australian Terry Dennehy, who scored a number of leader board placings in the Grand Prix series during 1969 and 1970, including a

fourth at Imola in 1969. Fellow special-builder Fritz Egli also built a full five-hundred twin. This was ridden by Florian Burki, who made an appearance at the international Brands Hatch meeting in October 1970.

South African Colin Lyster had been a racer in Continental Europe, but switched his attention to producing disc brakes and frames during the late 1960s. He also constructed a 450-powered racing bike, which featured a towering cambox housing a completely redesigned dohc arrangement and eight valves. Called the 'Revolution', the project was for both a racer and later a roadster funded by American Harry Glah. However, although the racing prototype appeared in 1969, the whole venture collapsed the following year.

The 750 Four

Like the 450 twin, Honda's CB750 (*see* Chapter 10) created quite a stir when it was launched in 1969. But unlike the smaller machine, the factory decided to take an official

Works type CR750 (based on production CB750), circa 1970. Note the twin discs, racing drum at rear, racing tank and seat. The bike was prepared for long-distance endurance racing.

racing interest. This led it to build a small number of racers based around the series production model especially for the Daytona 200 in early 1970. Riders were to be Ralph Bryans,

RIGHT: *One of the RC76 type Hondas prepared for the European Endurance Championship in 1977.*

Tommy Robb and the American star, Dick Mann. The last was the fastest of the Honda qualifiers at 152.67mph (245.65km/h) – 5mph (8km/h) short of Gene Romero's new record of over 157mph (253km/h) on a Triumph triple.

During practice, the Hondas had been troubled by oiling and cam-chain problems. After watching the race-kitted CB750s in action, puffing smoke with every gear change, no one expected them to go the distance. Robb was destined to retire early in the race with machine troubles, whilst Bryans' bike was destroyed after it caught fire in spectacular fashion. This left only one Honda circulating, with that wily campaigner, Mann, aboard. Throughout the race, everything except Honda led, but slowly the favourite runners dropped out, and by the end it was Dick Mann and the machine everybody had forgotten about, the CB750 Honda. Actually, as Dick Mann was to relate afterwards, he had decided to 'ride to finish', and whereas the other two Honda riders had revved their engines to the red line, Mann had not done so, thus achieving what he had set out to do; the victory being the icing on the cake.

The CB750 was also successful – in standard guise – in production sports machine events – until the Italians took over the class for the next few years with machines such as the Laverda 750 SFC and Ducati V-twin.

Then in the mid-1970s Honda brought out the Euro-styled CB400F and the CB500F fours, which were both used quite successfully in racing by privateers, either in production events or the newly introduced FIM Formula series (Formula 1 750cc; Formula 2 400–600cc and Formula 3 250cc).

In 1976 Honda had re-entered the sport, via the 750-based 941 RCB – which as a works-only special does not qualify in this history. The 941 RCB dominated European long distance endurance events (including the French 24-hour Bol d'Or) for several years.

For 1977, the company returned to building and marketing a production racing motorcycle. This, the MT125R, was a two-stroke and is covered in Chapter 14.

Formula Racing

Also in 1977, Honda made a successful return to the Isle of Man TT, Phil Read taking his works-prepared 750 4 to victory in the Formula 1 TT – and setting the fastest lap at 101.74mph (163.7km/h). In addition, Honda saw its machines take the Formula 2 (CB400F, Alan Jackson) and Formula 3 (CB250, John Kidson) races. As these events constituted the newly introduced World Championship in each category, Honda had scored a clean sweep in the Formula TT that year.

The following year, Read lost his title in sensational fashion to Mike Hailwood on a Ducati V-twin, but Jackson retained his Formula 2 crown, with Bill Smith becoming the new Formula 3 title holder on another Honda.

Right at the end of the 1970s, the company introduced the new CB900, and as Honda entered the new decade, it was to garner yet more success with its larger displacement machines from the 4-cylinder family.

Phil Read with one of the Honda Britain Formula 1 racers used in 1977/78. These were the forerunner of the dohc 750/900 series Hondas produced from 1978 onwards.

Later, in 1981, came the CBR1100 to carry on the tradition. But for many, the 1960s and 1970s were the most exciting times in what is now universally referred to as the 'classic era'.

A reunion of the Team Chisholm 125s. Bill Ivy's CB92 and CR93 with, left to right, the CB92's current owner, John Pitt, Mick Walker and Team Chisholm rider Roy Francis; Mallory Park, August 2003.

125

10   CB750

Edward Turner's Triumph Speed Twin of 1937 and the Honda CB750, which was launched just over three decades later, were, in this author's opinion, the two most influential motorcycles of the twentieth century.

Back in 1965 Honda had launched its CB450 dohc twin (*see* Chapter 5). But although it received massive publicity in the press it never really sold in the numbers that Honda had expected. It was in many ways the Japanese marque's first international failure.

The Rumours

After the arrival of the CB450, various rumours circulated regarding Honda's future plans, as prior to the 450 many observers had thought that Honda had reached its maximum engine size with the 305 twin. But, in truth, Honda was Honda – it had no limits combined with a massive Research & Development organization. And as for 4-cylinder engines, it already had considerable experience, albeit as a car manufacturer.

But would the rumoured bigger Honda be a twin or a four, as both had been mentioned as possibilities? There is no doubt that Honda's competitors, particularly the British, continued to be nervous – if for no other reason than the latter's main market was North America, where Honda already had a large presence and

a big dealer network. In August 1968 Honda's managing director, Kiyoshi Kawashima, revealed whilst visiting South Africa that in a bid to capture the United States' big bike market, Honda was 'developing a 750cc twin'.

Actually, this was something of a red herring. And Honda was not working on a twin, but instead a brand-new four.

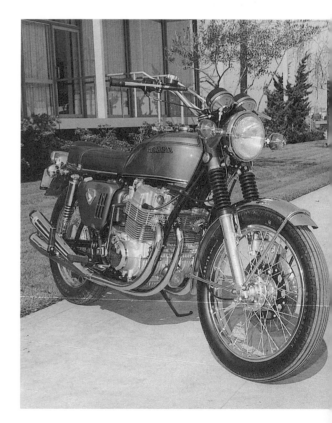

A very early pre-production CB750 outside the American Honda headquarters in Gardena, circa 1969.

A Tokyo Show Debut

Shortly before the Tokyo Show opened in late October, news began to leak out that the new-comer was actually an across-the-frame four with near-vertical cylinders and a single over-head camshaft. As *Motor Cycle* said in its 16 October 1968 issue: 'Expected to be on sale early in 1969, the Honda CB750 has been under development for at least two years.' At that time, the only other 4-cylinder roadsters in production were the 591.8cc Italian MV Agusta '600' and German 1085cc Münch Mammoth. But both of these were strictly limited production machines with large price tags, whereas the new Honda offered enthusiasts everywhere the chance to own what could truthfully be called a 'superbike' for a competitive price.

According to Japanese sources at the time, a double overhead camshaft layout was rejected 'to keep the power unit and frame as compact as possible'. The photograph published in *Motor Cycle* showed a pre-production prototype with a CB450 2LS drum front brake and a four-pipe black exhaust system, but otherwise it was largely as the production model displayed together with an engine unit at the fifteenth Tokyo Show, which *Motor Cycle* reported in its 30 October 1968 issue.

A Winner from the Start

Like all the best motorcycles, the CB750 looked right and was right, the Honda development team having come up with a machine that not only had the opposition on the ropes from day one, but boasted a specification which, at the time, simply couldn't be matched by any other series production bike. Not only was it a four, but a seven-fifty (when most 'big' machines were still limited to six-fifty). Not content with this, the CB750 featured sohc, five gears, a disc front brake (in an era when the opposition still had drum brakes!), a full duplex cradle frame (a first on a production Honda), a gleaming chrome-plated four-pipe exhaust, a quartet of CV-type carburettors, plus electric start, matching speedometer and tachometer, a host of warning lights, twin mirrors and a large dual seat.

But the arrival of the CB750 was more than just shattering news for the British motorcycle industry – Honda's Japanese rivals were also sent reeling. The biggest Yamaha street bike at the time was a 350cc two-stroke twin, whilst Suzuki had its T500 (another twin-cylinder two-stroke). But worst hit was Kawasaki, which had not only launched its Mach III two-stroke triple a month earlier, but had its own 750cc four under development. This latter bike was subsequently scrapped and big K went off back to the drawing board to design the 900cc Z1 (which debuted in 1972) and a 750cc two-stroke triple, the Mach IV. All-in-all, Honda floored the opposition with one heavy punch – this CB750 punch proving a knockout to the British and a pretty severe beating to the others.

As Roy Bacon said in his book, *Honda: The Early Classic Motorcycles*: 'The problem the Honda four gave the others was more than its specification; it was its keen price, availability worldwide and its sophistication.'

Another was that there was now a generation of riders who had grown up on Hondas and were ready to buy into the next stage of the company's motorcycle development. They knew that Honda on the tank meant a reliable machine with good performance, excellent electrics and a lack of oil leaks.

More show appearances followed. The first of these was in Las Vegas in January 1969, with Americans getting their first glimpse of the new Japanese 'Wonderbike'. European enthusiasts had their first sight of the brand-new 4-cylinder Honda on Saturday, 8 February 1969 after one of the new models had been flown from America to the Dutch importer's headquarters in Eindhoven. It was one of four that had been at Las Vegas, the CB750 arriving earlier that week, and was subsequently shown to Dutch dealers on Thursday, 6 February.

Honda had, in fact, forbidden Dutch Honda importer, Tom Riemersma, from starting the bike. Subsequent publicity shots showing manager, Rins de Groot, in the saddle had to be taken when he was free-wheeling. Asked what the price would be in Holland, Riemersma replied 'We don't know yet but we hope to get the first batch in August.'

Another of the Las Vegas machines was expected to arrive at Honda UK's London headquarters 'during the next week or so', reported *Motor Cycle* in its 12 February 1969 issue. This machine made its British debut in front of television cameras at Beaulieu, Hampshire, on Friday, 14 February.

With the new Honda, also in the UK for the first time was the Münch Mammut, as well as other large capacity machines lined up for a BBC *Wheelbase* recording session. Honda UK's technical manager, Alf Briggs, did start the four and provided the cameras with what were described as 'spectacular' wheel-spinning getaways. The bike was the one flown in from America and was the undoubted star at the Brighton Show that got under way on Saturday, 5 April 1969. As one pre-Brighton Show newspaper report said:

> Bewildering though Honda's lively policy of frequent changes can be, their new ranges are invariably exciting. And, for sheer thrills, the line-up to be unveiled at the Brighton Show on Saturday is the greatest yet. Star exhibit without question is Honda's first 4-cylinder roadster, the CB750, a 130mph smoothie with as much power (67bhp) as the world championship-winning MV Agusta big fours had only a few years ago.

Technical Details

The Power Unit

In many ways, the newcomer embodied Honda engineering practices, but transferred to a 4-cylinder configuration, with one notable exception, as the CB750 used a dry-sump lubrication system with a separate 6pt (2ltr) oil tank. Why? To keep engine weight low down and provide adequate ground clearance, as the engineering team believed the usual Honda wet-sump system would take up too much space at the base of the crankcases. The crankcases were sand-cast on very early production, but thereafter they were produced by conventional die-casting method. Cylinder heads went through the same evolution.

The basis of the engine assembly was a crankcase split horizontally along the shaft centre line, with a separate cylinder block and another one-piece casting for the cylinder head. The crankshaft of the 736.5cc (61 × 63mm) single overhead cam motor was a single forging

The mighty 736.5cc (61 × 63mm) sohc across-the-frame 4-cylinder engine. Note the four-pipe exhaust, ignition switch under the tank and horizontally split crankcases.

Rickman Engineering built small batches of machines (the CR) powered by the CB750 sohc engine. In this mid-1970s photograph, the Mayor of Christchurch, Hampshire, John Morgan (seated on the bike), is with Honda UK sales supreme, Eric Sulley, right (in the light suit).

and not a pressed-up affair, as was then usual Honda practice. This meant that the connecting rods were two-piece with end caps and the big-end bearings were white metal shells. The con rods were of forged steel construction with the gudgeon pins running directly in them and were retained in the three-ring pistons (two compression, one oil control) with circlips. The compression ratio was 9:1.

Five Main Bearings

The CB750 employed five main bearings. These were all of the plain type and were housed in the crankcase halves. There is no doubt that by locating the crankshaft, main bearings and transmission shafts on the centre line of the crankcase halves the engineering team provided maximum rigidity and oil-tight joints.

A 2-valves-per-cylinder set-up was enough for what, after all, Honda considered as a sports/tourer, not an out-and-out sportster. The valves operated in pressed-in guides, were retained by collars with split collets and

employed coil springs. The single camshaft ran directly in four split plain bearings formed on two camshaft holders with a quartet of separate top caps. These holders sat on the centre of the cylinder head and were machined as a half bearing at each end. They also extended fore and aft to support the rockers on a total of four pivot pins, each of these being locked in position by a single bolt.

Each pin supported two rockers, each rocker having an adjuster at its outer end. Valve adjustment was of the conventional screw and lock nut type. Access was obtained via eight large circular caps in the usual Honda style and were all screwed into the one-piece cambox cover. This cover also supported the rev counter drive, which meshed with a gear cut on the right (offside) centre of the camshaft.

The Camshaft

The camshaft was driven by a simplex chain from a centrally located bolted-up sprocket. There was also a matching sprocket on the

129

centre of the crankshaft. This passed through a series of tunnels cast into the cylinder block and head, with a chain tensioner located at the rear of the former and a guide roller lower down. In practice, this set-up proved reliable in service and was relatively cheap to manufacture; using a series of gears would have been much more costly. The centrally located chain was to remain a feature on later across-the-frame, 4-cylinder Honda designs.

The Lubrication System

As already mentioned, Honda chose to give the CB750 a dry-sump lubrication system. But otherwise it was a pretty straightforward high-pressure arrangement with the double (delivery and scavenge) trochoidal pump operating at 90lb pressure to the bearings. Trochoidal simply means an eccentrically rotating gear pump. This was actually a four-lobed inner rotor which rotated within a five-lobed outer rotor. The pump was mounted in the base of the lower crankcase half, with access being made by removal of the finned sump pan section. The pump was driven by a gear on the kick-start shaft. A valve prevented the oil from draining back through the pump and into the

sump – with pressure being held by a relief valve in the pump body. The lubricating oil went first to a full-flow car-type filler canister secured to the front of the crankcase and then onwards to an oil gallery running across the engine to the rear of the crankshaft. The end of this was sealed with a cap – the latter being removable so that a gauge adaptor could be fitted to check oil pressure.

From the gallery, oil was transferred to all five main bearings and from them to the big ends. Two feeds were taken up the cylinder barrel studs to lubricate the camshaft lobes and rockers, with the surplus draining down to the sump. There it was collected by scavenge pump, itself provided by a gauze strainer, and thence returned to the oil tank situated on the offside (right), below the dual seat.

The scavenge return included a take-off which fed both gearbox shafts; excess lubricant was collected in a tray which then fed through the output shaft to the final drive sprocket and chain. Honda recommended changing the oil and checking the filter every 1,860 miles (3,000km).

Offside view of the engine showing the cam-driven rev counter drive, kickstart lever and oil tank (under the side panel) for dry-sump lubrication.

Unlike other 4-cylinder Hondas, the CB750 employed a dry-sump lubrication system.

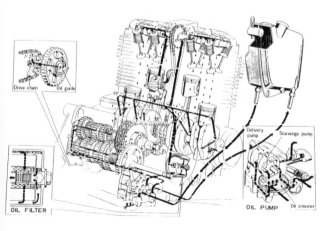

Ignition Details

The ignition of the CB750 was by two Toyo Denso double-ended coils, each fired by a set of Hitachi contact-breaker points. These two sets of contact breakers were housed under a circular chromed-plate on the offside (right) of the crankcase and were opened by a cam on the crankshaft end. Behind this was a centrifugal advance and retard mechanism. On the other side of the engine was a three-phase type Hitachi 210W alternator with an electromagnetic field coil. Output of this was controlled by an Hitachi electromechanical regulator and went via an Hitachi six-diode rectifier to a Yuasa 12V 14amp-hour battery.

The motor (manufactured by Mitsuba) for the electric starter had been relocated from its traditional Honda home at the front of the crankcase, to the top/rear of the cylinder block and was covered by another chrome-steel plate, but this time rectangular in shape. The motor was switched on by a relay and its armature was cut as a pinion which mated up with an idler set. This transferred the drive to a large gear set behind the alternator rotor, which featured a roller clutch at its centre.

The Transmission

The transmission was unusual, at least when it was introduced, as the primary transmission. There were two endless chains, which, like that of the camshaft drive, were situated centrally on the crankshaft. These dual chains drove the gearbox mainshaft, which in turn was supported on no fewer than four ball-bearing races – two at either end of the shaft and two either side of the chain sprocket. The chains ran close enough together to resemble a duplex component. The Japanese design team opted for a bushed instead of roller chain, this posing problems enough to ensure that duplex chains were impractical. Why chain drive instead of gears? Quite simply, the answer was cost and weight reduction.

The clutch, a wet multi-plate assembly, consisted of seven friction plates which were pres-

RECOMMENDED RETAIL PRICES
(incl. Purchase Tax)

	£. s. d.	£ . p
PF 50 Moped	70 – –	70.00
PC 50 K1 Moped	80 – –	80.00
C 50	105 – –	105.00
CZ 50 A	130 – –	130.00
ST 50	135 – –	135.00
SS 50 4 Speed	122 7 8	122.38½
SS 50 5 Speed	136 19 –	136.95
CE 90	147 – –	147.00
CD 90 Z	150 – –	150.00
CB 100 De Luxe	200 – –	200.00
SS 125	189 19 –	189.95
CB 125 De Luxe	260 – –	260.00
CD 175 K3	220 – –	220.00
CB 175 De Luxe	280 – –	280.00
CB 250 K2	330 – –	330.00
CB 450 5 Speed	470 – –	470.00
CB 750	695 – –	695.00

Plus Delivery Charge

HONDA (UK) LTD POWER ROAD LONDON W4.

The Honda UK 1970 price list, with the top-of-the-range CB750 listed at £695.

surized by single-coil, large diameter coil springs of comparatively low poundage. The friction plates drove the layshaft and the layshaft gear in turn drove the final drive shaft, on the nearside end of which was the rear chain sprocket. All were ball-bearing race supported.

The clutch centre was splined to the gearbox mainshaft, whilst the layshaft was situated behind and below it. Both shafts were supported by ball races and both carried five pairs of gears. These cogs acted as an all-indirect set and the various ratios were selected by a trio of forks controlled by a barrel cam. This in itself was operated by the positive stop mechanism, which was hidden under a cover on the nearside, from which the shaft for the gear lever protruded. The final drive sprocket was not fitted to either of the gear mainshafts; instead, it had one of its own that ran in separate bearings at the rear of the crankcase. It carried a single gear, this meshing with one splined to the layshaft. The sprocket itself was retained in the traditional Honda manner by a plate and two bolts.

Carburation

Four separate 28mm Keihin CV carburettors were employed and were located to each other by a plate. Each instrument had its own float chamber and individual settings, although in practice these settings were pretty standardized: main jet 120; idle jet 40; air jet 100; cutaway 2.5; and an idle speed of 900rpm. Figures apply to UK market machines, but others are similar.

It is worth noting that the pre-production machines were equipped with carburettor operation via rods and levers. This was not used for series production, probably on cost grounds.

All four carbs shared a common fuel supply and all four chokes were linked to a single lever (situated on the nearside of the machine). The four throttle cables ran into a junction box, with a single cable leading up to the twistgrip.

In addition, the carbs were connected to the cylinder head inlet stubs by short rubber hoses clamped into place, with a big air cleaner box on the intake side. The lower section of this was

detachable to provide access to the filter element contained within.

The Exhaust

As *Motor Cyclist Illustrated* said in its October 1970 issue:

> The Four is a big, bulky looking motorcycle. Four cylinders in front, and four exhaust pipes to the rear contribute an impression quite deliberately created by Honda of mass. Functionally necessary, exciting and complex, but instead of attempting to reduce and hide the multiplicity of fins, tubes, covers and castings, levers and ancillaries, Honda have exploited them to the full, on a motorcycle that, without a hint of modesty, lets the world know it has style as no other. Like a Morgan Plus Eight. Like a Land Rover. Like an ancestral home. Like a title.

And that four-pipe, chromed exhaust with its tapered megaphone-like mufflers was at the very forefront of the style with a capital 'S' factor on the CB750. As one commentator said: 'It gave the system a magnificent line set off by heat guards bolted to the top silencers.'

The header pipes were clamped to adaptors, which were bolted to the cylinder head and, like many other Honda models, the header

The CB750 4-cylinder was a good choice for long-distance endurance events, thanks to its excellent reliability. Here's one in action during the 1970 Barcelona 24 Hours.

pipes were double skinned – this helped to prevent discolouring from occurring. At the rear end of the mufflers (silencers) on each side they were connected by a short tube, but otherwise each system was isolated from the other cylinders.

The Chassis

Strangely, considering this was Honda's attempt to provide one of its mass production bikes with a full duplex cradle frame (except a single top tube), very few commentators or road testers said very much about it. This was probably because, as *Motor Cyclist Illustrated* commented, 'The frame of the Four is, like most motorcycle frames today, boringly conventional, just old fashioned and completely outclassed by the rest of the machine.' To cope with the class-leading power output figures the headstock was heavily braced with pressings, as was the rear swinging arm. The front suspension was by oil-damped telescopic front fork. The stanchions were protected by rubber gaiters – there being internal springs.

If the early CB750 had a fault, it was its high-speed handling. The experienced Dave Minton had this to say in 1970, and I can only agree with his findings: 'Handling was beyond criticism below 80mph. Line chopping was a delight, and roadholding on the longest, undulating curves utterly steady, but above this speed a slight deterioration set in.' He continued:

> The movement was suggestive of shallow fork trail, but as the Four's is 3.7in (94mm) it is unlikely. Fine until high speeds were reached and then something had to give, in this case the steering. Slowing down, time and time again from high speeds, I noticed a faint fork shudder, reminiscent of a sidecar machine on solo trait, and hard acceleration at speed on curves brought about an unwanted movement as well.

Honda had omitted a hydraulic steering damper, which would have helped.

Braking

The CB750 was the first Honda production bike to feature a disc front brake – and in fact the Japanese company claimed that this was a world first: the first use of a hydraulically operated disc brake on a production motorcycle. Mounted on the nearside (left), it consisted of a single 296mm stainless steel disc with a Tokico-made piston caliper. It should be explained that only one pad moved, with the other fixed in the caliper. This meant that some means had to be provided for the caliper as a whole to move laterally to the disc. Honda engineers solved this by mounting the caliper on an arm which could pivot on the nearside fork slider. It had a screw adjuster to regulate the clearance between the fixed pad and disc. As Mark Haylock says in his excellent book *Honda CB750: The Complete Story* (Crowood Press): 'This was unfortunate, because one of the main attractions of a normal disc brake is that it is self-adjusting, but here was one that did require periodic adjustment.'

Another weakness concerned the choice of a stainless steel disc. Worried about corrosion on a traditional cast-iron disc, Honda chose stainless steel to prevent the rusting problem. But as Mark Haylock explains: 'This was fulfilled, but unfortunately at the expense of reliably effective braking. Stainless steel does not have such good friction characteristics for brakes as cast iron, in particular when wet. It is also more prone to squealing.'

In contrast, the 180mm single-leading shoe full-width aluminium drum rod-operated rear brake came in for criticism for locking up, particularly in wet conditions. For example, *Motorcycle Mechanics* had this to say when testing a CB750 in its June 1970 issue: 'The rear brake was fierce and care had to be used to avoid locking the rear wheel. This applied even more on wet, greasy London roads.'

The wheels were built up on light alloy hubs with steel rims and wire spokes, while the tyre sizes were 3.25 × 19 front and 4.00 × 18 rear.

The Ancillaries

Where the CB750 really scored was as an overall package and value for money, one tester commenting: 'The CB750 is laden with "extras" like a Christmas tree – electric starter, flashing indicators, handlebar cut-out switch, oil and neutral warning lights, handlebar mirrors, stoplight operated by hydraulic, disc front brake and the snazziest speedometer and tachometer are among the many attractions offered on this "super-bike".'

The ND Denso speedometer and tachometer were both large and clear-faced with the speedometer reading 150mph and the tacho 11,000rpm. Lighting of the instruments was also excellent, as the dials were in black with light-green figures. At night, the instrument lights shone through the figures to give a luminescent glow.

All in all, Honda had hit the jackpot. The CB750 was a massive sales success, as figures would show over the next few years – at least until the other manufacturers got their acts together. But for the time being Honda had stolen a substantial lead.

A nice action view of an early CB750 under test.

A Racing Debut

The Honda CB750's race debut came at a Canadian meeting at Harewood, Ontario, in May 1969, when Mick Manley was third behind a Norton Commando ridden by ex-

1969 CB750 Specification			
Engine	Air-cooled sohc across-the-frame four, 10-degree inclined cylinders, 2-valves-per-cylinder, alloy head and barrel, chain-driven camshaft, one-piece crankshaft, two-piece con rods with shell big ends, horizontally split aluminium crankcases	Frame	Duplex steel cradle
		Front suspension	Oil-damped telescopic forks, with gaiters
		Rear suspension	Swinging arm, twin shock absorbers
		Front brake	Single 296cc hydraulically operated disc
Bore	61mm	Rear brake	180mm full-width SLS alloy drum
Stroke	63mm	Tyres	Front 3.25 × 19, rear 4.00 × 18
Displacement	736.5cc		
Compression ratio	9:1	**General Specifications**	
Lubrication	Twin pumps, dry sump	Wheelbase	57.3in (1,455mm)
Ignition	Two double-ended coils, two sets of contact breakers, 12V, electric start	Ground clearance	6.3in (160mm)
		Seat height	31.7in (805mm)
Carburettor	4 × Keihin 28mm	Fuel tank capacity	4gal (18ltr)
Primary drive	2 × independent single row chains	Dry weight	480lb (217kg)
Final drive	Chain	Maximum power	67bhp @ 8,000rpm
Gearbox	Five speeds; foot-change	Top speed	125mph (200km/h)

Yamaha works star, Mike Duff, and the 750cc Triumph Trident triple of Roger Beaumont. A period press report commented: 'The big Honda arrived from Japan too late for rider Mick Manley to cure handling problems, but the four led the race for the first two laps before being overhauled.' Details of the CB750's subsequent racing career are covered in Chapter 9.

The first man to fit one of the new 750cc 4-cylinder Honda engines into a racing sidecar outfit was the Australian, Lindsay Urquhart. This move paid off, for he won both 750 and Unlimited races in the Australian TT (in January 1970), beating his own 750cc lap record by 4sec and equalling the absolute three-wheeler record of 2min 22sec. It was reported that 'at least six other Australian sidecar men were switching to Honda units'.

Back in the UK the question was being asked 'who would be the first in Britain to follow the Australian lead?' The answer to this came in the 20 May 1970 issue of *Motor Cycle* when it was revealed that Kidderminster's sidecar racing brothers Roy and Doug Woodhouse were then 'putting the finishing touches' to a Honda-powered outfit which they intended racing in the Isle of Man TT. Its engine was a 'virtually-

The first UK racing sidecar outfit to be powered by the new CB750 engine was that of brothers Roy and Doug Woodhouse, details of which first appeared in spring 1970.

standard' CB750 unit taken from a complete machine purchased from Lincolnshire dealer, and ex-1949 350cc World Champion, Freddie Frith. The frame had a single, large diameter downtube with triple top tubes. The brakes on all three wheels were hydraulically operated by the same pedal.

A 1974 Japanto, converted to 970cc by the Paris-based tuning specialists. During the 1970s the French concern built both road and racing bikes based around the sohc Honda CB750.

CB750s came home eighth and ninth in the Production TT (Tommy Robb and John Cooper respectively), in a race won by Welshman Malcolm Uphill riding a 750 Triumph Trident, with the Norton Commandos of Peter Williams and Ray Pickrell coming second and third. But, as if to prove that although the Honda was quick, it didn't have the best handling, is to relate that the two CB750s were second and sixth through the speed traps – Cooper at 136.9mph (220.3km/h) and Robb 132.8mph (213.7km/h). Both bikes were equipped with non-standard dolphin race-type fairings.

In its unfaired, standard form the CB750 was capable of around 125mph (200km/h).

Deliveries Begin

Deliveries of bikes didn't arrive in the UK until January 1970, although supplies had been received in North America in mid-1969. The *Motor Cycle* dated 4 February 1970 reported:

> The first shipment of 125mph, 4-cylinder 750cc Hondas – all of them pre-sold – has been delivered to British dealers. Although Honda (UK) last week

refused to confirm the number, the consignment is believed to have contained 24 machines. It is also understood that 70 will be delivered this month and another 70 in March. Price of the bike, said Honda (UK) last week, is £679 19s – £30 more than was quoted at the Brighton Show.

Continuing Development

What may not have been widely appreciated, certainly at the time, was that there were many differences between the early bikes in 1968, those lent to the press for evaluation in early 1969, and later series production machines offered for sale. In fact, simply listing all of the changes to the CB750 during its ten-year life would take up more space than is available here; however, a total of around one million sohc CB750s were built and sold between 1969 and 1978 when production finally ceased. But of course even then the CB750 didn't cease, as it was replaced by the CB750K-Z with dohc engine. The K-Z has, incorrectly, been described as an updated CB750; in fact, it was a generally new design, with not

The Honda CB750K-Z. This replaced the old sohc 8-valve CB750K series and featured 748cc 62 × 62mm dohc and sixteen valves.

The Americans also got a C (Custom) version of the CB750K-Z. This is a 1980 photograph.

The new CB900 F-Z became the top of the range across-the-frame Honda four when it arrived at the end of 1978. Several were successfully raced in production events – for as along as they stayed together!

just a dohc roller-bearing engine but a frame with a removable section to assist engine removal. There was also the F-A750 and its bigger brother, the CB900F-Z. These were similar to the CB750K-Z, but with 4-into-2 exhaust systems and an increase in power. All three dohc machines are featured within this chapter (*see* Box overleaf).

Other Sohc Models

This leaves the other CB750 sohc models. The very first production CB750 four was simply that – no prefix. Next came the K1 (from frame number 1044650), which was released on 21 September 1970. This was the first major update since the CB750 had entered production twelve months earlier.

Engine changes were restricted to minor details such as the top breather pipe, cylinder head and carb mountings, cam-chain tensioner bar and locking bolt, clutch springs, crankcase mounting and tube for oil drain from separator in oil tank. Cycle parts saw alterations to the air cleaner box, seat, oil tank, battery side cover, glass instead of plastic on instruments and revised faces (from black to dark green), red zone on tacho reduced from

8,500 to 8,000rpm, modified front brake master cylinder/lever, 4mm narrower front hub and different speedo drive gearbox, modified front fork sliders (now 48mm instead of 46mm and the retaining circlip changed from 47 to 50mm), rear shocks now of De Carbon type, neater handlebar mirrors and modified centre stand.

The K2

The K2 was introduced on 1 March 1972 (from frame number 2000001). It is also worth pointing out that the engine number also began E2000001. This makes life easier in identifying exactly what bike you may own or be thinking of purchasing. One of the most noticeable features of the K2 compared with its earlier CB750 brothers is that the handlebar clamps were replaced by a new warning light display on a separate panel – which also doubled up as the handlebar clamp.

The American market K2 had a buzzer device telling the rider that his direction indicators were on (a button was also incorporated to cancel the sound on the nearside handlebar switch). The K2 also introduced a lock for the side-hinged seat (all CB750s had a steering

Double Overhead Camshafts

With sales of some one million, the original sohc CB750 (1969–78) had a ten-year production run and set Honda on the route to big-bike sales success. But by the end of production it had been caught and passed by rival manufacturers both in Japan and Europe. But Honda was loath simply to dump such a faithful servant and so came up with a new double overhead cam CB750. Actually it came up with two distinct models, the K-Z four-pipe 'tourer' and the F-A 'sports'. Both used a new 748cc (62 × 62mm) across-the-frame engine with wet-sump lubrication, sixteen valves and shim-set tappets.

The motorcycle that replaced the CB750F2, the dohc, 16-valve CB750 F-A.

Width was something of a problem compared with the models that came before, in that the engine was wider (plus the K-Z version had four exhausts) and so cornering clearance was restricted.

The 4-valves-per-cylinder layout offered many advantages, all due to the smaller size and weight of the valves. For the port area available they needed far less lift than a comparable 2-valve system and this, together with the lower mass of the individual valves, permitted higher engine speeds. Another advantage was that the (smaller) valve heads didn't protrude so far into the cylinder, which simplified piston design considerably. As a result, it was easier to obtain a high compression, without the usual problems of piston crown weaknesses or heavy pistons. And being able to use lighter pistons put less stress on the bottom end, notably the crankshaft.

The camshafts were driven by Hy-Vo chains, one from the crank to the exhaust cam and another from this camshaft across to the inlet. Both were equipped with slipper tensioners.

A third Hy-Vo chain took power off the centre of the crankshaft to a countershaft which drove the clutch via a shock absorber. The rest of the transmission followed normal practice, with an endless, O-ring chain driving the rear wheel.

The ignition system was electronic, with two pulsar coils at the crank and two electronic spark units feeding two coils. The voltage regulator was also solid state, so apart from the handlebar switches the electrical system was devoid of mechanical contacts. There was a 260W alternator and a 12V 14amp-hour battery. Carburettors were now four Keihin VB52A instruments.

There was more power, but also a wider spread of usable power. It was this that was the most noticeable comparing the old sohc and new dohc power units. But getting more power was only part of the story – keeping it was another matter. Here, Honda engineers used as much of the well-proven sohc technology as was possible – thus giving the advantages of both old and new, with the latter aimed at *increasing* reliability. The camshafts still ran in the head – a feature which demanded clean oil. Even so, Honda set the service frequency at 3,600 miles (5,800km), more than twice that recommended for the sohc models.

Besides the 748cc K-Z and F-A dohc models, Honda also offered the CDB900F. This was essentially the same motorcycle as the seven-fifty F-A, but with a larger displacement 901cc (64.5 × 69mm) engine. Both the 750 F-A and 900F had Comstar wheels (the K-Z had wire wheels). The nine-hundred four put out 95bhp at 9,000rpm. A 4-into-2 exhaust and the wide use of plastic kept the weight down to 512lb (233kg), which was lighter than the 750KZ.

But, unfortunately, the extra power of the bigger engines rather blighted the reliability that had been such a strong point on the 750s, with cam chains being known to fail after as little as 20,000 miles (32,000km). Honda set out to rectify this on later CB900s, by modifying both the cam chain and tensioner. Yet another 900 glitch was broken con rods, but this was confined mostly to the track for those racing the CB900F in production machine races.

lock from day one). A document holder was now mounted under the seat and two hooks were intended as helmet holders. The exhaust system was modified in line with more stringent noise regulations. The new, quieter type was stamped 341 on the outside of the silencer, instead of the original 300 coding.

The rear chainguard was redesigned, with the material changing from plastic to steel – in both cases finished in black. The K2 (and later version) chainguard extended further to the rear than the original. At the rear wheel, the quartet of bolts to mount the rear sprocket were replaced by studs and the rear brake pedal was modified, a 'stopper' being incorporated so that adjustment could be carried out. The rear shocks were totally redesigned and there was now a locking device multi-pin electrical connector where it joined the rectifier with the rest of the wiring loom. There were also cosmetic changes, including a range of new colour options including Candy Gold Custom (which was the only colour of the K2 in the UK). In addition, the upper fork shrouds, which doubled up as headlamp brackets, were now chrome-plated, instead of being painted.

The K3, K4 and K5 Models

The K3, K4 and K5 models were never sold in the UK and confusingly the model year CB750 was known in Britain during 1973–5 as the K2, whereas the Americans got the K3 (1973), K4 (1974) and K5 (1975) versions. But it should be noted that many of the mechanical changes incorporated by Honda were to be found in British bikes.

For the K3 (first released on 1 February 1973 – frame number 2200001) several engine modifications occurred. The cylinder head now featured different oil control orifices, which were easier to remove for cleaning during maintenance.

The camshaft holders were redesigned with a modified system of retaining the rocker-shafts – which themselves were changed accordingly. The valve guides had their guides modified to accept oil seals once more (very early engines in 1969 having had seals on the exhaust guides, which were then deleted).

The pistons were modified (with a larger groove for redesigned oil-control rings) – this being carried out to cure the CB750's appetite to use oil. And the cam-chain guide was modified.

There were also changes to the electrical system, whilst the clutch lever was redesigned to incorporate a switch. This was because the starter motor would now only operate if the clutch was disengaged and the gearbox was in neutral. There were also changes to components such as the switchgear and mirrors.

Once again, the rear shocks had been looked at. This time they were given better damping. The front forks were redesigned – again to improve damping. The front brake pivot pin had proved prone to seizure, so this had been redesigned with a different mounting on the fork slider. These brake components cannot be retro-fitted to pre-K3-type bikes.

Differences between the K3 and K4 were quite small. There were a couple of new colour schemes and a change in tank stripe design. Otherwise, the only changes to components other than the engine were the seat and front brake master cylinder.

During the production run of the K4, a few modifications were carried out to the engine. These were largely aimed at reducing oil leaks at the joint between the cylinder block and head. From engine number E2304501 onwards, the cylinder block was modified to accommodate a new type of O-ring to surround the two innermost rear studs.

Later, from engine number E2352923, the cylinder block was again modified. This concerned holes for studs between cylinders one and two, and those between cylinders three and four (in other words eight out of the total of sixteen). These were modified with a double counterbore. Each held a hollow dowel (Honda termed these as knock pins), surrounded by a seal in the form of a hollow rubber cylinder. In addition, the head gasket was modified with larger holes to accommodate the above changes.

The K5 arrived from frame number 2500001 (and engine number E2372115). And again there were a number of changes, these concerning the speedometer dial details, indicators (larger than before), throttle twistgrip and new-style fuel tap (with a completely new tap being fitted on the nearside of the tank, rather than the offside as before), side-stand (which now featured a rubber pad). But, as will become evident by late 1974, when the K5 was almost ready for production, Honda already had its eye on the next evolution of the CB750, the F Super Sports series, which is detailed later in this chapter.

A Tester's Opinion

My late friend, John Robinson, carried out a comprehensive road test and appraisal of the latest CB750 in the November 1974 issue of *Motorcycle Mechanics*. John began by outlining Honda sales successes in the big bike sector, which of course meant, largely, the CB750. But he then went on to say 'I find this mildly surprising, because I remember the first fours as big, heavy, admittedly powerful, but unwieldy, with some unfortunate habits in the handling department.' This statement was probably to be expected, because by the mid-1970s the CB750 was no longer the cutting-edge technology it had been when it first arrived at the end of the 1960s, as just about every other motorcycle manufacturer had its own superbike by now. This list included the BMW R90S, Laverda 1000, Benelli 750 Sei, Ducati

A 1975 CB750K5. This model was never officially imported into the UK.

A CB750F being put through its paces at Mallory Park in the 1977 Avon Tyres Production Racing Championship.

750 V-twin (to be joined shortly by the 900), Moto Guzzi 850, Suzuki GT750, Kawasaki Z1 – the list was pretty impressive!

John Robinson continued: 'This year's model looks pretty much the same as ever, but the changes are there all right, just waiting to be counted.' He was pleasantly surprised: 'I suddenly realized that the 750 was handling. Where were the wallows of yesteryear? I was interested mainly in chassis and suspension changes, expecting something fairly drastic to explain the newly found handling qualities.' But in this, as he said,

> Sadly, from my point of view, nothing dramatic has happened. The frame is basically the same and none of the major dimensions, wheelbase, head angle etc. have been altered. It is purely the result of five years of development, with many subtle changes adding up to the improved end product. The front forks incorporate different rates and the damping has been altered. They also have a new oil seal to overcome the problem of oil seepage. The suspension has been changed at least four times and now they have it just about right for a combination of comfort and roadholding. One other significant change

is that the disc brake has been moved inboard and is now some 6mm closer to the centre of the hub.

John also noted: 'The footrests are further back and the handlebar is flatter, which makes a much better riding position.' As for engine development: 'like all other Hondas, this has been towards a smoother silence and a compliance with existing or projected legislation. It doesn't seem to have suffered too much though. If the motor isn't as powerful as the early ones, it is a lot quieter, more flexible and generally less fussy.'

The New 750F

The new CB750F was released in the USA in April 1975. Because of the new GL1000 Gold Wing (*see* Chapter 12), Honda decided to make the F model more of a sportster, as it saw the role of the tourer being filled by the Gold Wing. And it was the American market that dictated how the CB750F turned out, with a prototype being evaluated by test riders in the States before actual production got under way. Feedback from these tests dictated a change in fork angle to improve handling, which was criticized on the prototype.

Both the rake (castor) and trail of the steering was changed, this giving an increased wheelbase (mainly due to a new swinging arm), which at last provided the Honda development team with the improvements it sought.

The production CB750F also had many other changes, certainly compared to the existing K series. For starters, the engine was fitted out with a number of new or modified components. For example, there was a new cylinder head and also higher compression pistons (up from 9:1 to 9.2:1). The camshaft was modified to provide a longer opening period for the inlet valves and a very slight additional valve lift. These improvements in power were confirmed by *Cycle*, which dyno-tested the old and the new engine – rear wheel figures were 58bhp on the F compared to 53.9bhp on the K. The gearbox was considerably modified, with both the main and layshafts being changed, as were six of the nine gears, which had the effect of lowering the ratios for fourth and fifth gears. The output gear was reduced from fifty-six to fifty teeth, whilst the final drive sprocket was changed from eighteen to seventeen teeth. The effect of these changes was to make the F lower geared overall than the K series, whilst giving the new gearbox closer ratios. The gear selector mechanism was also modified, including a new drum assembly, whilst the chain oiler in the final drive shaft was axed – the new shaft having a plain end.

Other engine unit changes were made to the clutch (the innermost of the seven friction plates was modified), whilst the clutch outer was retained on its shaft by way of a circlip. There was also a different breather (to comply with new anti-pollution laws) and minor changes to the carbs.

New Cycle Parts

But by far the biggest changes were reserved for the cycle parts. The tank, seat (with useful tail extension), exhaust (a 4-into-1), front forks, rear suspension and much, much more. The fuel tank capacity had been increased from 3.7gal (17 ltr) to 4gal (18 ltr) with a new type, flush-fitting fuel cap – although the fuel tap remained the same as the K5. There was also a new oil tank, although the capacity remained unchanged at 0.7gal (3.3ltr). The 4-into-1 exhaust might not have looked as dramatic as the original 4-into-4 system, but it was more practical and didn't suffer the problems of high replacement costs or limited accessibility, the final drive chain and rear wheel now being much easier to get at.

All-New Brakes

Braking was another area of change. Not only were the front disc and caliper new, but there was now a disc at the rear instead of the previous drum. Both front and rear discs were 272mm. The rear caliper was a two-piston affair, whereas the front still retained the single piston with a pivoting caliper. The calipers were of a new design and were manufactured by Nissin. A new, more modern-looking warning light console replaced the old K2-style set-up.

It is worth noting that no CB750F models reached the UK, and the bike was only in production for six months, after which came the F1 version for the new 1976 model year.

In truth, there was very little difference between the CB750F and the machine which replaced it, the CB750F1. The differences were purely cosmetic, with new colours of Sulphur Yellow and Candy Antares Red. The yellow was a plain, rather than a metallic or candy finish. The CB750F1 went on sale in Britain from October 1975.

CB750F2

The CB750F2 (also known in some quarters as the CB750F'77) reflected the greatly increased competition in the 750cc sports category – for example, Suzuki had joined the four-stroke, 4-cylinder stakes with its excellent first effort, the dohc GS750. Honda knew it needed a new bike, but the CB750F2 was very much an interim model – until the factory could bring out a new dohc version of the across-the-frame four.

New paintwork, a new exhaust triple disc brake (two at the front and one at the rear) and Honda's new Comstar wheels were the most noticeable changes. But actually the engine had received considerable work. The CB750F/F1 was a very slightly tuned version of the existing K series design, but with the F2 the Honda engineering team took things a stage further. For a start, larger valves were specified (inlets increased from 32 to 34mm; exhausts from 28 to 31mm), whilst the camshaft was reprofiled to suit. In fact, the F2 had the hottest cam profile fitted to any stock sohc Honda CB750, with 225-degree opening and 0.5mm additional lift for both inlet and exhaust. The valve springs were beefed up, which reduced the onset of valve bounce, the engine's red line now going up to 9,500rpm.

To make full use of these changes the port shapes and combustion chamber of the cylin-

der head had been altered and the compression ratio reduced to 9:1 (the figure used on the early K series engines). This meant, if Honda's own figures are to be believed, that power had gone up from 67bhp at 8,500rpm on the 1975 750F to 73bhp at 9,000rpm on the 750F2.

To cope with this additional power, the clutch springs were increased in strength and clutch lift increased from 2 to 2.4mm. The sump plate now had improved finning (to remove heat faster) and a larger oil filter was fitted. There were other more minor changes, notably to the cylinder block and the gearbox.

Much work had been carried out on improving the fitment and operation of the carburetors, as well as on choke operation and a form of accelerator pump (although only one carb had this device). A 630 size final drive chain was specified for the first time.

Two worthwhile improvements had been carried out to the electrical system. First, a quartz-halogen headlamp was standard and another first for the CB750 was the fitment of two (loud!) horns.

For the 1978 model year Honda produced

The CB750F2 was introduced n 1977 with several engine improvements, including larger valves and reprofiled cam. Also new are Comstar wheels and a heavier final drive chain.

the CB750F'78 (from frame number CB750F – 22000001). However, this was only available in North America and there were very few differences between it and the 750F2.

The Final K Series Models

The final K series of four-pipe models (as against the F series with 4-into-1 exhausts) ran from 1976 through to 1978. Actually, Honda's 'grand plan' had been to phase the K series out in favour of the 'new' F series. But just as BMW was to discover when it tried axing its long-running boxer twins in favour of the K range of fours and triples, the customer (who after all is the one who buys the product) objected so strongly, that Honda had to backtrack. And so the situation arose where the F and K machines ran alongside each other during the mid to late 1970s.

As a result, the K5 was not the last of the Ks and was replaced in October 1975 by the 1976 model year CB750K6, the latter running from

frame number 2540001 and engine number E2428762. And as the K6 was sold in both North America and the UK, the model series ran in parallel on both sides of the Atlantic, something that hadn't occurred since the K2.

Engine Details

Engine details of the K6 followed existing K practice, and were not uprated to F specification. This meant that the K6 retained the old cylinder head, camshaft and pistons. However, strangely, the transmission was a mixture of K5 and 750F components – and was different depending on the market where the bike sold. The gears and thrust washers were modified as in the F, apart from the countershaft top gear and output gears, which were K5. But as Mark Haylock points out:

> According to Honda's literature, the main and countershafts were the new F-type only in Europe, whereas bikes for North America and the UK had the old-type shafts and thrust washers. In

The 1977 CB750K7. Although the engine specification was very similar to the CB750F, the cycle parts owed more to the other K series machines.

CB750A (Automatic)

The CB750A (Automatic) which arrived for the 1976 model year was destined to be one of Honda's biggest-ever flops, certainly in the period 1946–80.

As *Cycle World* said in its September issue: 'A rider who enjoys snaking through the mountains or back roads will find the Hondamatic somewhat limiting, but the situation reverses itself when towns approach and traffic becomes a big part of the scene.' However, most riders wanting a town bike opted for a much smaller machine, even a moped or scooter. And this was where Honda got things badly wrong (as did Moto Guzzi with its V1000 Convert of the same era). People largely purchased big motorcycles for enjoyment and the riding experience – not for around-town transport.

The 1977 model year 750A (Automatic). First offered in 1976, production ended in 1978. Unlike any other sohc CB750, the automatic had a wet-sump lubrication system.

The Hondamatic (as the company liked to call it) was not, in the true sense of the word, an automatic. Rather, it was a semi-automatic, there being a simple two-speed gearbox with separate input and output shafts. The rider selected low or high ratio, with gear changing being made without the use of a conventional clutch lever. The torque convertor took care of the power delivery in the manner that provided the best possible acceleration.

Unlike any other sohc CB750, the Automatic had a wet-sump lubrication system. This was needed because the torque converter used engine oil as the transmission fluid, rather than the conventional ATF (Automatic

Transmission Fluid) found in most auto cars. So, in a sense, the CB750S's torque converter acted as the oil tank. And the Honda engineering team increased the oil capacity to 1.2gal (5.5ltr) to allow for this.

Power was transferred from the crankshaft centre by a Morse Hy-Vo chain. This replaced the twin roller chains used on all the other sohc CB750s. As Mark Haylock says: 'This was clearly in the light of experience with other Honda 4-cylinder bikes such as the CB400F and CB500. The mystery is why the new chain was not used on the later manual gearbox CB750s.'

The primary chain drove an intermediate shaft, which was geared to the gearbox mainshaft. An interesting point is that Honda used the same torque converter as it did on the small N600 car – so it saved on production and development costs.

The engine oil pump was in fact two trochoidal pumps, both of them drawing through a filtered scavenger from the wet sump. One pump was employed to feed the engine and lubricate the mainshaft and output shaft bearings. The other pump was slightly wider and was purely a pressure pump whose job it was to fill the torque converter and the pressure-activated clutch selected through the gear-change mechanism. Engine

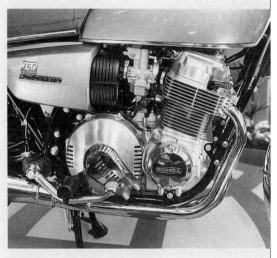

Close-up of the CB750A power unit. The torque converter is hidden beneath the large cover just above the brake pedal.

CB750A (Automatic)

pressure was normally around 70psi, whilst the pressure in the torque converter and clutches could be as high as 180psi.

The CB750A engine was tuned to provide maximum torque – the aim being low-speed power above all else. This was achieved by reducing the compression ratio to 8.6:1, fitting a milder lift camshaft and reducing the carburetter size to 24mm.

Because there was no transmission lock, a parking brake was specified. This was activated by pressing on the brake pedal and pulling a knob found under the nearside of the fuel tank. To release the brake, the rider pressed the brake pedal as well as a button in the centre of the knob.

As there was no oil tank, the engineering team was able to fit a larger 20amp-hour battery, which was charged by a more powerful 290W alternator.

The frame was much as the CB750F of the same era, but with the wheelbase increased by 10mm. Although the wire spoke wheel hubs were the same as used on the K6 model, the rims were totally different and were in fact the same aluminium components as used on the original GL1000 Gold Wing flat-four. The

rear was 17in diameter, with a 4.50 section tyre, with a 3.50 × 19 at the front.

The fuel tank was slightly increased in size to 4.2gal (19ltr), whilst the side panels were of a new design as the oil tank was no longer required. The seat was deeper – and of a more comfortable design than the stock CB750K of the period – was provided with an excellent pillion passenger grab rail (in bright chrome finish). Finally, a 4-into-1 exhaust was fitted.

The original 1976 model year CB750A began from frame number CB750A-7000001 and engine number CB750AE-7000001. Production of the CB750A series (the A'77) began from frame number CB750A-710001 and engine number CB750AE-7100001. The only changes concerned a new 4-into-2 exhaust and pinstriping for the fuel tank and side panels.

For the 1978 model year (coded CB750A/78), the automatic gained Honda's new Comstar wheels, but little else except a couple of new colour options.

Production ceased later that year following poor sales. Quite simply, even in its major market, the United States, customers had been hard to find. Honda's big-bike automatic mission had failed.

---

reverse fashion, North American and UK bikes had the new F-type output shaft, but European bikes retained the old one with the chain oiler.

Other features of the K6 were as follows:
• clutch as F-type, with new plate and circlip
• carbs mounted on F-type plate, with relocated throttle stop adjuster
• top yoke clamp bolts smaller diameter than both K5 and F (7mm instead of 8mm)
• new swinging arm, with F-type pivot and lubrication, but shorter
• old drum brake retained at rear, but hub modified mid-production run to incorporate improved chain-drive damper
• front disc brake mixture of K5 caliper and F disc
• UK and European machines used older, smaller direction indicators, rather than the newer one found on the K5.

All in-all, the K6 was something of a parts-bin special – and shows that Honda was caught on the hop, not having planned to produce the bike.

CB750K7

For the 1977 model year, Honda offered the CB750K7 (beginning frame number 2700009, engine number E2700009). By now, Honda had recommitted itself to the K series and this showed in the way it went about producing the bike. As further proof, the factory model code was changed from 341 to 405 – the former having served all CB750s from K2 to K6 inclusive.

The engine drew heavily on the CB750F – although, even then, it was not absolutely identical. This meant that the K7 had more power than the K6, thanks to its higher compression pistons and lumpier camshaft. The gearbox was the same as the F, meaning that the K7 had closer ratios than the K6 and the carbs were from the newly introduced F2, with enclosed mechanism and an accelerator in one carb.

Like the F2 and the new CB750A (Automatic), the K7 employed a most robust 630 final drive chain, which incorporated O-rings to help lubricant retention and was endless (in other words, without a spring link). There were also changes to the sprockets – the new ratio being 15:41, whereas the K6 used 18:48. The smaller (gearbox) sprocket was now held on the output shaft by a single 8mm bolt in the centre of the shaft with a larger washer. This replaced the traditional Honda layout of using a pair of 6mm bolts and a locking plate. The exhaust was changed to a new type, but still retained the 4-into-4 layout. And following the example set by other Honda models (including the K and Automatic), the front forks had no gaiters. This was, of course, in the modern style, but left the stanchions prone to damage and subsequent seal failure.

At the rear, the rear shocks had lost their shrouds, thus exposing the springs completely. The rear tyre was now a 4.50 × 17 – as on the Automatic, but the rims were chrome-steel, not aluminium. The fuel tank was new and had been increased in capacity to 4.2gal (19 ltr).

It is worth noting that during its production life, the K7 received quite a large number of updates. These included modifications to both engine and cycle components, involving items such as piston rings, connecting-rod bolts, cylinder block, camshaft holders, valve guides, clutch springs – even the crankcases. Changes to the final drive sprocket, a number of gearbox parts, the carburettors, wheel rims, chain adjusters, fuel tap and ignition switch also occurred.

K Production Ends

1978 was to be the final year of CB750K production. And only the USA and Canada actually had the K'78 model (from frame number 2800001 and engine number E3000001), whereas the rest of the world still had the K7 for another year.

And quoting Mark Haycock again: 'Although it has been said that the K'78 was merely a styling variation of the K'77, this is not correct as there were a few more changes.' These were as follows:

• cylinder head cover and breather altered
• new breather condensation chamber
• redesigned valve springs, cotters and spring retainers
• carb main jet reduced from 115 to 110 and other minor carburation changes to meet stricter emission controls
• front brake light switch now operated directly by handlebar lever, rather than under hydraulic pressure; this also simplified and reduced the number of brake pipes
• drive chain now DID 630V, instead of 630DL
• new seat based on that fitted to the CB750A.

And so came to an end the single overhead camshaft CB750, a decade on from when the first models had been exhibited at the Tokyo Show in October 1978.

Just as the 50cc Super Cub had been before it, the CB750 changed the face of motorcycling and was largely responsible for the word 'superbike'. What it certainly did was to give big motorcycles a level of sophistication unseen before. And even though Honda itself attempted to rewrite the script with other design layouts, including V-twins, V-fours, across-the-frame six and flat-fours and flat-six, the original across-the-frame six has proved the most popular of all superbike engine types. A fitting testament to one of Honda's greatest, the CB750.

11   Smaller Fours

In March 1971 Honda produced its fifteenth-million motorcycle, setting a world first. The 'Smaller Fours' all owed their existence to the fantastic sales success story of the CB750 (*see* Chapter 10) and resulted in Honda building and selling at various times during the 1970s versions in the 350, 400, 500, 550 and 650 capacity classes. But they certainly didn't arrive in that order.

The CB500

First to arrive was the CB500, which Honda placed on the market in April 1971, although not in the UK, where the new four was not displayed until January 1972 at the London Racing and Sporting Show. *Motorcycle Mechan-*

ics was the first British monthly magazine to test-ride the newcomer, at the same time as the show was getting under way. The magazine began its appraisal by saying:

> Is it really necessary? Four cylinders, electric starter, five-speed gearbox, flashing indicators, disc brake and four beautiful, burbling exhaust pipes to mute the 9,000rpm, 50 brake-horse-power motor. After all, the old single-cylinder Model 18 AJS 500 was smooth, fairly quiet and would lope along all day at 70–75mph and cover at least 60mpg into the bargain! It was a grand machine! But we can't live in the past…

Honda had, after all, reached its position of prominence in the early 1970s by always hav-

The CB500 was launched by Honda in spring 1971, but supplies did not reach the UK until early 1972. This M-registration machine dates from 1974.

Comedian Dick Emery was a keen motorcyclist and is seen here trying a new CB500 for size. Honda's John Norman (right) looks on.

ing recognized the importance of progress in motorcycle design. This made itself abundantly clear when you compared the latest Honda 500 with its twin-cylinder predecessor, the CB450. Customers had come to expect something completely new from the frame upwards – always the emphasis was on innovation and producing something which automatically made the last model instantly out of date. This was the Honda way. So, except for the top-of-the-range CB750, the new CB500 four had nothing in common with other existing Honda models.

Wet Sump

A major difference between the existing 750 and the new 500 fours concerned their lubrication system. The 750 had broken with Honda tradition and gone for a British-style dry-sump layout, but with the smaller four the company had returned to wet sumping. Both the 500 and 750s had a trochoid pump, but on the CB500 there was only a single pump, whereas the 750 had two.

Another difference was that the primary drive of the 750 was by two independent single-row chains, whereas on the 500 it was by a single Morse Hy-Vo silent chain. The cam-chain tensioning also differed in that the 750 employed a spring-loaded roller, whilst the 500 employed two flexible steel slippers. In the 750, the camshaft rotated in special 'stilts', whereas in the smaller engine the cam rested on a plain bushing machined directly into the head cast-

Jim Denholm, engineer and navigator, winner of eight of the fourteen stages of the London–Monaco Powerboat race in 1972, aboard his CB500 that summer. The bike is stock except for the three-point screen and Craven hard luggage.

ing. The oil pump was on the offside (right) in the big bike and on the left on the 500.

The sohc engine of the CB500 had vertical cylinders instead of inclined on the 750 and displaced 498.5cc (56 × 50.6mm). It ran on a 9:1 compression ratio and maximum power output, as already mentioned, was 50bhp (reduced to 48bhp from 1973) at 7,500rpm. Perhaps more important were the torque figures of 30.4 ft/lb (4.1 kg/m) at 7,500rpm – this compared with the CB750's 44.12 ft/lb (5.1 kg/m) at 7,000rpm. Carburation was by four 22mm Keihin (28mm on 750) instruments.

Like its bigger brother, the CB500 had a 12V 12amp-hour battery, two sets of contact-breaker points and dual twin-lead ignition coils, an alternator and voltage regulator.

Internal gear ratios of the five-speed gearbox on the CB500 were: first 2.35; second 1.64; third 1.27; fourth 1.04; fifth 0.90; with a final drive ratio of 2.80.

The Chassis

Whereas the 750 had a triple top tube and double downtube cradle frame, the CB500 featured a single top tube, but retained the remainder of the basic layout. However, the rake and trail was different: 26 degrees, 4.1 in (27 degrees, 3.7in).

Although the same 180mm SLS drum was retained at the rear, the single front disc size had been reduced from 296mm to 260mm in diameter. The front forks were still of the double-damping, internal springs, rubber dust-cover type, and at the rear were Showa three-position adjustable shocks.

The American *Motorcyclist* magazine, when doing a comparison test of the 350, 500 and 750 4-cylinder Hondas, found 'The 500 is the sweetheart of the trio, manageable, smooth, powerful enough to feel a punch when accelerating and a dreamy handler. It makes more sense than the less powerful 350 and the more bulky 750 – a perfect compromise.'

On the other side of the Atlantic, *Motorcyclist Illustrated*'s Dave Minton discovered virtually the same things as his American counterpart: 'The 500 is everything the 750 isn't. The smaller is sweeter, less harsh, gear changing is marginally smoother. The larger machine's disc was

Club racer Eunice Evans racing her CB500, circa 1973. Modifications include racing seat, clip-ons and double front discs.

Customizing king Paul Dunstall's CB500 four café racer conversion, with alloy rims, 4-into-2 exhaust, rear sets, Girling rear shocks, clip-ons and race bodywork including fairing.

just as powerful, more so, but in turn required a higher lever pressure.' But an even bigger surprise greeted Dave when he considered the handling of the 750 'elephantine'. He was to become an admirer of the 500's roadholding, even though he reported 'the merest hint of wallow crept in over long sweeping 85mph bends'. But as he went on to point out 'The machine is intended as a touring motorcycle, erring on the side of softness and comfort. If fast road work is your pleasure, Koni or Girling units would be preferable, though not essential.'

From personal experience, I can relate that all of the early Honda fours (CB500, plus CB750 and CB350) were very much touring rather than sporting. And excellent in many ways that they were – and not forgetting their truly impressive specifications and lengthy list of standard equipment – they were rather bland motorcycles. However, these thoughts are based on the fact that at the time I was mainly involved, at my own bike dealership, with the Ducati range, which at the time com-

prised the overhead singles in both Desmo and valve spring guises and the 750 V-twin (GT and Sport).

Whereas the Ducati were very much basic machines with a definite sporting character with racer-like handling and minimum weight, the Honda fours of the early 1970s were quiet, smooth, reliable and generally well finished with features such as electric start, comfort, decent electrics, four cylinders and the like, which none of the Ducati range had at that time. But I can still remember my first ride on a CB500 Honda four. It was a revelation in many ways, super smooth, without the rawness of the Ducati. However, and this is what struck me most, the instant I handed back the keys of the Honda to its owner I began to lose the sensation of having ridden the bike, whereas the Ducati, for all its faults and lack of creature comforts, left one with a picture of what it was like days, or even months later. To sum up, the Ducati (single or V-twin) had *character*, whereas a ride on the CB500,

Bill Smith is seen here having his Yoshimura-tuned CB500 refuelled ready for the 1973 Senior TT. A few days earlier the same bike/rider combination had taken part in the Production race. It was then stripped of all its road kit and fitted with an open 4-into-1 exhaust. It was timed at 133mph (214km/h).

CB750 or CB350 in 1972, though you would have been mightily impressed by its easy-going nature, specification and smoothness, didn't excite in quite the same way.

The CB350 Four

The smaller Honda four of its era, the CB350, arrived in June 1972, just over a year after the five-hundred. Whereas the CB750 and CB500 had originally had no prefix after the engine size, from day one the newcomer was official-ly known as the CB350F. This was to avoid confusion with Honda's existing and best-sell-ing CB350 twin (*see* Chapter 6). Rarely did Honda get it wrong. But unlike the larger fours it was to prove a poor seller – being more expensive and slower than the twin.

There is no doubt that the model was built because, at the time, the 350 class was the biggest-selling displacement class in America. Honda reasoned (wrongly!) that four cylinders could only help it to compete in what they described as the 'ultra-sophisticated' market which was already represented by the Kawasa-ki S2350 triple and the Suzuki GT380 triple. But as *Motorcyclist* reported on the CB350F's launch:

> In reality it's a docile performer which has more technical appeal than appeal from the saddle even though it performs all the duties of a motorcycle well. There is no flair. It's a good, but bland motor-cycle, superior to the Honda 350 twin for touring because it is smoother, but certainly not the accel-erator or price bargain of the twin.

Specifications

Technically speaking, the new CB350F fol-lowed the CB500, not the CB750, in its gen-eral design and layout. Like the others, it was a sohc across-the-frame four and like the CB500

The smallest of all Honda's air-cooled fours of the 1970s, the CB350F. Mainly intended for America, it wasn't sold in the UK.

1971 CB500 Specifications

Engine	Air-cooled sohc across-the-frame four, vertical cylinders, alloy head and barrel, chain-driven camshaft, one-piece crankshaft, two-piece con rods with shell big ends, horizontally split aluminium crankcases	Rear suspension	Swinging arm, twin shock absorbers
		Front brake	Single 260mm hydraulically operated disc
		Rear brake	180mm full-width SLS alloy drum
		Tyres	Front 3.25 × 19 (18in from 1973), rear 3.50 × 18
Bore	56mm		
Stroke	50.6mm		
Displacement	498.5cc		
Compression ratio	9:1		
Lubrication	Single pump, wet sump	**General Specifications**	
Ignition	Two double-ended coils, two sets	Wheelbase	55.3in (1,405mm)
of contact breakers, 12V, electric start		Ground clearance	5.5in (140mm
Carburettor	4 × Keihin 22mm	Seat height	31.in (787mm)
Primary drive	Single Morse Hy-Vo silent chain	Fuel tank capacity	3gal (14ltr)
Final drive	Chain	Dry weight	407lb (185kg)
Gearbox	Five peeds; foot-change	Maximum power	50bhp @ 9,000rpm (48bhp from 1973)
Frame	Duplex steel cradle		
Front suspension	Oil-damped telescopic forks, with gaiters	Top speed	110mph (177km/h)

employed vertical cylinders. Displacing 347cc, usually for a Honda, it had long-stroke dimensions of 47 × 50mm. With a compression ratio of 9.3:1 (slightly up on the 500 or 750), the CB350F put out 32bhp at 9,500rpm and there was a quartet of 20mm Keihin carburettors. But to put that into context, the CB350 twin (actually 325.6cc) produced 36bhp at 10,500rpm and had a dry weight of 328lb (149kg), compared with the four's figures of 373lb (169kg) – and the CB350F was 25 per cent more expensive than the twin in the States! These figures really tell the story as to why the smaller four was largely unsuccessful.

So who would buy the smaller four? Well, it came down to only two sets of people. The first must own a four, but couldn't afford the two larger models, and the other customer was the guy (or gal!) who was too small to handle the CB500 or CB750.

The control layout of the CB350F. This particular bike is a German market machine.

Riding the Small Four

The CB350F was never officially imported into the UK. However, in the September 1984 issue of *Motorcycle Enthusiast*, the late Don

1972 CB350F Specifications			
Engine	Air-cooled sohc across-the-frame four, vertical cylinders, alloy head and barrel, chain-driven camshaft, one-piece crankshaft, two-piece con rods with shell big ends, horizontally split aluminium crankcases	Frame	Duplex, steel cradle
		Front suspension	Oil-damped telescopic forks
		Rear suspension	Swinging arm, twin shock absorbers
		Front brake	Single hydraulically operated disc
Bore	47mm	Rear brake	160mm full-width SLS alloy drum
Stroke	50mm	Tyres	Front 3.00 × 18, rear 3.50 × 18
Displacement	347cc		
Compression ratio	9.3:1	**General Specifications**	
Lubrication	Single pump, wet sump	Wheelbase	53.3in (1,354mm)
Ignition	12V battery/coil, electric start	Ground clearance	5in (127mm)
Carburettor	4 × Keihin 20mm	Seat height	29.8in (757mm)
Primary drive	Single Morse Hy-Vo silent chain	Fuel tank capacity	3gal (14ltr)
Final drive	Chain	Dry weight	373lb (169kg)
Gearbox	Five speeds	Maximum power	32bhp @ 9,500rpm
		Top speed	87mph (140km/h)

Upshaw tested an example owned by Martin Eustace. This bike was originally sold in West Germany (and probably brought home by a British serviceman). As Don said, 'The bike looks every inch a smaller brother to the 750-4 and 500-4, from the chrome plated front mudguard to the tip of the four silencers. First to hit Don Upshaw was that the 'clutch was, oh, so light and easy, the gear lever's action short and precise, quickly snicking through the cogs'. He went on to say:

> There's no real power below 6,000rpm, just a perceptible pulling power, but the engine note takes on a nice muted snarl about that figure, and by 8,000rpm the engine is getting into its stride.' There is no doubt that the 350 four motor needs to be kept on the boil with constant use of the five speed gearbox – and a sixth gear wouldn't have been amiss. If one expected to find this bike a 4–cylinder flyer than you'd come unstuck.

But probably the most unexpected feature of the CB350F was vibration – most coming through the handlebars, with less through the

seat and footrests – the 350 had more vibes than either the 500 or 750!

Again, the CB350F's redeeming feature was its lack of size, with *Motorcycle Enthusiast* say-

Mini four-pot Honda with its enthusiastic owner, Martin Eustace, in 1984.

ing: 'When riding the bike it feels physically quite small, certainly of more manageable proportions than, say, a 400 Dream.'

A Winner – The CB400F

If the 350 four proved a disappointment, the machine which replaced it, the CB400F, was just the reverse and proved a real winner for Honda. The four-hundred was launched in December 1974 and came just over a year after both President Soichiro Honda and Executive Vice President Takeo Fujisawa had retired in October 1973; that same month, Kiyoshi Kawashima became President.

The new CB400F was unusual, in that it was produced in two engine sizes: on the Japanese home market it had a capacity of 398.8cc (51 × 48.8mm), whilst for export markets the engine size was upped to 408.6cc (51 × 50mm). As for power output figures, the home market got 36bhp at 8,500rpm, whilst the larger engined model put out an additional 1bhp, but with the engine revolutions unchanged.

The Best Honda Yet?

'Is this the best Honda yet?' So asked tester John Robinson in the June 1975 issue of *Motorcycle Mechanics*. He set out the reason why he made the statement:

The howl from the four-into-one exhaust is more subdued than ever but it doesn't disguise the nature of what is probably the best Honda yet. Behind the high level of silencing is an equally high level of performance; the stuff that made Honda the world's largest motorcycle manufacturer. Since those days back in the sixties when Honda amazed everyone, they seem to have gone downhill. Development reached its peak with the CB450 – the stir caused by the 750 was due more to its size. Most models, in particular the twins, deteriorated as they developed, the only real improvements being the handling of the later 750s. Now Honda seem to have retraced their steps and are once again on the right path. The 400, developed from the 350-four, is smaller and more comfortable than the 500 and the design is

If the CB350F didn't prove a success, the machine which replaced it certainly was, the CB400F, which was put on to the market in December 1974.

less cluttered. While I like the sheer power advantage offered by the 750, the 400 is more compact, manageable, gives a better ride and more precise handling, and, in my opinion, wins on points.

That was one man's view, but it was shared by many. And again, from personal experience, I can only concur. The newcomer looked and felt very small (even more so than the 350F, due to the 4-into-1 exhaust and lower, narrower handlebars).

John Robinson, continuing the introduction to the *Motorcycle Mechanics* test, said: 'Since the early, ultra-sporty, high revving lightweights, Honda have degenerated each model, getting woollier than the last with handling to match. The signs are that they are rethinking just what makes a motorcycle; at least the 400 points the way.'

The Engine

The engine was a particularly neat blend of the old and the new, providing crisp responses and using revs more than muscle. As with Hondas of old, this engine could be revved, and if the rider did this it was transformed into a super sports model. But unlike many Hondas of the early 1970s, the CB400F's biggest advantage was its suspension, which had been transformed into a system that was able to cope with all sorts of road surfaces – and most importantly was able to provide taut and predictable handling. As one tester said: 'The 400F is the kind of motorcycle you feed into corners rather than throwing it about, relaxed in the knowledge that it will tell you when you've gone far enough.'

Another ace in the 400F's pack was the riding position. When you are in a natural position, able to reach all the controls blindfolded, you know things are right, and that's how it was with the 400 four. As John Robinson describes: 'your weight is balanced against the force of the airstream; it's as if your body becomes part of the suspension'.

Styling

Styling was another key to the 400F's success. It was nice, clean and simple, and promoted a slim, compact nature to the machine. Although at the time of its launch several journalists criticized the 4-into-1 exhaust as being a gimmick, it was in fact something of a masterpiece of design style. Not only did it perform well, look super-stylish, but it also relieved the machine of the previous bulk shown by the earlier Honda 4-cylinder roadsters. The 400 four almost looked like a single, such was the compact nature of the machine.

Engine-wise, the 400 was quite simply a 350, but with more power and a six- speed gearbox – a first for Honda. But this was another secret in the success of the design. Believe you me, the 400F needed all those six ratios. Although it was able to cruise at the legal limit in top, there was little acceleration possible. To keep speeds up you needed to use the gears almost continually to cope with hills, headwinds or when overtaking – more so if a passenger was being carried. In fact, two-up into a headwind, the 400F was actually quicker in fifth than in sixth and quite often needed fourth. As the three higher ratios were spaced quite closely together, it was possible to extract the model's full potential. But this

The 400F was built in two engine sizes. For the Japanese market it was 398.8cc (51 × 48.8mm), whilst for export the engine displacement was increased to 408.6cc (51 × 50mm).

The CB400F was also widely used for production machine racing, being a class winner, including the Isle of Man.

had quite a drastic effect on fuel consumption; again, two-up only made things more so.

A Solo Bike

In truth, the CB400F was a solo machine – and was infinitely more enjoyable when released from the burden of carrying a passenger.

Motorcycle Mechanics achieved an electronically timed 103mph (167km/h), whilst the standing quarter-mile was achieved in 15.2sec, with a terminal speed of 85mph (138km/h).

Like the 350F, the 400 had 18in wheels (the 750 and early 500s had 19in at the front) and a single disc at the front and an SLS drum at the rear. John Robinson rated the brakes highly:

1974 CB400F (Europe) Specifications

Engine	Air-cooled sohc across-the-frame four, vertical cylinders, alloy head and barrel, chain drive camshaft, one-piece crankshaft, two-piece con rods with shell big ends, horizontally split aluminium crankcases	Front suspension	Oil-damped telescopic fork
		Rear suspension	Swinging arm, twin shock absorbers
		Front brake	Single hydraulically operated disc
		Rear brake	160mm full-width SLS alloy drum
		Tyres	Front 3.00 × 18, rear 3.50 × 18
Bore	51mm		
Stroke	50mm		
Displacement	408.6cc		
Compression ratio	9.4:1	**General Specifications**	
Lubrication	Single pump, wet sump	Wheelbase	53.30in (1,355mm)
Ignition	12V battery/coil	Ground clearance	5.90in (150mm)
Carburettor	4 × Keihin 22mm	Seat height	31.10in (790mm)
Primary drive	Single Morse Hy-Vo silent chain	Fuel tank capacity	3gal (14ltr)
Final drive	Chain	Dry weight	170 kg (375lb)
Gearbox	Six speeds; foot-change	Maximum power	37bhp @ 8,500rpm
Frame	Semi-double (single front down tube) cradle	Top speed	103mph (167km/h)

The brakes are also among the best. I hesitate to call anything perfect but if these were any better it would need an extremely skilful rider to take advantage of them. The disc loses efficiency in the wet but less so than others [with stainless steel disc material]. And the 400 stayed controllable even under ten-tenths braking, which is more important than having super-powerful brakes.

Another area of praise was the clutch – as with the 350F it was both extremely light in operation, yet entirely reliable in use.

John Robinson ended his test:

There are just two improvements I would like to see. A decent throttle operation and a fairing. A fairing would enable several things to happen: top end performance would improve; the 400 could pull slightly higher gears, which usually means an even nicer feel to the bike; fuel consumption ought to improve and the rider might avoid some of the weather. In a perfect world I would add more engine torque (pulling power) at low- and mid-range throttle openings. But even so, most observers, including myself, view the CB400F as probably Honda's best all-round series production roadster of the 1970s.

Praise indeed. The 400F (in F2 guise from late 1977) remained in production until late 1978.

The CB550

Actually, the CB550 came before the CB400F, certainly as regards its arrival, being put onto the market eleven months earlier than the smaller four, in February 1974. But it didn't mean the end of the existing CB500, as this latter model continued to be available until the end of 1975. Like the 400, there were two distinct versions, but unlike the small four, the 550 was produced as the CB500K – essentially a larger engined CB500 with four silencers – and the CB550F, which had a more sporting appearance and a 4-into-1 exhaust, although the latter model did not arrive until the end of 1975.

The original CB550K1 was, essentially, simply a CB500 bored out to 58.5mm, thus becoming 544cc, an increase of 45.1cc. Strangely at 50bhp, albeit produced at 8,500rpm (500rpm less than the CB500), it was, at least on paper, no more powerful than the original 500's figure, also of 50bhp (reduced to 48bhp from 1973). Where the 550 scored was by increased torque – up from 4.1kg/m to 4.4kg/m at 7,500rpm.

Tony Rutter getting down to it at Silverstone in 1975 on his Mocheck-entered CB400F.

The Castrol Racing and Rally Service used a kitted-out CB400F for communications.

On the road, this showed up by increased smoothness and the ability to pull low down the engine speed range. The gear change, clutch and front forks had also been subject to changes, which only helped to improve over what in any case had been a popular machine.

The more sporting CB550F arrived in mid-1975 and was very much in the same style as the CB750F, which had been launched earlier that year (*see* Chapter 10). The F series attempt-ed to repeat the style of the 400, but, it has to be said, not with the same level of success.

The remainder of the CB500F was clearly very much based on the existing CB550K. Detail improvements included a new warning light console which was located between the instruments, with the ignition switch below it. The latter (transferred from an under-tank position) doubled up as a steering lock, thus making it a simple task of turning off the ignition and locking the bike in one action. There was also a cut-out device to prevent the machine being started in gear.

The fuel tank was revised, like the CB750F, with a thinner line, whilst the filler cap was now hidden behind a hinged flap, the whole concept providing a flush-fitting appearance. However, a mistake was not taking the opportunity to provide security by way of a lock.

The 550F slotted nicely in-between the small 400F and heavyweight 750F, with its touring brother, the 550K, remaining in production for those not only wanting a traditional four-pipe Honda but a more laid-back rider style.

The two 550 continued into 1976, with the touring model becoming the K2, but with little change. For 1977 the K3 arrived, which ran through to the end of production in early 1979. Meanwhile, the 550F1 became the F2 midway through 1977, with production halting at the end of 1978. In July 1978 production of Honda motorcycles exceeded thirty million units. Reached in a little over three decades, this was a fantastic achievement.

The CB650

The final series production 4-cylinder Honda motorcycle of less than 750cc produced during the 1970s was the CB650, which was

The CB500 grew into the CB550. This was achieved by boring out the cylinders to 58.5mm, thus increasing the engine size to 544cc. Two distinct versions were sold; the K and the F. A CB550K3 is shown here, circa 1976.

marketed for the first time in January 1979. Actually, the newcomer was not really a 'six-fifty' at all, because it displaced 626cc (59.8 × 55.8mm). Although it never became a top seller, the CB650 was quite a decent bike. So why had Honda decided to launch another sohc four, when the rest of the Japanese industry seemed firmly switched onto dohc? The answer has to lie in the sales success of Kawasaki's budget-priced Z650.

Compared with the latest dohc CB750/900 models, the new 650 might have seemed tame, at least on paper. But where it scored was in being small and blessed with decent handling. The CB650 weighed in at 436lb (198kg) – not much different from the 550F, whilst the engine felt more like a 750. Compared with the 550, the bore had been increased by 1.3mm and the stroke by 5.2mm. Inlet and exhaust diameters had been increased by 4mm and 3mm respectively, whilst the carburettor size had increased to 26mm. This, combined with a power output of 63bhp at 9,000rpm (against the 550's 50bhp at 8,500rpm), meant a considerable improvement in overall performance. Honda claimed a top speed of 120mph (192km/h). Maximum torque was 11.2lb/ft (5.4kg/m) at 8,000rpm.

As with other 1979 multi-cylinder Hondas, the 650 had fully transistorized ignition, a seat height of 31.3in (795mm), tubeless tyres (3.25 × 19 front; 3.75 × 18 rear), Comstar wheels, 240mm double front disc brakes and a 180mm rear drum brake.

Peter Kelly, then editor of *Motorcycle Mechanics*, writing in the November 1978 issue (following the official press launch of the 1979 Honda range in West Germany), was certainly fired up: 'Far from being an anti-climax, the CB650 showed all the promise of becoming a classic in the handling and performance stakes, as delightful to ride as the much-loved CB400F.'

The Industry Hits the Buffers

But then, of course, the motorcycle industry hit the buffers as the 1980s dawned, with a sales slump that hit rock bottom in 1981 and 1982. This not only saw the end for many, many dealers, but also hit the Japanese industry hard; Yamaha was nearly forced out of business after

1975 CB550F Specifications

Engine	Air-cooled sohc across-the-frame four, vertical cylinders, alloy head and barrel, chain-driven camshaft, one-piece crankshaft, two-piece con rods with shell big ends, horizontally split aluminium crankcases	Front suspension	Oil-damped telescopic forks, with gaiters
		Rear suspension	Swinging arm, twin shock absorbers
		Front brake	Single 260mm hydraulically operated disc
Bore	58.5mm	Rear brake	180mm full-width SLS alloy drum
Stroke	50.6mm	Tyres	Front 3.25 × 19, rear 3.75 × 18
Displacement	544cc		
Compression ratio	9:1	**General Specifications**	
Lubrication	Single pump, wet sump	Wheelbase	55.3in (1,405mm)
Ignition	12V battery/coil, electric start	Ground clearance	6.3in (160mm)
Carburettor	4 × Keihin 22mm	Seat height	31.7in (805mm)
Primary drive	Single Morse Hy-Vo silent chain	Fuel tank capacity	3gal (14ltr)
Final drive	Chain	Dry weight	423lb (192kg)
Gearbox	Five speeds; foot-change	Maximum power	50bhp @ 8,000rpm
Frame	Full duplex steel cradle	Top speed	108mph (174km/h)

1979 CB650 Specifications

Engine	Air-cooled sohc across-the-frame four, vertical cylinders, alloy head and barrel, chain-driven camshaft, one-piece crankshaft, two-piece con rods with shell big ends, horizontally split aluminium crankcases		exposed stanchions
		Rear suspension	Swinging arm, twin shock absorbers
		Front brake	2 × 240mm hydraulically operated discs
Bore	59.8mm	Rear brake	180mm full-width SLS alloy drum
Stroke	55.8mm	Tyres	Front 3.25 × 19, rear 3.75 × 18; both tubeless
Displacement	626cc		
Compression ratio	9:1		
Lubrication	Single pump, wet sump	**General Specifications**	
Ignition	12V electronic; electric start	Wheelbase	56.30in (1,430mm)
Carburettor	4 × 26mm Keihin	Ground clearance	6.10in (155mm)
Primary drive	Single Morse Hy-Vo silent chain	Seat height	31.30in (795mm)
Final drive	Chain	Fuel tank capacity	4gal (18ltr)
Gearbox	Five speeds; foot-change	Dry weight	436lb (198kg)
Frame	Duplex steel cradle	Maximum power	63bhp @ 9,000rpm
Front suspension	Oil-damped telescopic forks,	Top speed	119mph (192km/h)

record losses. Honda, thanks to its diversification, no longer relied on two-wheel sales and thus escaped the worst of the depression. But for the CB650, it was a different matter and sales never reached expectations. A pity, because it was a decent bike that had deserved to succeed.

On a wider front, motorcycling itself went through massive changes. And when it recovered, in the mid-1980s, the era of the motorcycle for transport had largely died, except in the Third World. Instead, there was to come the age of the motorcycle as a rich man's toy. And this demanded huge technical and performance leaps. Although the across-the-frame Honda four survived, it was now liquid-cooled, with advanced electronics, single shock rear suspension, anti-dive forks and much more. The age of the air-cooled, twin shock Honda fours was over, but their place in history is not forgotten.

The final series in the sub-750cc Honda across-the-frame 4-cylinder models was the CB650, which arrived for the 1979 season. With a capacity of 626cc (59.8 × 55.8mm), the CB650 came just as sales were to go into decline.

12   Gold Wing

The introduction in 1969 of the world's first modern superbike, the 4-cylinder CB750, gave Honda a lead on the rest of the industry, but it also gave everyone else a target, and this produced a flood of new designs from other manufacturers, including Kawasaki, Suzuki and Yamaha, plus the major European brands.

Honda felt it had to respond to this challenge by coming up with a new, even more impressive design – with a larger displacement engine and more power than its existing CB750.

King of Kings

The original idea was for what Honda labelled a 'king of kings' motorcycle, development of which got under way in 1972. The brief was for a grand touring bike which had to be superior to Honda's competitors in both smoothness and performance. Another priority was that it had to have a totally new engine configuration, other than the existing across-the-frame, 4-cylinder layout of the CB750. Finally, it had to have its

There is no doubting it, but any Gold Wing, even the very first GL1000 model of 1974, is a big piece of hardware.

162

Although it was a heavy machine, a low centre of gravity helped to lighten the load once under way and the GL1000 handling was better than might have expected.

own unique character – something which would endear itself to existing and future generations. This in itself was a hard task, as previously most Hondas had had a relatively short production life of only a few years, the exception to this being the C100 Cub step-thru which had not only sold in millions, but developments of which were still going decades later after its initial launch back in 1958.

The AOK Flat-Six Prototype

The first creation of what was ultimately to arrive in the mid-1970s as the Gold Wing, was a flat-six, codenamed AOK. At first, Honda thought it could build a single machine to fulfil both super sports and grand touring roles. And the AOK, of which only a single prototype was built, had a cubic capacity of no less than 1,470cc; at the time this would have been the largest displacement, series production roadster of the modern era. It weighed in at 500lb (227kg) and Honda sources state it could achieve 130mph (210km/h). However, the development team soon realized that in the AOK it had a tourer, not a sportster. It was then

decided that two entirely different designs would be needed at the top of Honda's motorcycle range, which led to the GL1000 Gold Wing (essentially with two of the AOK's flat-six cylinders lopped off) and a sportster. The latter, not to emerge until the 1978 model year, as the CBX, was to employ an air-cooled across-the-frame, 6-cylinder engine (*see* Chapter 13).

Other details of the AOK prototype included an 8:1 compression ratio, a power output of 80bhp at 6,700rpm, a double-barrelled single carburettor (one Venturi having a 29mm bore and the other 27mm) feeding into a cast inlet manifold as was common practice in the car industry; another automobile feature was a single-plate dry clutch.

The Gold Wing Finally Arrives

What was to become known as the GL1000 Gold Wing was finally introduced at Honda's dealer convention in Los Angeles in late 1974. Its displacement was 999cc. Actually, its bore and stroke measurements of 72 × 61.4mm were virtually the same as the AOK prototype. And, in fact, as Honda was to discover, the newcomer's 1-litre flat-four power output of 80bhp (at 7,500rpm) was virtually the same as the near 1.5-litre 6-cylinder prototype!

The Los Angeles show bike was best described as a pre-production prototype, as it sported a host of handmade parts. Despite boasting several features which indicated a more than decent performance, most of those present still assumed that the machine was a soft, luxurious and mild-tuned straight-line tourer. Actually, as events were to prove later, larger engined Gold Wing's were exactly that, but the original 1975 GL1000 production version still retained a sporting side to its character.

Four 32mm Carbs
The four 32mm Keihin CV (Constant Velocity) carbs should, as *Cycle* reported 'have been a tip-off' as to the prototype's nature. There were also triple stainless steel discs with two-piston calipers, Bridgestone's new H-rated tyres (good for a sustained 131mph (211km/h) speed), suggesting something more than simply touring aspirations. An early tester commented: 'Power response in any gear at virtually any speed is incredibly smooth and silent. The motor feels as if it's winding itself up and then releasing a flood of power, rather like a jet as it surges along the runway on take-off.'

Another thing to praise was that there was absolutely no vibration – mirror images stayed perfectly clear – and no torque reaction even with violent blips of the throttle. Silencing was also excellent.

So what were the drawbacks? For a start, the sheer bulk of the Gold Wing took some getting used to, and although it was surprisingly easy to lift onto the centre stand, the same could not be said when it came to pushing the thing around when it was stationary – well, it did tip the scales dry at 647lb (294kg). But once moving, the weight wasn't such an issue due in part to the low centre of gravity.

As the late John Robinson was to write in *Motorcycle Mechanics*' July 1975 issue:

The suspension almost copes but allows too much wallowing, especially on the Island's bumpy roads [John was in the Isle of Man]. On the straights at speed the bumps were bad enough to lift me from the seat several times, but steady revs showed that the suspension, at least, keeps the wheels on the road. It seems that the springs are soft enough to give reasonable comfort and roadholding, but that there isn't enough damping to control them. Through turns, as well as wallowing, the suspension movement allowed prop stand and footrest to ground too easily.

Another issue was that although the riding position was 'quite comfortable at least up to 80–90mph', the lack of a fairing limited comfortable progress above these figures.

But, as with all Gold Wings since that time, as one journalist was to comment when first seeing a 1975 GL1000 model in the metal, so to speak, 'Whatever you think you can't ignore it.'

The Engine
As *Cycle* magazine explained in its April 1975 issue:

Rumours have been dive-bombing us for a couple of years regarding the size and layout of the new Honda engine. It was obvious that it had to be bigger: the Z-1, R90S and GuzziV7 (not to forget the H-D 1200) dictated this. But how would it look? Where would the cylinders be? How much power would it make?

Hearsay described a huge V6 and then there was talk of an enlarged conventional power plant much like the CB750. What we got was an incredibly compact and marvelously smooth horizontally opposed water-cooled four. In locating and connecting the components, Honda's engineers studied the best ideas from makers such as Porsche, BMW and Chevrolet.

It was also Honda's first production liquid-cooled motorcycle engine.

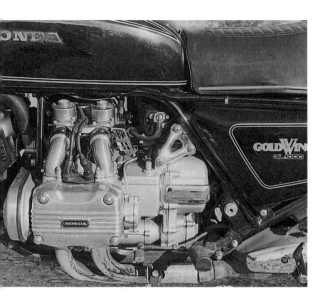

The GL1000 liquid-cooled 1000cc (72 × 61.4mm) sohc flat-four, with staggered cylinders, plain big ends, belt-driven camshafts and aluminium heads and barrels.

The Crankcases

The crankcases came together like a Porsche. However, the crankshaft fixing method was unique to Honda. One half of the main bearings were in unit with the offside (right) crankcase. The caps held the crankshaft to that offside case with three bearings: one at each end and one in the centre. When the engine was stripped, the nearside (left) case half came off with the pistons exiting from the base of their cylinders. Should the offside pistons need to be removed, the positions of the main bearing bosses required that the connecting-rod bearing caps be first unbolted and the piston/rod assemblies removed from the top of the cylinder. It should be pointed out that the cylinders (one per side of the engine) were one-piece with the crankcase halves.

A Morse-Type Hy-Vo Chain

Immediately behind the rear main bearing was a sprocket to drive a Morse-type Hy-Vo chain. This chain ran straight down to a matching sprocket which drove the outer clutch hub through a transmission shaft. The inner clutch hub then drove the transmission mainshaft through the countershaft and forward directly under, and parallel to, the crankshaft. A shock absorber cushion was built into the centre of the mainshaft Hy-Vo sprocket. The layshaft was to the right of, and meshed with, the mainshaft. The rear gear of the layshaft drove a gear directly above it to rotate the output shaft. Incorporated in the output shaft was a spring-loaded cam-type shock absorber, which, as *Cycle* described was 'almost identical to that used by BMW.

A Multi-Plate Clutch

The GL1000's clutch was a multi-plate, wet-type affair, with seven friction and eight plain plates. Most of the features of the transmission were identical to those found on the existing CB750 four and except for the Hy-Vo chain drive system a trained Honda mechanic would feel at home working on the gearbox and clutch of the Gold Wing.

Immediately behind the Hy-Vo sprocket on the crankshaft was a spur gear to drive the alternator and counterbalance shaft. The matching gear on the counterbalance shaft was divided in half, with each half independently coupled to

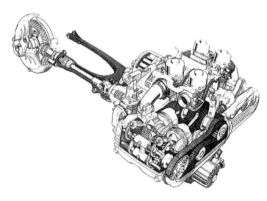

GL1000 Gold Wing engine and transmission, including final drive and rear bevel box.

the shaft via splined carrier plates and rubber cushions. This cushioning was necessary to rid the engine of the gear howl that inevitably accompanied such arrangements. The idea of using a counter-rotating mass to oppose the torque reaction of the engine was the most technically interesting aspect of the GL1000 design.

Beating Torque Reaction

Honda engineers went to great pains to point out that cylinder placement and disposition of the crankshaft had nothing to do with the cause of torque reaction – they only governed which way it affected the machine. In all cases, the reaction was opposite the direction of engine travel. On motorcycles with the crankshaft set across the wheel's centre line, the reaction compressed the rear shocks as it tried to rotate the whole bike around the crankshaft centre.

This had proved a major reason why prospective BMW buyers had been put off owning one of the German flat-twins. But, in truth, the dreaded torque reaction was not too much of a problem except when the throttle was blipped at a standstill, or full-power quick shifts were made, or the throttle was chopped shut whilst cornering at race-type speeds. But how many of the touring-oriented BMW owners did any of these things?

However, the Honda engineering team didn't want to take a chance and decided to counteract torque reaction. Since the alternator shaft was directly gear-driven by the crankshaft, its rotation was opposite the crank's. An extra flywheel was attached to the rear of the alternator and the shaft was driven at slightly higher speed than the crankshaft.

With the CB750, Honda introduced what was called the excited-field alternator, which only generated the amount of electricity actually needed. But in what at first appeared a backward step, the GL1000's alternator output was at a fixed rate and varied only with engine speed. The unneeded electricity was returned into the frame and dissipated as heat through an

electronic valve. Why? Well, because any sudden variation in the effect of the anti-torque device could be felt by the rider as a lurch sideways.

Keeping Down Costs

As mentioned previously, the cylinders were cast into the crankcase halves in the same manner as any watercooled car engine and many outboard motors. This resulted in a considerable manufacturing cost reduction but meant that any piston work required would entail the engine being removed. Very thick iron liners were cast into the blocks.

Prior to this water-cooled engine, all previous Hondas had been equipped with the piston gudgeon pin holes placed one millimetre to the rear of the piston centre line. This was done to achieve less piston noise, which was caused by the additional clearance dictated by an air-cooled engine. With the thermostat controlling the rate of expansion of the cylinder and keeping the operating temperature of the coolant almost constant, tighter clearances could be employed and so offset gudgeon pins were unnecessary.

About the only obvious unorthodox feature of the piston/rod pairing was the lack of any gudgeon pin retainer. Instead, the pins were a press fit in the rod eyes and a press had to be used to centre the pin during assembly. Naturally, that meant the pins had to be a good floating fit in the piston bosses. The offside (right) cylinders got enough lubrication from oil slung off the crank, whereas the nearside (left) bank required extra squirts through holes in the rods. The same rods were used on both sides, and a plain bearing without a feed hole blocked the squirt on the right side. The compression ratio was finalized at 9.2:1, giving the pistons a decided dome.

The Cylinder Heads

Apart from the water-circulation passages, the other noteworthy feature of the GL1000's cylinder heads was the generous breathing areas of the ports and valves. The 37mm inlet and 32mm exhaust valves fed ports correspondingly large for the 250cc cylinder size. In order to squeeze these valves (2-per-cylinder) into the combustion chamber of the 72mm cylinder, the valves were offset to opposite sides of the chamber centre line, as they were in the existing CB750. The Gold Wing's proportionately larger valves were allowed thanks to its bore/stroke ratio of 1.2:1, compared to a figure of 0.97:1 for the 750 four.

Like the transmission, the valve and camshaft arrangement was virtually identical to that of the CB750. Pairs of shafts held the inlet and exhaust valves for each bank of cylinders. The cam – best described as like the CB750 assembly but cut in half – rode in aluminium plain bearings, sharing the same high-pressure oil feed with the rocker spindles.

Rocker arm clearance was set by conventional screw and lock nut. The cams were driven by a pair of toothed Gilmer belts in a separate (dry) chamber at the front of the engine. A pair of spring-loaded idler pulleys set tension on the belts when their lock bolts were released (recommended at 24,000-mile (38,600km) intervals in Honda's service schedule. The belts, said Honda, were the same as those used on the Civic car engine.

Constant Velocity Carbs

Feeding the cylinder heads were individual 32mm Keihin CV (constant velocity) carburettors for each pot. The fuel-metering needle in this type of instrument was not linked to the throttle, but to an independent slide which moved according to the inlet tract vacuum and Venturi air speed. Even if the rider completely opened the throttle in a higher gear at low rpm, the Venturi air speed would not drop to an inefficient level as it would with conventional carburettors.

All four carbs were fastened to a common air box and the entire assembly could be removed for servicing purposes in a matter of minutes by disconnecting the air cleaner, fuel supply hose

and the eight manifold acorn bolts. Once off, the carburettors could be mechanically synchronized. The rubber hoses leading to each instrument from the air box were sensors for the low-speed air bleed systems. All fuel to the carbs passed through drilled passages in the air box casting. An automotive-type inline fuel filter was employed between the fuel tank valve and the carburettor group inlet.

A Dummy Tank

A distinctive feature of the GL1000 Gold Wing was its dummy tank – there being no fuel at all in the space normally occupied by the tank on most motorcycles. In fact, the 4.8gal (23ltr) tank on the big Honda flat-four was to be found in the space under the seat between the frame tubes. There were two good reasons to put the tank there; *Cycle* explained what these were: 'It is the safest place for the tank to be, and its placement helps to lower the centre of gravity.' The resulting fuel level was near enough to the carburettor's float level that a fuel pump was needed to provide a stable supply. This was a car-type, driven off the rear end of the offside camshaft.

The handlebar layout followed similar lines to other big Hondas of the era, but the tank-mounted fuel gauge was entirely fresh.

Oil Pump

An Eaton-type trochoid oil pump was driven via a small, double-row chain, connecting the clutch hub to a long, slender power shaft which ran the length of the engine. This high-pressure system for the engine and gearbox was augmented by a smaller pump which scavenged the clutch cavity. There was also a water-circulation pump at the lower nearside front of the engine.

As in car practice, the water pump kept coolant flowing on a closed loop course within the engine until it reached a predetermined temperature: 176–182°F for the Gold Wing. Then the thermostat allowed just sufficient coolant from the radiator to enter the engine loop to keep within this range. If the coolant temperature rose above 210°F, in slow traffic for example, a thermo-switch operated an auxiliary electric fan. The fuel gauge was set in the dummy tank. A plastic overflow tank under the false tank's right cover allowed inspection and replenishment. Honda's official recommendation was a mixture of 50 per cent water and 50 per cent Ethylene Glycol-type radiator coolant. The temperature gauge was situated in the tachometer.

A small sprocket on the engine side of the Hy-Vo sprocket led down to a conventional electric starter near the rider's left foot.

The Exhaust System

What appeared to be a neatly contoured individual 2-into-1 exhaust system on each side of the motorcycle was actually a welded-up system that had to be unbolted and lowered to change the rear tyre and removed completely before the engine was taken out of the frame. Removal of the engine for repairs was facilitated by taking out a section of the lower left frame tubing. American Honda's service division made up an adaptor for an automotive transmission jack to make engine removal much simpler. Once the engine bolts, control cables, wiring and UJ (Universal Joint) spline were loose, the engine could be slid straight out on the nearside (left) of the frame without any need for lifting or prying. The engine's assembly weight (without oil, but with carburettors) was 212lb (96kg).

Removing the Driveshaft

The removal of a circlip with special pliers allowed the UJ and driveshaft to slide back on a splined rear carrier connection for engine removal. Like the BMW flat-twin, the Gold Wing's driveshaft ran through the centre of the offside swinging arm tube. The UJ was a smaller version of a conventional car unit. This component was *Cycle*'s 'single cause for service-orientated concern' on the entire machine. This was because 'The needle bearing assemblies are held by stacking the U-joint body against them, and there is no provision for greasing the bearings. Granted, the assembly is under a protective rubber boot, but still, U-joints don't last forever. It should have a grease fitting, and the bearings should be retained with removable circlips.'

Bevel Gear Rear Drive Unit

The spinal bevel gear rear drive unit (with a ratio of 3.4:1) was very similar to the BMW design, but on the Honda the pinion shaft was equipped with Timkin-type tapered roller bearings instead of the ball-race ones found on the German machine. Different thickness shims were available to set the spacing between the ring and pinion gears.

The swinging arm pivots were fitted with needle bearing assemblies. A notable feature was the hardened pins screwed into the frame boss on each side to provide precise alignment for the drive shaft's universal joint.

A massive 20amp-hour battery was housed in a shock-mounted carrier under the nearside plastic side cover.

The Front Fork

At the front there was an entirely new telescopic fork assembly. Compared to the CB750 the stanchion tube diameter had been increased from 35mm to 37mm – to handle the increased weight loading of the Gold Wing. The floating calipers for the dual disc front brakes were mounted at the rear of the fork legs, thus reducing weight that would otherwise have been concentrated more forward, thereby assisting steering.

For its day the 1975 GL1000 had an exceptionally wide rear tyre, with a 4.50 section. To keep the machine low the rear rim and tyre was 17in in diameter. Honda had come up

with a new wide aluminium rear rim featuring a novel square-sectioned hollow around each side of the rim's bead area. This, Honda claimed, provided the correct shape and strength without adding a lot of unnecessary weight.

Instrumentation

As usual, Honda had provided comprehensive 'standard' equipment – including a neatly designed instrument console. This featured readable instruments day or night, and between these was a bank of warning lights for oil pressure, high beam and when the transmission was in neutral.

The dummy tank opened up (a three-way hinged affair), the ignition key unlocking the spring-loaded top lid. Access was provided to the fuel tank filler cap, a small plastic storage tray and the tool kit. The sides also folded down to reveal an array of electrical components (left) and radiator (right).

Accessories

Right from the start many owners soon started decking their 'Wings with an array of accessories, including fairings, panniers, top boxes, engine protection bars and the like. There is no doubt that the long straight roads found in the States were the Gold Wing's natural habitat. However, it wasn't just in America that the design became popular, but with a hard core of touring riders in Europe too. Enthusiasm for this unique design showed by the number of national owners clubs which were soon formed.

Model Update

The first major update came for the 1978 model year. The full list of changes was as follows:

Rear view of a 1976 GL1000.

1974 GL1000 Gold Wing Specifications

Engine	Liquid-cooled sohc horizontally opposed four, with staggered cylinders, plain bearing big ends, belt-driven camshafts, alloy cylinder heads and barrels		nearside (left) frame rail detachable
		Front suspension	Oil-damped telescopic fork
		Rear suspension	Swinging arm, twin shock absorbers
Bore	72mm	Front brake	Twin 280mm hydraulically operated discs
Stroke	61.4mm	Rear brake	Single 280mm hydraulically operated disc
Displacement	1000cc		
Compression ratio	9.2:1	Tyres	Front 3.50 × 19, rear 4.50 × 17
Lubrication	Twin pumps, wet sump		
Ignition	Twin contact breakers, battery/coil 12V, electric start		

General Specifications

Wheelbase	60.9in (1,546mm)
Ground clearance	6in (152mm)
Seat height	30in (762mm)
Fuel tank capacity	4.2gal (19ltr)
Dry weight	647lb (294kg)
Maximum power	80bhp @ 7,000rpm
Top speed	115mph (185km/h)

Additional engine specifications:

Carburettor	4 × Keihin CV 32mm with fuel pump
Primary drive	Inverted tooth chain/duplex chain
Final drive	Shaft
Gearbox	Five speeds
Frame	Duplex tube of all-welded and gusseted construction with bottom

The GL1000 circa 1979 with aftermarket touring saddle and wraparound engine 'bars.

- smaller carburettors, softer valve timing and revised ignition to improve low- and mid-range engine power
- brighter headlamp
- more comfortable, stepped dual seat
- Comstar wheels (with tubeless tyres)
- revised suspension
- wet weather braking improved.

Increased Displacement

Then, in 1980, came an increase in engine displacement to 1085cc. This was achieved by increasing the bore size by 3mm to 75mm, the stroke remaining unchanged at 61.4mm. With a quartet of 30mm CV Keihin carbs and a compression ratio of 9.2:1 the newcomer wasn't much more powerful, but offered a definite improvement over the original. According to *Superbike* magazine: 'The new engine had just made the Wing a lot nicer to ride. Its earlier incarnations were too peaky. This one combines fair bottom end with plenty at the top in a civilized and fuss-free combination.'

Another improvement was the suspension. *Superbike* again: 'By adopting air-suspension front and rear, Honda have made the hippo ride comfortably – at last. Where a freeway bump would have had the last bike first bottoming harshly, then wallowing while trying to recover its poise, and finally weaving disturbingly along a straight piece of road, the new bike just soaks up the bumps.'

Honda also offered, for the first time, a fully dressed version of the Gold Wing. This was known as the Interstate in America and the De Luxe in Europe. As Roland Brown said in his 1991 Crowood Moto Classics *Honda* title, 'After years of sitting back and watching while accessory manufacturers got rich pandering to riders who bought fairings, hard luggage and crashbars for their Gold Wings, Honda finally designed a bike with all those things included as standard – and immediately sold every one they could make.'

Aspencade

Two years later came the Aspencade, named after the hugely popular American rally which had become dominated by Gold Wing riders. The newcomer added to the Interstate/De Luxe the luxuries of a sound system, passenger backrest and an on-board compressor with

In the early 1980s the Gold Wing became the 1200D (Aspencade), with the engine size increased to 1182cc (75.5 × 66mm) and many styling and technical changes, including not just the engine, but the suspension, brakes and much more.

which to adjust the air suspension. I can well remember testing one of these machines during the summer of 1984, when I attended one of the very first rallies organized by the VJMCC (Vintage Japanese Motor Cycle Club) in Norfolk. And I well remember how, with my late son Gary (then aged 11) on the pillion, I experienced at first hand the pleasures of riding this excellent touring mount.

Yes, it was a big, big bike. But, once aboard, much of the weight when stationary disappeared. It was also super smooth and extreme-ly comfortable – both the seating and the suspension. Quite honestly, road bumps were a thing which the Aspencade simply ironed out. In fact, if Harley-Davidson hadn't already registered the 'Glide' name it would have been an instant choice for the big Honda.

Bigger Still

Yamaha then introduced its own Wing-type machine, the XVZ1200 Venture, with a V4 engine and similarly lavish level of equipment. Honda's response was to redesign its flat-four and relaunch it as the GL1200. This had a capacity of 1182cc. This time the stroke was increased (from 61.4mm to 66mm), whilst the bore was upped very slightly to 75.5mm. Not only did the '1200' have the advantage of more power (94bhp at 7,000rpm) and torque, but also maintenance-free hydraulic tappets and clutch. A new frame, suspension, fairing and seat resulted in improvements to handling, comfort and ground clearance (a notable problem with earlier Wings).

The anti-dive system and linked braking arrangement (the foot pedal operating the rear disc and one of the front pair) that had been introduced for 1983 were retained.

Six Cylinders

Then, when I attended the international Milan Show in November 1987, came the launch of the first 6-cylinder Wing, if one discounts the prototype-only AOK of the early 1970s.

This machine is really outside the scope of this particular book, but suffice to record its basic details, which included not only adding two additional cylinders to the transverse flat layout, but also an increase in displacement to 1520cc (71 × 64mm). A pair of 33mm Keihin carburettors, which ran on a compression ratio of 9.8:1, gave a claimed 100bhp at 5,200rpm. With a dry weight of 796lb (362kg), Honda claimed a maximum speed of 125mph (200km/h).

And today, more than three decades after the launch of the original 999cc 4-cylinder GL1000 in late 1974, the Gold Wing retains its spot at the very top of the de luxe touring motorcycle chart, with its only real challengers coming from BMW and Harley-Davidson.

13 CBX Six

By early 1977 it had become quite obvious that the Honda Motor Company was preparing for a major two-wheel sales offensive. Not only was a return to GP racing being mentioned almost weekly by the press, but also that top-secret testing was taking place back in Japan of a new top-of-the-range multi-cylinder machine, probably, said the Americans, with a 1-litre V6 engine. As events were to prove, those early reports were not very far away from fact.

A Return to the Big Time

A year later, in March 1978, *Motorcycle Mechanics* carried a news story headed 'Honda Stirs', going on to say:

> So far as Honda are concerned their return to GP racing [with the ill-fated NR500 oval-piston 500cc four-stroke] and their decision to join the bhp rat race with the CBX six [using a 1000cc across-the-frame dohc engine] are but the tip of the iceberg and are merely considered to be two prestige moves in a massive programme designed to re-establish Honda as the world's most technically advanced and biggest bike builder.

Some three years earlier, Honda had at last seen that complacency and the demands of its automobile division had left the company extremely vulnerable. So it decided that the motorcycle operation needed to have its own research and development facility. This was subsequently set up at Osaka and stopgap

models such as the CB750F2 and GL1000 Gold Wing were introduced, whilst an entire new range of motorcycles was planned. The proposed newcomers included new 3-valves-per-cylinder 250cc and 400cc twins, a 500cc V-twin (to emerge as the CX) and the 1000cc CBX six. Honda's plan was for a total of twelve new models to be introduced by the end of 1978, and would also include new 16-valve 750cc and 900cc fours.

European Influence

A feature of these new designs was that their styling should be influenced by the demands of the European market, with Honda basing two stylists permanently in Paris. They were briefed to report back directly to Japan – this being seen in the 250T and 400T twins (*see* Chapter 6), which arrived in the late summer of 1977.

So why had Europe suddenly become so important? Colin Mayo (Editor of *Motorcycle Mechanics*) had this to say: 'First of all they don't want all their eggs in one American basket. Second, and probably more significantly, domestic sales are expected to fall this year as inflation tops the 10 per cent level and the Japanese Government take measures to deflate the home economy.'

An Inside View

It is, at this stage, worth giving the reader an inside view of the Suzuka plant in which many of the new models, including the 6-cylinder

CBX, were to be built, as it shows how Honda operated at the time. Constructed in 1961, Suzuka was a model of industrial efficiency. As one journalist described it: 'Quite literally, raw materials, or component parts, arrive at one end of the works and bikes emerge at the other. There are no facilities at the factory for stockpiling and within an hour of its arrival, a component or piece of sheet steel will be exiting at the other end of the factory as a part of a complete machine. From there it is put straight on a lorry for delivery to the docks or showroom.'

The CBX1000 Super Sport was designed by a team led by Soichiro Irimajiri – the man responsible for the legendary 250cc and 297cc 6-cylinder GP racers. And just by studying the CBX one could immediately see the connection. Some 24,000 CBX Super Sports were to be built in total.

In an era when the British car industry was suffering massive problems with its industrial relations, Suzuka's efficiency was not only a tribute to the precision and speed of its mass-production techniques and its modern machine tools, but also to Honda's efforts to maintain good labour relations. The management saw that by providing working conditions which were as pleasant as possible and instilled corporate loyalty, it would be better for the company. And so it had proved, even though by the late 1970s the Japanese unions had become more well-organized. There was more militancy than before, but by the British standards of the time this was pretty harmless stuff. Generally, worker/company relations at Honda were good.

So how did Honda set out to keep its work-force 'on side'? Well, boredom and fatigue on

The cylinders of the CBX were inclined forward by 30 degrees from the vertical. Motor Cycle Weekly *achieved a timed 139.2mph in a 1977 road test.*

the production line were minimized by switching personnel around and also by giving everybody working on the lines an equal opportunity for promotion. New employees at the Honda Motor Company didn't just walk in and become chief executives (as still happens in Western corporations!). Instead, everybody had to begin on the production line. Interestingly, at the end of the 1970s formal qualifications still meant very little in the Honda organization, where a man being considered for promotion was judged mainly on his performance and ability. Actually, this had been a Honda policy right from the beginning, the top jobs going to men who had worked their time, proved their ability and helped the company to grow. It simply wasn't possible for outsiders to grab plum jobs; it was a formula which worked, as Honda's continued growth was to prove.

The CBX Design

Like the CX500 (*see* Chapter 14), the CBX was the work of a design team headed by Soichiro Irimajiri, the man also responsible for the legendary World Championship winning 250cc and 297cc 6-cylinder GP bikes of the 1960s and Honda's Formula 1 and Formula 2 car racing engines.

In fact, the CBX used much of the technology of the racers, with its air-cooled dohc, 24-valve, across-the-frame layout. Like the GP racers, it also employed a diamond frame, allowing the engine to be inclined 30 degrees forward. This, said Honda, provided greater strength to the frame and more space behind the engine for the positioning of the six 28mm Keihin VB carburettors.

Displacing 1047cc, with bore and stroke dimensions of 64.5 × 53.4mm respectively, the

The cylinder head and cylinder block castings were each single assemblies; note the oil cooler above the cam cover and below the steering column.

CBX engine had no fewer than seven main bearings. Running on a compression ratio of 9.3:1, the first examples which arrived in early 1978 produced 105bhp (crank reading) at 9,000rpm. *Motor Cycle Weekly* achieved an electronically timed 139.2mph (224km/h) when testing one of the very first bikes off the line in Japan during the last days of 1977. Lubrication was taken care of by a wet–sump system with a dual pump and oil cooler; its capacity was 1.21gal (5.5ltr).

Hollow Double Overhead Camshafts

The hollow double overhead camshafts were driven by chains, whilst a centrally located Hyro chain drove the alternator from the crankshaft. The engine itself was a truly impressive sight. It actually appeared wider and bigger than it was, the design team having done an outstanding job in keeping it so narrow; in fact, it was only 2in (50mm) wider than the existing CB750 power plant. This was achieved by mounting the CDI ignition and alternator to the rear of the crankshaft and by clever placement of the carburettors.

Lightweight pistons helped to ensure that the engine could be revved to 10,000rpm and still remain within the safe piston speed level

From the side view the CBX 1047cc six (64.5 × 53.4mm) looks quite compact. Engine width was reduced by locating the CD1 ignition and alternator to the rear of the crankshaft and by clever placement of the carburettors.

of 17.8m/sec. And in traditional Honda fashion the cylinder head and cylinder barrel assemblies were one-piece affairs, whilst the crankcase split horizontally.

A particular development issue centred around combustion problems, which led the engineering team to plump for a state-of-the-art transistorized ignition circuit triggered by magnetic pick-ups. This type of system provided an 'automatic' advance curve, because the pulser circuit's rise-time was faster at high engine speeds. The degree of advance could be tailored, but it stayed proportional to engine speed.

The CBX also employed a mechanical advancer with three bob-weights and the advance 'curve' being stepped. The ignition was advanced steadily through 25 degrees up to 2,000rpm. Then the advance was cut off, and in fact it was retarded by a degree or two until the engine got somewhere between 6,000–7,500rpm, when the advance began again. It then went on to between 31 and 34 degrees at peak rpm and then got chopped off again.

There is little doubt, although Honda wouldn't admit it, that without these devices the combustion process would have been interfered with by pinking or flat spots – in fact, the latter did interfere on the first series of machines, before being attended to for the 1980 model year (which is explained later).

Combustion problems take designers into rather grey areas. And Soichiro Irimajiri's development team had compensated by attending to features they did know about – mechanical stresses.

The 4-Valve Layout

Another technical area was the 4-valves-per-cylinder layout. This, Honda said, provided 'sufficient valve area but with valves and springs which are light enough to be used at 10,000rpm'. Honda also claimed that the 6-cylinder design resulted in less overall piston weight and, of course, the individual pistons

A CBX engine specially cut away and on display at The Classic Motor Cycle Show, April 2002.

were much smaller than would have been needed in, say, a 3- or 4-cylinder engine.

Finally, the stroke had been made extremely short, this being intended to keep the piston speed well within safe limits, Honda considering that the 'whole unit should give the necessary power but still be as bullet-proof as its predecessors'.

The Chassis

Besides its spine-type tubular frame, the CBX sported telescopic front forks with triple-rate springs and 160mm of travel. At the rear were Honda-made FVQ dampers, with five pre-load settings and variable bump and rebound damping. In fact, the original rear shocks came in for the most criticism when the American *Cycle* magazine listed the changes for the 1980 model year CBX in November 1979.

Like the CX500, the CBX was a pioneer in the use of tubeless tyres. On the six, a 3.50V19 was fitted at the front, a 4.25V18 at the rear; in both cases the rim profile on the Comstar wheels was specifically designed to suit tube-

French-built Moto Martin CBX1000 with monoshock rear suspension and Forcella Italiana inverted front forks.

less tyres. With a wheelbase of 58.9in (1,496mm), castor of 62.5 degrees and trail of 4.7in (120mm), the steering and handling of the 549lb (249kg) machine could only be described as borderline. There is no doubt that

with the CBX, Honda's engine development had outpaced its chassis. But, to be fair, the CBX was a sports/tourer, not an outright sports bike or road racer. According to one tester at the time:

Even more extreme was this Moto Martin turbocharged CBX – the performance was stunning!

1978 CBX 1000 Super Sport Specifications			
Engine	Air-cooled dohc across-the-frame, 4-valves-per-cylinder, alloy head and barrel, 6-into-2 exhaust system	Rear suspension	Swinging arm, twin shock absorbers
Bore	64.5mm	Front brake	Twin 296mm hydraulically operated discs
Stroke	53.4mm	Rear brake	Single 296mm hydraulically operated disc
Displacement	1047cc		
Compression ratio	9.3:1	Tyres	Front 3.50 × 19, rear 130/90V × 18
Lubrication	Twin pumps, wet sump, oil cooler		
Ignition	CDI, 12V, electric start		
Carburettor	6 × Keihin VB 28mm with accelerator pump	**General Specifications**	
		Wheelbase	60.43in (1,535mm)
Primary drive	Chain	Ground clearance	6.1in (155mm)
Final drive	Hyvo chain/gear	Seat height	31.89in (810mm)
Gearbox	Five speeds	Fuel tank capacity	4.8gal (22ltr)
Frame	Spine-type, with engine as a stressed member	Dry weight	545lb (247kg)
		Maximum power	105bhp @ 9,000rpm
Front suspension	Telescopic fork, with air assistance	Top speed	140mph (225km/h)

The ride on open roads was most noticeable for its comfort and the mental effort in keeping somewhere close to the speed limits. It has the kind of handling that you don't really notice; you put it into a corner and it goes round. Half way through the roundabout the guy in front does something daft, you put the brakes on and the Honda stops. There were no problems and nothing to notice or raise comment.

However, as John Robinson pointed out in 1978, 'At higher speeds, particularly the long fast turns around the test track, the six started to weave.' Some lighter riders even found that the big Honda would weave along a straight piece of road (when using all the performance) at high speeds.

But, in contrast, at slower speeds the handling was quite pleasant – with light steering – though it was still a heavy bike to hustle around at over 100mph. John Robinson again: 'The wind force and the strain on the arms caused by braking from speeds in excess of 130mph soon make the rider tired.' Of course, the original CBX was, like most Japanese bikes

of its era, naked without any form of rider protection.

Another problem associated with using all the performance of the six was tyre wear. A 1978 *Motorcycle Mechanics* test commented: 'After 1,200 miles, most of them pretty hard ones for the tyres and transmission, the back tyre needed replacing and the front one was well on its way.'

Touring Abilities

Except for potential pitfalls such as those described above, and relatively poor fuel economy, the 6-cylinder Honda made a pretty good stab as a serious touring mount. As well as adding to the bike's comfort the big tank held 5.4gal (24.5ltr), whilst the seat was a pretty plush affair, fully capable of holding two with ease.

The clutch was particularly light and as one tester said: 'At last Honda seemed to have found a decent throttle. It has a reasonably quick action and, although it is opening six carburettors, it is pretty light to use. Even after half a day of stop–go riding through heavy traffic, I had no aches or pains.' Another said: 'Out on the open road, the Honda can be both an ultra-rapid sportster or a superb long-range tourer. It's got everything you need for both roles and it does it so well that you can make touring more like a sporty blast along the lanes.'

Comparing Prices

In comparing prices in the UK (October 1978), the list price was £2,578 with twelve months warranty and unlimited mileage. This compared with £2,005 for the Yamaha XS1100 shaft drive four and around £1,900 for the brand-new Suzuki GS 1000 (4-cylinder, chain final drive). Both rivals only came with a six-month warranty with a limit of 10,000 miles (16,000km), and although it was a real crowd-puller, an MV or BMW would have cost you more.

A Number of Changes for 1980

At the end of 1979 Honda brought out a catalogue of detailed changes for its flagship model. The original 1978 model year CBX had a more than healthy appetite for petrol – *Cycle* commenting: 'You might need a Mercedes-Benz budget if gasoline mileage is of any concern, because the CBX consumes fossil fuel at an amazing rate.'

And poor fuel economy wasn't the CBX's only shortcoming. As introduced, the bike had plastic swinging arm bushes, shock absorbers that didn't do their job properly and an aggravating lean spot that disrupted the flow of mid-range power, which, as one commentator put it: 'created the impression that the big-muscle CBX had weak knees in the mid-range'.

Less Power

The 1980 CBX made less horsepower. This was because during 1979 the Germans had adopted a horsepower ceiling: 100bhp at the crank-shaft. If a motorcycle had more, it wasn't going to be imported for use on German public highways. As Honda's claimed peak crankshaft figure was 105 for the first CBX, it therefore came up against the German limit. Concerned with the possible spread of the limit to other European countries, the Japanese decided to detune the CBX. According to Honda, the crankshaft horsepower was reduced to 98, a loss of just over 5 per cent. But when *Cycle* tested a 1980 model, it said that the drop 'in terms of rear wheel horsepower was 16 per cent'.

Honda America's spokesperson at the time stated: 'CBX production is so small by Honda standards that it made no sense to produce separate models for the United States and other countries.' And although a horsepower ceiling was a German problem, emissions were an American one. The carburettors had therefore been re-jetted to help make it possible for the 1980 CBX to pass the 1981 emission tests. But in reality there was no reason to believe that jetting was responsible for the latest CBX's power loss.

The shortfall could be found in the 1980 CBX's lower lift cams, which opened the inlet valves 7.8mm and the exhaust valves 7mm. These figures were 0.5mm less than previously. But the biggest influence to muting the six had come from revisions in valve timing. Specifically, this was done by advancing the exhaust cams 5 degrees and thus closing the exhaust valves at TDC (Top Dead Centre) instead of leaving them open further into the intake cycle. This shortening of the 'overlap' phase reduced the time during which fuel droplets could escape past the exhaust valves and become those unburned hydro-carbons that the American legislators were so worried about. More crucially, it also shortened the CBX's breath – which certainly didn't do any favours to its performance potential.

Besides modifications to the carburettors, the Honda engineering team had redesigned the CBX silencer baffles, thereby allowing the system's back pressure to match the altered cam timing and carburettor jetting.

Full List of Changes

The 1980 CBX changes were as follows:

• altered cam timing, carb jetting and exhaust modifications as detailed above
• air assistance for the front fork
• a stronger swinging arm, together with a pivot pin which operated on needle and ball bearings
• strengthened frame gusseting
• wider rear wheel rim
• Showa shock absorbers with thirty different damping/spring pre-load combinations. These shock absorbers provided for 3.9in (99mm) of travel at the rear wheel spindle
• red and black were now the available colours, the previous silver and black combination having been discontinued
• a lockable tail section had been added to the dual seat.

A 'Grand Prix' Sports kit was marketed by American Honda of Gardena, California, for around US$180. This comprised lower han-dlebars (still forged aluminium alloy I-beam clip-ons), but lower, shorter choke and clutch cables, a short front brake hose and rear set foot controls.

The CBX-B and -C Models

1981 and 1982 saw the arrival of the CBX-B and CBX-C models respectively. Both of these models were equipped with a comprehensive fairing; also available were cost-option matching hand luggage. Another major difference was the all-new 'Progressive-Linkage' (Pro-Link, as Honda termed it) rear suspension. This featured a massive chromed alloy box-section swinging arm. The air-assisted monoshock (28–57psi) also featured three-way adjustable oil damping, but its position between the engine and rear wheel stretched the wheelbase by 1.5in (38mm). The front forks were stiffened – going up from a flexible 35mm diameter to a more sturdy 39mm, further improved by air assistance (7–13 psi) and a balance pipe.

Brakes, never a problem on the CBX-A (1978–80) versions, were also improved. Two twin-rotor (Honda called them 'turbine

A CBX1000C Pro-Link. This was the later touring version of the CBX and was produced during 1981–2. It did not have the power of the original Super Sport.

cooled') vented discs with four-piston calipers at the front were rated as excellent for the period, when virtually every other production bike had two-piston calipers and solid unvented discs. Controls were much as before, no LCD (Liquid Crystal Display) in sight. But a fairing-mounted clock was an addition; there was also a rear suspension warning light and the steering now locked with the ignition switch. The engine (and Comstar wheels) were now finished in black, outlined in polished alloy. Honda said the clutch had been modified (in an attempt to cure tickover rattles).

All of the changes added up to a huge weight of 611lb (277 kg) – 66lb (30kg) up on the old unfaired A version. And performance was down – by some 10mph (16km/h) to around 128mph (206km/h). This was a combination of the increased weight penalty and a reduction in overall gearing.

In all, some 6,000 B and C models were built and sold before production came to an end in 1982, but only 289 of these were sold in the UK, most of the remainder going to the USA and Canada. Although much rarer than the original CBX-A series (of which some 24,000 were built), the B and C versions do not command such a high price today.

Ownership Problems

All CBXs are expensive to own, not just the purchase price for a pristine example, but running costs such as fuel, tyres and servicing. O-ring final-drive chains are recommended as they boost life considerably.

Dropping out of fourth gear is not uncommon on CBXs and is usually due to tolerances along the gear stacking up against full engagement. Once the dogs start to wear, it jumps out; the repair bill can be large as the job involves splitting the engine casings to get at the gears.

Other components needing checking over on otherwise immaculate low mileage bikes are battery problems and rot around the ends of

Rear wheel and brake view of the CBX 1000C. In all, 6,000 were produced, but only 289 were sold in the UK, most going to the USA and Canada.

both silencers. Pattern exhaust systems can drop the value of the machine quite considerably. As mentioned earlier, tyre wear was a major problem; CBX tyres were tubeless as standard.

So which CBX to choose? Well, the original CBX-A Super Sport is much easier to find and is preferred by many, but the later B and C versions have superior brakes and handling, although that fairing does them no favours, not only adding extra weight but also not working very well and throwing up a lot of noise.

Either way, the CBX marked the pinnacle for Honda in its pre-liquid-cooled hi-tech model range, which really kicked in after around 1983 and as such is the range-topper of the various models covered in this book. It's also the nearest the factory got to building a road-going version of Mike Hailwood's legendary 1960s GP models. And for many this has been the deciding factor in their ownership of probably the most glamorous Japanese motorcycle of the 1970s.

14 CX Series

In many ways, the design of the CX500 V-twin marked a major step forward for Honda (together with the CBX 1000 six). As is fully related in Chapter 13, by the mid-1970s Honda had become seriously concerned at the inroads that Yamaha, and to a lesser extent

The CX500, which took no fewer than three years to reach the market, was finally launched in a blaze of publicity at the beginning of December 1977.

Suzuki, had made into Honda's sales – particularly when both their rivals set about introducing four-stroke models.

So in early 1975 the company decided to set up a new R & D facility at Osaka to design only motorcycles (previously this function had been a combined car/motorcycle operation at Waco). And yet another facet of Honda planning was that, at last, it had realized the importance of the European market to overall sales.

The CX500 Makes its Bow

The CX500, which took no fewer than three years to reach the market, was finally launched in a blaze of publicity at the big Tokyo Show of December 1977.

As with the CBX six, the CX500 was the brainchild of Honda's then director of R & D, Soichiro Irimajiri, who had previously designed the fabulous 6-cylinder racer campaigned by Mike Hailwood in the 1960s, the Formula 1 and 2 racing cars, the CVCC car and the CB400T, which had been released earlier that year.

This is what Irimajiri had to say at the European launch press conference, held in the South of France:

> The CBX1000 six has been realized purely for sporting riding. But like the CB400T, the CX500 has been built to satisfy the majority of riders. We were looking for four things on the CX500; it should be comfortable and fatigue free – it's no good if the rider is tired after just several hundred kilometres riding; it should be very reliable; it should be sporty; it must be easily manipulated by all riders.

Soichiro Irimajiri continued:

> Up until now it has not been possible to satisfy all of these points. So we checked through all the possible mechanisms, ignoring our past ideas. The water-cooled V-twin was chosen because it would be well silenced and smooth. For smooth touring we gave the crankshaft 50 per cent more flywheel mass. Soft springs were used for the suspension for a good ride. But we also wanted to cut out many of the black spots of motorcycling such as chain problems, spoke loosening and ignition troubles.

Priorities were, Irimajiri said: 'Shaft drive, Comstar wheels and CDI ignition', which 'eliminated all this'. Other important considerations were: 'We also wanted more power to give sporty performance and used the same specification as the Formula 1 and 2 racing cars with a short stroke and 4-valves-per-cylinder.'

But he also pointed out:

> There was, however, a disadvantage of using the high specification on the transverse V-twin. For good gas flow the carburettors would interfere with the rider's legs. So the cylinder heads were twisted by 22 degrees so that the two carbs were close together. This made the pushrod valve opening necessary. For ease of handling we lowered the polar moment of inertia by concentrating as much of the mass as close to the centre of gravity as possible. And to minimize the torque reaction from the crankshaft, the clutch runs the opposite to the crank. The 80-degree included angle between the cylinders was chosen because the cylinder heads interfere with the rider's knees with the more common 90 degrees. Vibration is only one tenth of that on a parallel twin. Watercooling provided reliability with quietness and the ability to use a high-compression ratio necessary for high power while still running on regular grade fuel.

The Engine

The heart of the newcomer was a shaft drive, liquid-cooled 496.9cc 80-degree transverse V-twin with 4-valves-per-cylinder. Bore and stroke were 78 × 52mm, the same as Honda's Formula 1 V12 racing car which the company had built several years earlier.

The use of small valves and lightweight stainless steel pushrods meant, said Honda, that the engine was safe up to 10,000rpm. Maximum power was quoted as 50bhp at 9,000rpm, with maximum torque just under 32lb/ft at 7,000rpm. Honda sources also said that the engine developed as much as 80 per cent of its maximum torque as low as 3,500rpm.

The reason given for the use of pushrod valve operation was that overhead cams would have been impossible to fit because of the twist of the cylinder heads. This was done to straighten the gas path from the two 35mm

ABOVE: *A rocker cover removed, showing the disposition of the four valves, rocker arms with lock nut adjustable tappets and centrally located spark plug.*

LEFT: *The transverse V-twin layout was very much like the Moto Guzzi V35/V50 series, which also made its bow at around the same time as the Honda model.*

LEFT: *The heart of the liquid-cooled 496.9cc 80-degree transverse V-twin with 4-valves-per-cylinder; bore and stroke were 78 × 52mm.*

BELOW: *View of the CX500 pushrod valve operation layout. There were 4-valves-per-cylinder, lightweight stainless steel pushrods and a single camshaft.*

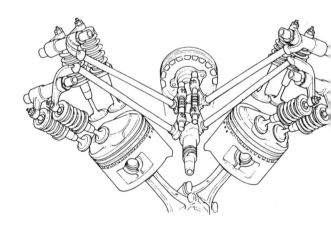

Keihin CV carburettors into the pentroof combustion chamber and exhaust pipes, providing maximum torque and power.

Two exhaust valves, instead of 1-per-cylinder as on the CB400T, were employed due to the critical amount of reciprocating weight offered by the pushrods. The valves were operated by a single camshaft mounted between the vee of the cylinders. This was driven by a Morse chain at the rear and had a water pump to the rear and a cooling fan for the radiator at the front.

The Transmission

Mounted in line with the wheels, the engine was supported in a frame using a single large diameter spine and the drive was taken by gears from the front on the crankshaft to the clutch. A feature of the CX500 was the exceptionally light operation (disengagement) at the handlebar lever.

A five-speed gearbox was to the right and slightly below the crankshaft, whilst the final drive was by means of a Hook joint and shaft running in the offside swinging arm tube to the rear spiral bevel gears in the wheel.

Electrics

Interesting features of the 12V electrical system were the CDI point-less ignition, an alternator mounted on the rear of the crankshaft,

which charged a 14amp-hour battery – even at tickover – and the mounting of the fuses between the handlebar mounts on the top of the upper fork yoke. As was to be expected of a Honda, there was also a full complement of electrical components, including an electric start (no back-up kick-starter), 50W headlamp, direction indicators and the like.

Tubeless Tyres

Tubeless (Bridgestone or Yokohama) tyres were used for the first time on a production motorcycle. John Nutting, *Motor Cycle,* 17 December 1977, said: 'They grip nicely and as well as offering slightly lower unsprung weight are claimed to be more resistant to sudden punctures.' These new tyres were able to remain on the rims at pressures as low as 3psi. The wheels were the by-now familiar composite Comstar units.

The suspension was best described as soft, with triple-rate springs in the forks, with the original equipment twin shock absorbers coping better than Honda-supplied units of earlier years. John Nutting again: 'The handling is just like the smaller CB400T' (*see* Chapter 6), and going on to say: 'The steering doesn't drop in hairpins at low speed and is light but with stability in faster bends. The centre of gravity is high and with the low self-centring action, the feel of the CX500 takes some getting used to.'

Another view came from Brian Crichton in *Motorcycle Mechanics* dated July 1978:

The components of the CX500 shaft final-drive system.

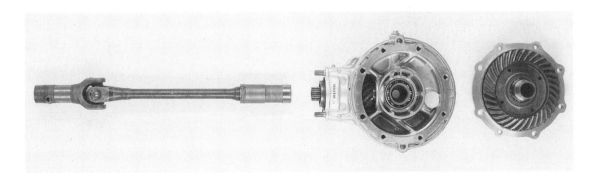

1978 CX500 Specifications			
Engine	Liquid-cooled, ohv transverse V-twin, 4-valves-per-cylinder, short pushrods, cylinder heads twisted by 22 degrees, 80-degree included angle between the cylinders, pentroof combustions chambers, single camshaft located in crankcase, shell big-end bearings	Frame	Single large diameter spine-type
		Front suspension	Oil-damped telescopic fork
		Rear suspension	Swinging arm, twin shock absorbers
		Front brake	Twin 240mm hydraulically operated discs
Bore	78mm	Rear brake	Single 180mm SLS drum
Stroke	42mm	Tyres	Front 3.25 × 19, rear 3.75 × 18
Displacement	496.9cc	(both tubeless)	
Compression ratio	10:1		
Lubrication	Trochoid pump, wet sump	**General Specifications**	
Ignition	CDI, 12V, electric start	Wheelbase	57.3in (1,455mm)
Carburettor	2 × Keihin 35mm CV	Ground clearance	5.9in (150mm)
Primary drive	Gear	Seat height	30in (762mm)
Final drive	Shaft and bevel gears	Fuel tank capacity	3.7gal (17ltr)
Gearbox	Five speeds; foot-change	Dry weight	441lb (200kg)
		Maximum power	50bhp @ 9,000rpm
		Top speed	108mph (174km/h)

The supple suspension offering over five inches of movement at the forks worked over the slightest irregularity and the rear suspension gave comfort and stability. The rear shocks could be bottomed on the softest spring preload setting with a passenger on board. Going from the hardest to the softest setting for riding solo on the road gave a slightly softer ride at the rear, while handling remained excellent. This says a lot for the Honda FVQ dampers.

Performance

Honda claimed a top speed of 112mph (180km/h) at the launch. *Motorcycle Mechanics* electronically timed its test bike at 105.5mph (169.7km/h), with the tachometer reading just short of the 9,750rpm red line. Later when the machine was put on the dyno it gave a top reading of 42bhp at 8,300rpm at the rear wheel. The Honda 50bhp figure was probably a crankshaft figure.

Even so, *Motorcycle Mechanics* said:

This is tremendous performance when it is considered that the pushrod engine is driving a shaft,

water pump, fan blade at half crankshaft speed, and has all this as an extra weight penalty. If it weighed less and had chain drive it could be a real flier. But then it would not be the CX500.

Countering Torque Reaction

On the CX500 the clutch mounted at the front of the engine rotated in the opposite direction to the crankshaft to counter torque reaction. As *Motorcycle Mechanics* said:

BMW owners have lived with torque reaction for over 50 years. Honda has evidently decided it was a problem and have almost completely cancelled it out by this neat move. The only way you realize that there is some torque reaction left is to search it out by taking your hands off the bars. The bike then rolls to the left slightly. Honda's shaft drive set-up is also neatly executed, with only one 90-degree turn, at the rear wheel.

However, as the magazine continued, 'Owners may not be quite so enamoured with the idea that if you want to take a piston out, the engine has to be removed from the frame and then the transmission has to come out because the barrels are cast as part of the crankcase.'

Mechanical Glitches

There is no doubt that in the main the CX500 got off to a flying start: it received rave reviews in the press and sold by the thousand from day one. But there were two potential mechanical glitches. The first was premature big-end failure, particularly on early examples. This is what Brian Crichton had to say in July 1978:

> Reverberations of high praise created by Honda's new CX500 V-twin have sent on such an impressive reputation that when one came my way I was expecting to have to repeat everything that had been said so many times before. Big-end trouble changed those preconceptions. If it surprises you to hear that the otherwise brilliant CX500 suffered from big-end knock I can assure you that it hit me the same way. I read as many road tests on the model as I could find and none of them came near the subject. When the same thing happened to a second engine and Colin Mayo [the then editor of *Motorcycle Mechanics*] said that one he tried at the model launch in Italy blew its big ends, we scored a three out of three failure rate.

After the problems experienced by *Motorcycle Mechanics*, Honda UK sent out a bulletin to all Honda dealers. The official explanation was that 'there was not enough clearance between the crankshaft and the shell big end bearings'.

Another early problem was dropping out of top (fifth) down to fourth gear. As Brian Crichton explained:

> At first it would, on the odd occasion, drop into a false neutral and then fourth. As the test proceeded it started to prefer going straight to fourth and omitting the warning neutral. This only happened a few times. But when accelerating in top and the bike suddenly drops into fourth, the suspension takes a dive, and then the bike surges ahead

> because it takes you so by surprise that you don't have chance to ease the throttle, it makes you very wary.

If all this was not enough, Crichton found:

> One other peculiarity started to show itself. Clutch slip. This first happened at the second track session. The clutch was fine for the standing quarters, but then slipped slightly on a fast left-hander. It repeated itself two or three times later in the test, only in top. Yet when I tried to make it slip by opening the throttle hard in top gear at the bottom of the hill, it drove perfectly. The phenomenon was as unpredictable as the transmission problem.

Finally, some early CX500s suffered from cam-chain problems. But Honda worked hard on these faults and by the 1980-model year they were largely a thing of the past.

Big for a Five-Hundred

In appearance, the CX was big for a five-hundred. It was also quite bulky and you could feel its weight of 441lb (200kg) dry. But this was counteracted by the comfortable arrangement of its riding position. The seat and handlebars gave just the right stance; the CX500 was a machine that you sat in rather than on. The footrests were placed back by the swinging arm pivot and with the large 3.7gal (17ltr) fuel tank the riding position was excellent for most conditions.

Brakes were considered good for the late 1970s, with rain grooves in the pads of the twin front discs – 240mm, the same diameter as the CB550 four – and there was an SLS drum at the rear. These were described by one tester of the day as 'offering excellent feel from high speeds with really good bite, yet free from the fear of locking up'. It was generally agreed that a single disc at the front would not have been enough.

Developments

Besides the mechanical teething troubles out-lined above, the CX family (which later includ-ed the larger engined CX650E) was to evolve as a true workhorse; in fact, London dispatch riders swore by the model, often clocking up huge mileages during the 1980s and 1990s.

The first development came for the 1980 model year with the CX500A. This differed from the original model by way of a cockpit fairing complete with screen (virtually the stock headlamp surround with a tinted screen) and a redesigned radiator.

Then, for the 1981 model year, came the CX650C (Custom) with styling changes

From the 1980 model year the CX500A gained a small screen and a redesigned radiator. Besides the CX500A, there was also the CX500C (Custom), with many differences outlined in the main text.

which included rear swept handlebars, smaller 2.6gal (12ltr) tank, 3.50 × 19 front and 130/90 × 16 rear tyres, additional chrome and sepa-rately mounted instruments, plus new mud-guards, shocks, saddle, side panels and the like.

Then in mid-1981 came the first news of the CX500 Turbo (again also later produced as a '650'). This featured what Honda said was the smallest turbocharger in the world, made by IHI (Ishikawajima) with a 50mm turbine and 48mm compressor. As *Motorcycle Mechanics* stated 'The 500 that knows it's a 900' – this being in response to a test where both the CX500 Turbo and the CB900FZ reached close to 130mph (209km/h). The newcomer sported notable differences from the existing CX500A/CX500C model, with new (gold) Comstar wheels, Pro-Link (single shock) rear suspension, a wind-tunnel-developed fairing and all the technical changes needed to trans-form a tourer into a fire-eating sportster. There

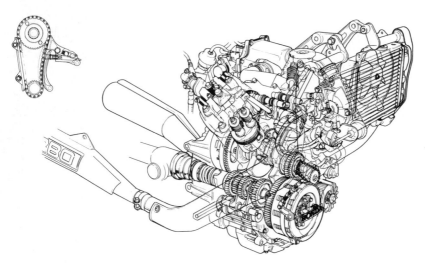

ABOVE: The high performance Turbo version arrived in September 1981, but although technically interesting it – and the other Japanese turbocharged bikes – were not a sales success.

LEFT: CX500 Turbo engine and transmission details.

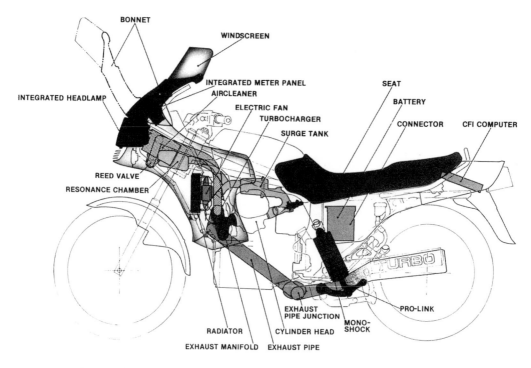

BONNET
WINDSCREEN
INTEGRATED METER PANEL
AIRCLEANER
SEAT
BATTERY
INTEGRATED HEADLAMP
ELECTRIC FAN
TURBOCHARGER
CONNECTOR
CFI COMPUTER
SURGE TANK
REED VALVE
RESONANCE CHAMBER
EXHAUST
PIPE JUNCTION
MONO-
SHOCK
PRO-LINK
RADIATOR
CYLINDER HEAD
EXHAUST MANIFOLD
EXHAUST PIPE

ABOVE: Layout installation of the various components associated with the CX500 Turbo motorcycle.

BELOW: There was even a Honda CX Cup single model race series in some European countries.

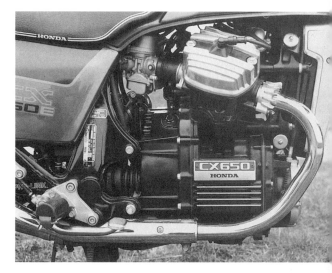

RIGHT: *The final development of the CX series was the '650'. This displaced 674cc (82.5 × 63mm) and was offered in various guises including the Turbo and E (Europe) sports/touring model.*

ABOVE: *The IHI (Ishikawajima) RHB51A turbocharger, which Honda claimed was the smallest such device in the world. It revolved up to an incredible 180,000rpm, helping the CX500 Turbo generate 82bhp.*

were other changes, including a longer wheelbase, bigger section tyres and revised wheel sizes (18in front, 17in rear). As for power output figures, Honda put a figure of 80bhp for the 500 Turbo – and 90bhp for the CX650. Honda also brought out the CX500E (Euro Sport) for the 1983 model year.

Finally, for the 1984 model year Honda introduced the CX650E (Euro Sport). My comments at the time in a road test for *Motorcycle Enthusiast* regarding the 674cc (82.5 × 63mm) machine, was 'At £2,290 the CX650E is good value if you want a motorcycle to use both as everyday transport and for long-distance touring.' This was with the following proviso: 'but whatever you do, don't buy it if you want a sports/tourer, because it just does not like being pushed around in a sporting manner.'

The CX 'E' series featured (like the Turbo versions) Pro-Link rear suspension, plus TRAC anti-dive (but on the nearside fork leg only). Silencer rot was a problem on the earlier CX500 models, but the 500E and 650E models had an aluminium end cone in the rear of each silencer, in an attempt to solve this problem.

Overall, the CX series of V-twins were, with the exception of the Turbo models (which were a sales disaster, like all the similar bikes from the Japanese factories), easy-to-live-with, comfortable touring bikes with a unique character all of their own. Some derided the design, but thousands of enthusiasts voted with their wallets, making the CX, at least in 500cc guise, a top seller during the late 1970s and early 1980s.

15   Two-Strokes

Although the Honda Motor Company began its career with two-stroke power, it soon gave up the type in favour of the four-stroke. However, by the early 1970s it had reluctantly realized that the 'stroker was a necessary evil. Not only had the modern two-stroke – thanks in no small part to the design genius of the German engineer, Walter Kaaden – largely taken over in most forms of motorcycle sport (road racing, motocross and trials), but was also a more economical power plant (at least from a manufacturing standpoint, if not fuel economy for the owner!) than a small displacement four-stroke. And so it was that Honda, the champion of the four-stroke, entered the ranks of a modern two-stroke engine designer and manufacturer.

Motocross

Even by the mid-1960s it was becoming obvious that if one wished to win in dirt bike racing – motocross – a two-stroke was needed. For example, Britain's biggest marque, BSA, spent a fortune to retain the world titles that Jeff Smith had won on his unit construction works Victor motocrosser. The Birmingham company built an ultra-lightweight 500cc model in 1967, but to no avail, as the two-stroke challengers from the likes of CZ, Husqvarna and Maico simply swept the BSA away.

Then came the entry, at the end of the 1960s, of Suzuki and Yamaha into the motocross arena. Suzuki, with Roger de Coster aboard, won the 500cc World Championship

for the first time in 1971, after taking the 250cc title a year earlier in 1970 – in fact, the team took the first three places in the championship with Joel Robert, Sylvain Geboers and Olle Pettersson. With riders such as de Coster and Robert, Suzuki went on to score more world crowns as the 1970s unfolded.

As for Yamaha, it made a later start. After a 'development' season in 1971, it entered the GPs in 1972, with victory first coming in the 250cc Swedish round towards the end of that season with Hakan Andersson. And it was the same rider who gave Yamaha its first title, the 250cc, in 1973.

Belated Action

Even though Soichiro Honda was actually on record as having said: 'Honda will never build a two-stroke', Suzuki's and Yamaha's progress in motocross stung the Honda company into belated action. Finally, in 1971 Honda recognized the need for a *competitive* motocross machine in its line-up, which of course meant that it had to be powered by a two-stroke engine.

The man who was largely responsible for Honda's entry – and subsequent dirt bike racing success, was Soichiro Miyakoshi. Having served his apprenticeship in the Honda Corporation with exclusively four-stroke power plants, this talented research engineer actually taught himself about two-stroke design. As Mick Woollett describes in his 1983 book *Honda* (Temple Press): 'We can guess that the

194

rival factory's machines were all methodically stripped down in his workshop, meticulously examined, measured and analysed.'

Soichiro Miyakoshi then set about the task of creating Honda's first modern two-stroke motorcycles. He applied the principle of low weight and maximum power. By the winter of 1971–2 he had succeeded in creating an extremely compact, ultra-lightweight, and very powerful 250cc class motocrosser. Coded 335C, this machine had radical port timing, and bore and stroke dimensions of 70 × 64.4cc, giving a displacement of 247.8cc.

Perhaps as an omen Soichiro Honda had retired from heading up the company's R & D department in April 1971 …

Track-Testing the 335C

The 335C had been extensively track-tested (without any Honda marking) several times in Japanese championship motocross races during October, November and December 1971; a sole example of the 335C was also shipped to the USA for testing. Then in February 1972 riders Hirokazu Ueno and Taichi Yoshimura were signed to contest the 1972 Japanese national series.

By the spring of 1972 the new 250cc Honda motocross had been officially designated RC250M. Then a few weeks later in June 1972, a 125cc class machine, the RC125M , was announced.

The big problem with these early machines was that in the search for an ultra-lightweight design, Miyakoshi and Honda had not built in enough strength. When the bikes were campaigned in California, they suffered a spate of

An early production CR125M Elsinore motocrosser, which was air-cooled with a five-speed gearbox.

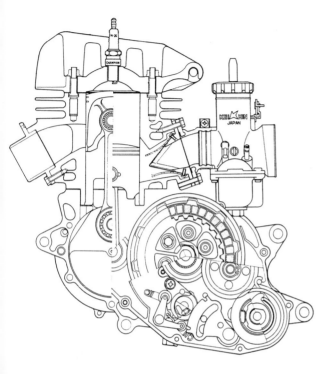

A factory engineering drawing of an early CR250 production motocross engine, with reed valve induction.

retirements. As one reporter said: 'Frames bent after 20 or 30 minutes and stones pierced the fuel tanks. Wheels broke and swing arms bent.'

Also, although probably the fastest bikes in their respective classes at the time in the States, the bikes had road racing, rather than dirt bike priorities. For example, the frame geometry was way out and simply didn't handle as it should have off-road.

Production Gets Under Way

But, as with the early racers, Honda back in Japan responded quickly and positively to the feedback provided from the American Honda arm, with the result that by the end of 1972 the bikes were much improved and the production CR250 models that went on sale in the States in the spring of 1973 were largely bullet-

proof. But when they went on sale the CR250 was still a pretty lean machine tipping the scales at only 213lb (97kg) dry.

Production of the CR250 had begun back in Japan late the previous year, followed shortly thereafter by the CR125 (123.1cc – 56 × 50mm), the smaller dirt racer tipping the scales at 178lb (80kg). Both were generally known as the Elsinore – named not after Shakespeare's Hamlet's castle, but after the American city where the well-known Stateside cross-country event was staged annually.

CR125/250 Details

In an attempt to save weight, the production CR125/250 machines made extensive use of aluminium. The frame, a conventional single downtube semi-duplex affair, was manufactured in a chrome-molybdenum alloy, whilst the engine was of all-aluminium construction, with magnesium side covers. The deeply finned head and cylinder barrel – the latter featuring an austenetic steel liner, six transfer ports and a newly devised combustion chamber shape (the latter to improve scavenging) – helped the CR250 produce a claimed 33bhp at 7,500rpm (the CR125 put out 21.7bhp at 9,500rpm).

On both CR models a five-speed gearbox was built into the engine, unit construction having been a Honda feature since the early days of the company. The first production models were finished with a green and silver fuel tank. It was not until 1974 that the distinctive 'fire engine' red finish became a trademark for Honda's dirt bike racers.

The Enduro Models

Following on from its successful CR motocrossers, Honda soon developed the MT250 and MT125 enduro models. Both leaned heavily on the existing bikes, being essentially very similar except for details such

1972 CR250 Motocross Specification

Engine	Air-cooled single-cylinder two-stroke with piston-port induction, alloy head and barrel, unit construction, vertically split crankcases, magnesium outer covers	Front suspension	Oil-damped telescopic forks
		Rear suspension	Swinging arm, twin shock absorbers
		Front brake	SLS 140mm drum
		Rear brake	SLS 140mm drum
Bore	70mm	Tyres	Front 3.00 × 21, rear 4.00 × 18
Stroke	64.4mm		
Displacement	247.8cc		
Compression ratio	7.2:1	**General Specifications**	
Lubrication	Petroil mixture	Wheelbase	56.5in (1,435mm)
Ignition	Flywheel magneto	Ground clearance	7in (178mm)
Carburettor	Keihin	Seat height	32in (813mm)
Primary drive	Gear	Fuel tank capacity	1.5gal (7ltr)
Final drive	Chain	Dry weight	213lb (97kg)
Gearbox	Five speeds; foot-change	Maximum power	33bhp @ 7,500rpm
Frame	Single full loop, chrome-moly tubing	Top speed	75mph (120km/h)

as state of tune, carburettor size, gearing and so on. Bore and stroke dimensions on both engines remained unchanged. The MT series, which entered production in 1973, had power outputs of 13bhp at 7,000rpm (125) and 23bhp at 6,500rpm (250).

By 1974 both the CR series and the MT series were firmly established in their major market, the USA. When the American magazine *Motorcyclist* tested the latest Honda 250 enduro mount in its February 1975 issue, the headline read 'The Year of the MT250'. Although the journal went on to explain that the Honda was 'Primarily a street machine with off-road leanings', it also explained that by spending only '$50 dollars more, it can be a winner'. This had in fact been proved by the same magazine only the previous month, when the MT250 had bested seven other Japanese enduros in a giant off-road test.

The main problems of the 1975 (and the 1974 bike, which was virtually identical) came down to what *Motorcyclist* described as 'too tall a gear ratio and terrible rear shocks'.

The *Motorcyclist* team set about curing these

faults: 'So we installed a 14-tooth countershaft sprocket up front [the stock gearing being 15/44] and a brand-new set of Honda's CR rear shocks. The pieces bolt on, just move the wheel back to take up slack in the chain gained because of the smaller sprocket. Now the bike works off-road.' One has to ask why Honda didn't offer the MT250 in this guise. It probably felt that most MTs wouldn't be seriously campaigned off-road and tried to save a few dollars on the shocks.

Improved CR125 and CR250 Models

For the 1976 model year, Honda produced much-improved CR motocrossers. This was because although its original machines had proved a big success and had sold in huge numbers, by 1974 the Suzuki TMs and Yamaha YZs were in the hunt, followed soon afterwards by the Kawasaki KX. By 1975 Honda sales had dropped like a stone.

But as the April 1976 issue of *Cycle World* was to report: 'This year, however, Honda returns with more than a few new 'doodaas' to dazzle the buyers. This year they've got a completely new machine, and from what we discovered during the weeks we thrashed it, they've done their homework well.'

The actual bike that *Cycle World* had tested was the CR125M2. Typical of the improvements was the engine. For 1976, the cylinder finning was much greater, so as to give better heat dissipation – a problem that had plagued earlier Honda CR models. There was also increased volume for the exhaust port and a larger Keihin carb (up from 28mm to 30mm). The cylinder head was a totally new design. The squish area had been tightened up to improve combustion, whereas the compression ratio had been dropped slightly (from 7.6: to 7.5:1). As before, a wet multi-plate clutch transmitted the power from the straight-cut primary gears to the gearbox (which now had six ratios). Sparks were provided by a CDI internal rotor unit. The cycle parts had been uprated with new, heavier forks, plus a new frame and swinging arm – the 1976 CR125M weighing in at 198lb (90kg).

The scene was now set for the rest of the 1970s, with Honda's development team making enough changes to keep the company abreast of the opposition, whilst the CR250/125 series was joined by 80cc and 100cc versions. This picture was to remain until, for the 1981 model year, Honda (quickly followed by the other Japanese marques) introduced the first of its liquid-cooled models with monoshock rear suspension. And so the day of the air-cooled, twin shock motocrosser (and enduro bike) was at an end.

MT125

In 1977, Honda made a return to road racing, but not at works level. Instead, it at last decided to design, build and market a competitive, relatively cheap to maintain machine for sale to private customers through its normal dealer outlets.

Coded the MT125R, this machine was powered by a tuned version of the air-cooled piston-port single-cylinder CR125 Elsinore two-stroke motocross engine. The 1977 MT125R produced 25bhp at 10,500rpm and featured lots of magnesium and aluminium, seven intake ports, CD1 ignition, a 34mm Mikuni carburettor and a six-speed close-ratio gearbox.

The single downtube, twin cradle frame was manufactured from chrome-moly tubing, with

A line-up of nineteen brand-new MT125 single-cylinder two-stroke racers awaiting delivery at Honda UK's London headquarters; circa 1977.

Interestingly, the 124cc (54 × 54mm) MT125R had been under development for some three years prior to its release, and so with the added advantage of the motocross connection it was a generally excellent little machine, which was to have quite a long life – and in fact even today Honda still builds yearly batches of what is now known as the RS125, but obviously with many improvements including liquid-cooling, aluminium frame, monoshock suspension, inverted forks and the like.

Championship Series

The British MT125 Championship series was the brainchild of the then Honda UK chief executive, Gerald Davidson, himself a former racer. Gerald foresaw the value of a one-model formula with identical specification for every motorcycle, each of which was to be sponsored by one of Honda's dealerships.

The concept was to revitalize 125 racing, which, with the withdrawal of much factory interest, had gone into decline. One major difference with the Honda series was that with

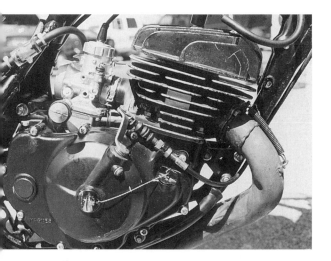

The air-cooled MT125 engine, which was essentially a reworked CR125 motocross unit featuring seven intake ports, CDI ignition, 34mm carb and six-speed gearbox. It put out 25bhp at 10,500rpm.

standard equipment including a single hydraulically operated front disc brake, a rev counter, racing tyres and a dolphin fairing. Dry weight was 154lb (70kg), with Honda claiming a top speed of 115mph (185km/h).

1977 MT125R Road Racer Specification

Engine	Air-cooled, piston-port, single-cylinder, two-stroke, alloy head and barrel, unit construction, vertically split crankcases, magnesium outer covers	Front suspension	Oil-damped telescopic fork
		Rear suspension	Swinging arm with twin shock absorbers
		Front brake	Single hydraulically operated disc, two-piston caliper
Bore	124cc	Rear brake	SLS drum, full width
Stroke	54mm	Tyres	2.50 × 18 front and rear
Displacement	54mm		
Compression ratio	8:1	**General Specifications**	
Lubrication	Petroil mixture	Wheelbase	48in (1,219mm)
Ignition	CDI	Ground clearance	6in (152mm)
Carburettor	Mikuni 28mm	Seat height	N/A
Primary drive	Gear	Fuel tank capacity	2gal (9ltr)
Final drive	Chain	Dry weight	154lb (70kg)
Gearbox	Six speeds; foot-change	Maximum power	25bhp @ 10,500rpm
Frame	Chrome-moly tubing, single front downtube, twin cradle	Top speed	115mph (185km/h)

THE MACHINE

ABOVE: Left to right, Bob Blakely (team owner), Tony Smith, Chuck Downs and Art Blight with the 1977 MT125 which was raced by Englishman Tony Smith; Daytona, 5 March 2002.

LEFT: The 1979 MT125 R111/W; now liquid-cooled and with more power.

200

each machine precisely the same as the next, racing would be intensely close. Only rider skill would separate winners from losers – and here was the nub of the attraction of what was to become known as 'the Honda 125cc Championships'.

A lot of money was poured into the 1977 MT125 series, with £1,000 for the overall winner and £200 for the victor of each round, more than was being paid out to other major motorcycle racing events at the time. By 1979, the first prize had risen from £1,000 to £1,250 with the series' runner-up winning £750, third £450, fourth £300, fifth £250, sixth £172, seventh £125, eighth £75, ninth £50 and tenth £25. The prize money overall was £11,235.

In its first year (1977), the series saw many 125cc lap records falling, including some set by works Yamaha riders, Phil Read and Bill Ivy (both riding V4s!).

Clive Horton, winner of the original series in 1977, was sponsored by Manchester dealers, Fosters. Bernard Murray, backed by another Manchester dealership, Derek Johnson Motorcycles, came second.

Then during 1978, the improved MT125III proved faster still. Outright lap records were beaten and, with a season's experience behind them, both riders and dealers were even more focused than before. The series gained even more public recognition and Cadwell Park and Scarborough were added to the list of famous venues including Brands Hatch, Mallory Park, Oulton Park and Snetterton.

With many of the bigger names committed to Grand Prix action, the championship became a two-man battle between out-of-retirement Rod Scivyer (Hartford Motorcycles) and Dave Hunter (Granby Motors).

After the final round at Brands Hatch in October 1978, Rod Scivyer found himself richer by £2,000 – half for the title outright, the other half for winning five of the nine rounds. Dave Hunter was runner-up, with the

Englishman Graham Noyce was signed by Honda in January 1978. He is seen here competing in the 500cc British Moto Cross GP at Farleigh Castle that year; the following year he took the title.

1977 champion, Clive Horton, third, even though he missed several rounds due to 125cc World Championship duties. It is also worth noting that Bernard Murray not only finished fourth in the MT title hunt, but also took the 125cc British Championship with his Honda single, with Leigh Notman coming third in the same series on his MT125III.

The British MT125 Honda Championships, 1979, Ron Haslam (4) leads Rod Scivyer (82) and a gaggle of other series riders.

Into 1979 and although Scarborough was not included, Donington Park took its place on the fixture list. To enable entrants and riders to make the most of their MT125s, Honda UK provided a back-up van at each meeting in the series, giving a comprehensive parts service. Additionally, a complete spare machine was taken to every circuit to provide under normal circumstances the possibility of putting a machine back into

The new CR250R went on sale in October 1979 and incorporated lessons learned by Honda works mounts in GPs.

full racing specification should a major incident occur.

All of this preparation and back-up made the Honda MT125 series one of the most successful one-model race championships ever. And for the 1979 season, the machine had been updated once again. Not only did the MT125 RIII/W (W – for water-cooled) sport a red rather than white paint job, but the previously square 54 × 54mm bore and stroke dimensions had given way to new 56 × 50mm ones, making the engine short-stroke and the displacement 123cc.

The Two-Stroke Mopeds

Another facet of the modern Honda two-stroke was its use in a family of ride-to-work commuter mopeds, which were first introduced during the early 1970s.

The first of these was the 49.8cc (39.6 × 49.8mm) PM50 Novia, which was manufactured for the European market in a Belgian

Probably Honda's best two-stroke moped of the 1970s was the NC50 Road Express (known in some markets as the Roadpal). It went on sale at the beginning of 1978.

factory owned by Honda. The specification of this machine included piston-port induction single-speed automatic clutch, 2.00 × 17 tyres, leading link forks and swinging arm with a single shock rear suspension; maximum power output was 1.8bhp at 4,000rpm.

Next, in 1975, came the PF50 MR Amigo – again using the same basic 49.8cc engine and single-speed transmission, but slightly more power (1.93bhp) and new suspension (telescopic front forks and twin shocks at the rear). A year later, the PA50 Camino (again built in Belgium) appeared with automatic transmission and toothed belt drive. It was also much more modern in the styling department and featured a horizontal cylinder in place of the 30-degree declined layout of the earlier mopeds. The Camino put out 2.3bhp.

The Road Express

Probably Honda's best two-stroke moped-type ultra-lightweight was its NC50 Road Express (also known in some markets as the Roadpal). This scored because it had conventional motorcycle-type footrests and a kick-starter, rather than pedal (the former now being legal for restricted 50cc machines in the UK). Like the Camino, the Road Express featured a horizontal cylinder and automatic transmission. Standard specification included steering lock and carrier. Shopping baskets were a popular optional extra. Also the Road Express featured smaller (14in) wheels.

By the beginning of the 1980s, Honda's ultra-lightweight two-stroke line-up comprised: the NS50 Melody miniature scooter (another UK sales success), which came with 12V electrics, an automatic gearbox and comprehensive weather protection; the NX50 Caren (with scooter styling, 12V and auto transmission); the MB50S (a miniature road-race styled motorcycle with a high-performance engine and noval balancer shaft), race-type beam frame, disc front brake and Comstar

203

The 1980 H100 used a 99cc (50.5 × 49.5mm) single-cylinder engine of advanced design with a balancer shaft, anti-backlash gears and an innovative oil system which matched oil injection to throttle opening.

speed MB/MT 50cc unit, featured a number of new ideas: a balancer shaft, anti-backlash gears and an innovative oiling system that matched oil injection to throttle opening. The H100 was known as the MB100 in some markets and, again depending upon the market, came either with a fully enclosed final drive chain or a far less 'open' chrome-plated guard option.

Three Million for the First Time

As for Honda itself, 1980 was the year in which its annual motorcycle production topped three million for the first time. The actual output for the year from the Japanese-based Honda factories was 3,087,471 – more than 11,000 every working day! And of course this didn't take into account overseas production such as the Gold Wing in the USA and mopeds in Belgium, for example. Or for that matter the thousands of cars, industrial engines, outboard motors, agricultural machinery and generators which the Honda Motor Company was now turning out in ever-increasing numbers. In just over three decades Honda had risen from little more than a one-man operation producing a handful of auxiliary-engined bicycles to a major industrial power – a fantastic achievement. And since then, Honda has simply grown and grown into the vast international corporation it is today, with worldwide production and sales facilities.

wheels); and the MT50S trail bike. Both the MB and MT models featured a five-speed gearbox, whilst the controversial NV50 Stream three-wheeler had a 4bhp two-stroke engine and electric starter.

The H100

A complete departure for Honda came in 1980 with the launch of its new H100 99cc (50.5 × 49.5mm) single-cylinder two-stroke engine, with a tubular beam-type frame. This engine, said to have been based on the five-

Index